4/2/12
#24.95

QUEST FOR EQUALITY

QUEST FOR EQUALITY

THE FAILED PROMISE OF
BLACK-BROWN SOLIDARITY

Neil Foley

HARVARD UNIVERSITY PRESS
Cambridge, Massachusetts
London, England
2010

Library of Congress Cataloging-in-Publication Data
Foley, Neil.
Quest for equality : the failed promise of black-brown solidarity /
Neil Foley.
p.   cm.
Includes bibliographical references and index.
ISBN 978-0-674-05023-5 (alk. paper)
1. African Americans—Relations with Mexican Americans.   2. United
States—Race relations.   I. Title.
E185.615.F567 2010
305.896'073–dc22   2009044455

For Sabina, Bianca, and Sophia
—and young activists everywhere

"I believe deeply that we cannot solve the challenges of our time unless we solve them together . . . we may not look the same and we may not have come from the same place . . . [but] working together we can move beyond some of our old racial wounds, and . . . in fact we have no choice if we are to continue on the path of a more perfect union."

—Barak Obama, 2008

"To those who believe the battle against discrimination has been won, I say, look at the realities of paychecks and power."

—Linda Chavez-Thompson, 1997

CONTENTS

ACKNOWLEDGMENTS

I would like to express my gratitude to Henry Louis Gates, Jr., and Evelyn Brooks-Higginbotham for inviting me to give the Nathan Huggins Lectures and for the opportunity to engage the faculty, staff, students, and friends of the Du Bois Institute of African and African American Research. For their insightful comments and criticisms, and generous hospitality during my stay, I would especially like to thank Skip Gates, Evelyn Brooks-Higginbotham, Werner Sollors, Larry Bobo, William Julius Wilson, Marcyliena Morgan, Vera Grant, Mira Seo, Barbara Rodriguez, and Faith Smith.

Over the years I have been fortunate to receive a number of grants and fellowships for this book project and another one, *Latino USA,* forthcoming from Harvard University Press. For providing time away from my teaching duties and to travel to archives, I would like to thank the John Simon Guggenheim Foundation, the National Endowment for the Humanities, the Woodrow Wilson International Center for Scholars, the Fulbright Senior Research Scholars Program in Mexico City, the American Philosophical Society, the American Council of Learned Societies, and the College of Liberal Arts at the University of Texas. I have also had the good fortune to work with Joyce Seltzer, senior executive editor at Harvard University Press, who has enthusiastically supported these projects from the start and offered wise counsel along the way.

Many scholars have been instrumental in shaping my understanding of African American, Afro-Latino, and Latin American history. Among these scholars I wish to acknowledge the work of Ben Vinson, Ariel Dulitsky, Thomas Holt, Gerald Horne, Alan Knight, Mauricio Tenorio, Erika Gabriela Pani, Rebecca Scott, Werner Sollors, Henry Louis Gates, Jr., Bobby Vaughn, Anani Dzidzienyo, Amilcar Shabazz, Tanya Katerí Hernández, Lani Guinier, Gerald Torres, David Roediger, Juliet Hooker, Frank Guridy, and many others too numerous to name. I have also benefited from the work of scholars in comparative interracial history in regional, national, and transnational context, including the work of Arlene Dávila, Michael Phillips, Laura Gómez, Lauren Araiza, Zaragosa Vargas, Brian Behnken, Rebecca Anne Montes, Natalia Molina, Gordon Mantler, Richard White, Vicki Ruiz, Martha Menchaca, Peggy Pascoe, George Sanchez, Gary Gerstle, Ramón Gutiérrez, Gabriela Arredondo, Nancy MacLean, Ariela Gross, Thomas Guglielmo, Michael A. Olivas, David Gutiérrez, and Shana Bernstein. Sadly, rising costs of publication and space limitations have made it impossible to cite the abundant scholarship upon which this work builds and from which I have learned so much.

The work of historians bears an enormous debt to the archivists who generously assist us in our research. For help in locating documents and guiding me to useful collections, I thank the archivists at the Library of Congress and National Archives in College Park, Maryland, and Region X, National Archives, in Fort Worth, Texas. I am grateful to Dr. Michael Hironymous at the Nettie Lee Benson Collection in Austin, Texas; Tim Ronk at the Houston Metropolitan Research Center; Alejandro Padilla Nieto at the Archivo Histórico Genaro Estrada, Secretaría de Relaciones Exteriores, Mexico City; and Raymundo Alvarez at the Archivo General de la Nación also in Mexico City. I would like to thank Paul Rascoe, Don Gibbs, and Janice Duff at the Perry-Castañeda Library at the University of Texas for their able and timely assistance.

Family and friends have done more to sustain my spirits over the years than I can adequately acknowledge. To my sisters Teresa Foley and Rita Foley Yaroch (and husband Steven), I owe a debt of gratitude for offering me their homes and warm company on my frequent trips to the National Archives and Library of Congress. Teresa regularly hosted family gatherings for me and our five other brothers and sisters, their spouses, and fourteen nieces and nephews. I thank her for all the delicious home-made enchiladas picantes and the peaceful afternoons and evenings in her garden. On the West Coast my brother Patrick Foley has offered a unique perspective on race relations in southern California, ground zero for so many paradoxes and ironies as the new Ellis Island of America. His insights have clarified my thinking and emboldened me to let the historical chips fall where they may. My good friend Nickey Bishop has helped me in more ways than he knows or than I can adequately express. I am grateful for his friendship over the years.

Finally, for everything good that has ever happened to me, I am most indebted to my family: To Angela Hinz for the many years of hard work and commitment to making the world a better place, beginning at home with our mostly grown daughters—Sabina Eva Maria Hinz-Foley, Bianca Anneliese Hinz-Foley, and Sophia Luisa Hinz-Foley—and in her work at the Austin International High School for immigrants, where for years she has taught mainly Mexican immigrant students and helped them adapt and succeed in their adopted country. To Sabina, Bianca, and Sophia, who have challenged my thinking on virtually every subject from the moment they began to talk, I am thankful and encouraged. They have become strong-willed, independent young women with definite ideas about how we need to live differently in the world. With a growing interest in and commitment to human rights around the world, particularly immigrant rights and criminal justice reform in our own country, they give us hope for a better future. To them and their generation of young activists I dedicate this book.

QUEST FOR EQUALITY

Introduction

In May of 2005 Mexican President Vicente Fox said before an audience of Texas businessmen in Mexico, "There is no doubt that Mexicans, filled with dignity, willingness and ability to work, are doing jobs that not even blacks want to do in the United States." Jesse Jackson called the remark "a spurious comparison" of Mexicans and African Americans with "ominous racial overtones" because it reinforced the stereotype of black Americans as poor when the majority of poor people in the United States, Jackson reminded Fox, are white. A spokesman for the State Department also called the remark "insensitive."[1] It's difficult to know exactly what Fox's comment was meant to imply. Had he said that Mexican immigrants do the jobs that Americans won't do, no one would have raised an eyebrow. Fox likely meant to suggest that blacks were unwilling to do the jobs Mexicans did because of the harsh nature of the work and the low pay—and because these jobs represented the only kind of employment that African Americans were entitled to for over a century. To be sure, African Americans have done their share of the gardening, ditch-digging, and domestic work now mostly provided by Mexican labor. But the phrase "not even blacks want to do" suggests that most menial labor is performed by blacks in America and implies, however unintentionally, that African Americans are perhaps not as committed to hard work and economic advancement as Mexican immigrants. Whatever his intentions, Fox's racially fraught comment raised questions about the way Mexicans in general view black Americans, not to mention their own citizens of African descent.[2]

The following month an even more serious question was raised when the Mexican Postal Service issued a stamp featuring the comic book character Memín Pinguín, a caricature of an African with thick lips and simian features. His mother, *doña* Eufrosina, is a mammy-like washerwoman reminiscent of Aunt Jemima. Putting these images on Mexican stamps was deeply offensive to African Americans and other Americans, including leaders of the NAACP, the Rainbow/PUSH (People United to Save Humanity) coalition, and the National Council of La Raza (NCLR).[3] David Pilgrim, the curator of a Michigan museum that collects Jim Crow memorabilia, called the Memín Pinguín caricature a classic pickaninny. "It's disappointing," he said, "when you find a government putting its stamp on racism." The White House issued a statement declaring that "images like these have no place in today's world."[4]

Most Mexicans saw no racial connotations, much less racism, in a caricature that for many Americans was reminiscent of blackface and the minstrel show tradition. For Mexicans, Memín Pinguín was a hero—intelligent, loyal, generous, and courageous.[5] In one episode Memín Pinguín and his friends visit an ice cream shop in Dallas, Texas, where the waitress serves Memín's four light-skinned friends but refuses to serve him because, as the waitress explains, "In this place we do not give service to Negroes." Outraged by the racism of the waitress and storeowner, Memín's friends break the store's mirrors, causing hundreds of dollars of damage, and scuffle with the storeowner until the police arrive and arrest them. The racist people of Texas are the villains in this episode, while the courageous boys of Mexico defend the honor and rights of their "negrito" friend. From the writings of prominent nineteenth-century Mexican liberals like Justo Sierra to Mexico's postrevolutionary ideology of *indigenismo* (the

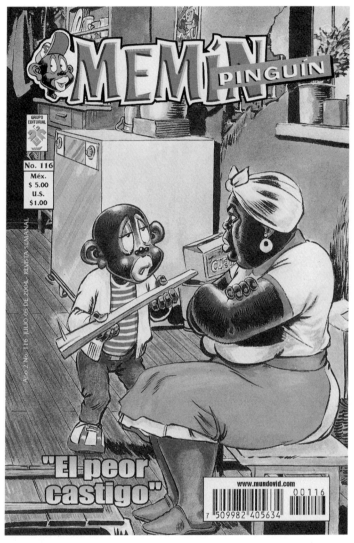

Memín Pinguín, "El Peor Castigo" (the worst punishment). Grupo Editorial Vid.

Mexican postage stamps featuring Memín Pinguín. Courtesy of Michael Hironymous, Nettie Lee Benson Library, Austin, Texas.

incorporation of indigenous peoples into a unified nation-state), the moral superiority of Mexico over the United States has been a recurring theme in the discourse of Mexican intellectuals and government officials; and despite Mexico's long tradition of defending the rights of its resident nationals in the United States against discrimination, Mexico mostly ignores discrimination and exploitation of its own citizens at the hands of its predominantly white, economic elite.[6]

A spokesman for the Mexican Embassy, Rafael Laveaga, said the stamp should "not be interpreted on a racial basis in Mexico or anywhere else." He compared Memín Pinguín with the Looney Toons cartoon character Speedy Gonzalez, who he claimed

Memín Pinguín, "Líos Gordos" (big trouble). Grupo Editorial Vid.

had "never been interpreted in a racial manner by the people in Mexico." President Fox refused to apologize, calling Memín Pinguín a lovable character embraced by all Mexicans. Sambo or not, the image of Memín did not signify for Mexicans what it apparently did for black Americans, and Foreign Minister Luis Ernesto Derbez bluntly declared that the U.S. reaction to the stamp showed a lack of respect for Mexican culture. One Mexican blogger wrote: "Gringos talking about racism when they shoot our people who cross the border—what a joke!" Mexicans turned out in droves to purchase the stamps, and the run of 750,000 stamps sold out in just a few days.[7]

Memín's racial blackness was thus incidental and even irrelevant to any cultural understanding of the popularity of Memín, since most Mexicans have had little contact, and even less awareness, of the Afro-Mexican population, which has been dismissed as

Cartoon character Speedy Gonzales. Warner Brothers Entertainment, Inc.

Mexican President Vicente Fox apologizes to African Americans for his insensitive remarks. Courtesy of Lalo Alcaraz.

tiny and mostly rural despite the fact that by 1821 most cities in colonial New Spain had substantial numbers of *negros* and *mulatos*.[8] And despite obvious prejudice based on skin color and phenotype in Mexico and virtually all Latin American countries, Mexicans continue to insist that discrimination against their indigenous and Afro-Mexican population is grounded in social, cultural, and class distinctions, not race.

Like most things that differentiate Mexico and the United States—language, religion, economic wealth, and so forth—racial regimes in the two nations have evolved along sharply different paths. Indians and mestizos figure prominently in Mexican history and national ideology, whereas in the United States, the principal divide has been between whites and blacks, with Asians and Latinos often straddling the color line—sometimes as (honorary) whites, although more often not—and American Indians, who at under 2 percent of the population, are barely mentioned at all, except in their leading role as native Americans. Until the emergence of a Mexican-style multiculturalism in the 1990s (mainly as a result of the decline of the welfare state and the indigenous uprising in Chiapas in 1994), Mexico continued to promote a national ideology of *mestizaje*—the fusion of indigenous peoples and Spanish colonizers into a new and stronger race, *la raza cósmica* (the cosmic race), a phrase coined in the 1920s by José Vasconcelos, Mexico's most prominent intellectual of the first half of the twentieth century. Noticeably absent from that mixture, however, are *afromexicanos*, notwithstanding that many leaders of Mexican independence—Vicente Guerrero, Juan Alvarez, José María Morelos, Valerio Trujano, and Mariano Tabares—are acknowledged to have had African ancestry.[9] Indeed, Vasconcelos's idea of the cosmic race rests upon the white supremacist assumption that "The lower types of the species will be absorbed by the superior type. In this manner . . . the Black could be redeemed, and step by step, by voluntary extinction, the uglier stocks will give way to the more handsome."[10] Mestizaje redeems blacks essentially by obliterating them.

As a major player in the slave trade in the sixteenth and seventeenth centuries, Mexico was home to around 200,000 African slaves who labored on sugar plantations, silver mines, and cattle ranches.[11] Most Afro-Mexicans intermarried with mestizos and Indians, and only remnants of their culture survive today in the state of Veracruz and a 200-mile-long stretch along the Pacific Ocean (the Costa Chica) in the states of Guerrero and Oaxaca. The Mexican census discontinued the practice of classifying citizens by race after the 1910 Revolution and therefore it is difficult to know what percentage of the Mexican population is of African heritage. Added to that is the tendency of many Mexicans to deny any African ancestry and to downplay their presence in Mexico.[12] In 1810 about 10 percent of the Mexican population was classified as Afro-Mexican. When, more than a century later in 1943, the Afro-American News Agency asked the Mexican ambassador, Francisco Castillo Nájera, whether a person of "Negro blood" had ever held a high office in Mexico, the ambassador responded that it would be impossible to say with any certainty because "racial differences are no longer significant in Mexico." He estimated that less than 1 percent of the population was "Negro" and explained that social distinctions corresponded to "economic levels" rather than racial categories.[13]

The category of mulatto was removed from the Mexican census in the nineteenth century, just as it was in the United States in 1930. The Mexican census folded the category of mulatto into mestizo, whereas the U.S. census eliminated the only mixed-race category, mulatto, in favor of the so-called one-drop rule for determining the boundaries of blackness. While Mexico sought to erase the category of blackness in the nineteenth century, the United States sought in the first half of the twentieth century to more clearly define it, broaden its boundaries, and stabilize it as the measure of all things whites supposedly were not. And both countries viewed the Chinese as threats to the formation of nationalist states: the United States, founded on the principle of white supremacy, excluded Chinese immigrants in 1882, while postrevolutionary Mexico, founded on the principle of mestizaje, forcibly deported them in the early 1930s.[14]

Thus when an official of the Mexican Postal Service, Carlos Caballero, claimed that Memín Pinguín was not a racist depiction but "a traditional character" that reflected "part of Mexico's culture," he was alluding, in part, to the small and virtually unknown black population of Mexico.[15] But if Memín Pinguín represents a part of Mexican culture, as Caballero claims, it is not because of his race, as any Mexican will tell you, but rather his many positive character traits. Mexican pundits on the left and the right went all out to defend the caricature and accused the United States of confusing its own racist Jim Crow history with a country that abolished slavery in 1829 and never enacted any Jim Crow laws. Indeed, the Mexican reply to the American response to the caricature was something akin to the old adage that people who live in glass houses should not throw stones.

The image of the pickaninny and Little Black Sambo were, after all, U.S. exports that could be found in countries around the world, not just in Mexico. One U.S. journalist visiting Hong Kong in the late 1980s was astonished to find a tube of toothpaste called "Darkie" that carried the image of "an Uncle Tom-like character from the Old South."[16]

In Mexico Aunt Jemima pancake mix still goes by the brand name "La Negrita," and a 1995 commercial on national television featured a dark-skinned man in a white tuxedo telling viewers that at Comex, a Mexican paint company, "they're working like niggers to offer you a white sale." No one complained about the ad "because we don't have a racism problem—that's the key to it all," said Marisela Vergada, an account executive at the Mexican advertising firm that produced the twenty-second spot. "It is simply an expression that everyone uses." Colin Palmer, a historian of slavery and Afro-descendant peoples in Mexico, explained that Mexico's racial hierarchy "is based on skin color, with white the higher value as opposed to those who are brown and those, God forbid, who are black. In that regard . . . [Mexico's racial hierarchy] is worse than in the United States, where it is recognized and a lot of people of good will are trying to change it. By and large in Mexico it is unrecognized and unaddressed, which leads to a perpetuation of the status quo and a continuing assault on people of African or Indian descent."[17]

But if prejudice against Afro-descendant citizens in Mexico is relatively trivial compared with that in the United States, it is nonetheless true that the minority light-skinned citizens of Mexico have viewed the majority dark-skinned citizens of Indian and African origin as their social inferiors for centuries.[18] Although racism officially does not exist in Mexico, Mexicans continue to deploy a specialized language to describe skin color. Among the most frequently used are *güero* (white), *negro/negrito* (black), and *moreno* (brown).[19] As a descriptor of color that distinguishes the majority of Mexicans, *moreno* encompasses those who are light brown (*moreno claro*), as well as dark brown (*moreno oscuro*) or *prieto* (dark-skinned, black), often used in a derogatory manner, except in some cases, as in *mi prieta linda* (my beautiful morena, which is the title of a popular Mexican tune from the mid-1900s).[20] The term *indio* (Indian) always implies dark skin and low social status and is not used in polite company. Like other Latin American countries, Mexico embraces the idea that, unlike the United States, it is a "racial democracy" where citizenship, not race, forms the bedrock of national identity and belonging—and class, not race, the bedrock of inequality. In other words, race may not matter in Mexico, at least not officially, but skin color and social class most certainly do.[21]

The controversy over ex-president Fox's comment and the issuance of a postage stamp featuring an Afro-Mexican "Sambo" caricature recapitulates in important ways the just-below-the-surface tension that has periodically characterized relations between African Americans and Mexican Americans in states like California and Texas, where both groups have lived and worked in close proximity throughout the twentieth century. Mexicans and blacks in these states—like African Americans, Dominicans, and Puerto Ricans in New York, and Cubans, Haitians, and African Americans in Miami, Florida—have distinct histories of cooperation and conflict that embody, in broadly generalized terms, the transnational and diasporic histories of Afro-Latinos in countries like Brazil, Colombia, Panama, and Venezuela, as well as Afro-Caribbean cultures in Puerto Rico, Cuba, Santo Domingo, and other West Indian islands.[22]

Although Mexicans freely acknowledge and officially celebrate their indigenous roots, they do not seem to regard Afro-descendant people as kith or kin on either side of the U.S.-Mexico border.[23] Mexico's racial amnesia thus provides a useful backdrop for understanding the ways that Mexican Americans in general have been slow to recognize African Americans as strategic allies in the struggle for equality in the mid-twentieth century. In many cases they tended to distance themselves from African Americans and the stigma of blackness to a degree that other Latinos in the United States, for example, Puerto Ricans and Dominicans, have not.[24]

Mexicans and African Americans were nevertheless keenly aware of the presence of the other and at times worked in close proximity, sometimes cooperating where it seemed useful and other times regarding each other suspiciously as potential adversaries in the competition for jobs. An editorial in the African-American newspaper, the *Pittsburg Courier*, titled "And Now the Mexicans," observed that the influx of "little brown men" from Mexico placed the "Negro in a most awkward position," especially because the whites-only American Federation of Labor (AFL) and Mexico's national union, Confederación Regional Obrera Mexicana (CROM), held their annual meeting in 1925 on the border in El Paso and Ciudad Juárez to exchange delegates and explore the possibility of a transnational partnership. "It begins to look," the editorial concluded, "as though the Mexican will be our next competitor for American labor."[25] Many African Americans feared Mexicans, as they had the Irish and Italians, as yet another immigrant group scrambling for footing on the bottom rung of the economic ladder. They viewed Mexicans, regardless of their citizenship status, as foreigners who did not deserve to cut in line ahead of long-suffering, long-struggling African Americans.

Black Americans capitalized on the Anglo-American perception of Mexicans as foreigners in order to stake their own claim to rights as homegrown American citizens who had fought and died for their country since the first black patriot fell during the Revolutionary War. The Field Secretary for the NAACP, William Pickens, forcefully expressed this view in 1923, when he was required by law to sit in the Jim Crow section of the El Paso train station while, to his amazement, "Not only the 'white people,' but all the non-American 'colored peoples'" were permitted the luxury of sitting in the White Only section: "Yellow Chinese, brown Japanese, and the many-colored Mexicans, some dirty with red handkerchiefs around their necks and carrying baskets and bundles with fruits, vegetables, and live chickens. These Mexicans are the people whom the colored soldiers of the Twenty-Fourth Infantry held off those white people some years ago . . . Any Mexican, however, . . . can ride on any train. Any foreigner . . . can travel freely, but not the mothers or wives or sisters of the black Americans who fought, bled, and died in France."[26] Pickens deeply resented that African Americans, the "most loyal of all Americans," were forced to use Jim Crow cars, "while the rest of the world," whether "an unlettered Mexican peon, an untrammeled Indian, or a representative of the uncivilized 'white trash' of the South" could ride on any train and on any Pullman car he chose.[27] Picken's observation echoed Justice John Marshall Harlan's dissent in *Plessy v. Fergusson* that Americans regarded Chinese as belonging to a "race so different from our own that we do not permit those belonging to it to become citizens of the United States." But under the Louisiana statute, Harlan noted, a "Chinaman" would be permitted to ride in the same passenger coaches as white citizens, while black citizens would face criminal charges for attempting the same.[28]

It's probably fair to say that many African Americans, like Pickens, held stereotypical views of Mexicans as poor, dirty, and foreign, just as many Mexican Americans, and many Latin Americans, regarded African Americans as racially inferior. Given the racial regime of the United States during the first two-thirds of the twentieth century, with whites at the top and blacks at the bottom, it should not be surprising that many Mexican Americans, as an intermediate group, looked down on blacks, while African

Americans felt hostility toward "many-colored Mexicans" and other nonwhite resident nationals who received more favorable treatment than loyal black citizens.

Most European immigrant groups, whether Russian Jews, Sicilian Catholics, Irish, or Germans, sought to shed the stigma of their Old World roots by reconstituting their identities as white Americans. It would have been crazy not to. "Who can blame the Irish steward or the Sicilian hatmaker for wanting to be white? White in America," author Richard Rodriguez reminds us, "was the freedom to disappear from a crowded tenement and to reappear in a Long Island suburb, in an all-electric kitchen, with a set of matching plates."[29] It rankled Mexican Americans in the Southwest that the vast majority of Anglo Americans refused to accord them the same rights and privileges as whites, no matter how many generations their families had been in the United States. But in demanding their full citizenship rights as whites, many Mexican Americans, like other immigrant groups, often reinforced the color line rather than crossed or subverted it. Meanwhile, African Americans since the nation's founding witnessed successive waves of immigrants undergo the transformation from despised groups of foreigners to fully franchised American citizens, often in just a few generations.

Not all Mexicans claimed a white identity. Unlike many middle-class Mexican Americans, Mexican immigrant workers rarely identified themselves as white or Caucasian, certainly no more than they would have in Mexico where their identity was inextricably linked to nationality, social class, and the postrevolutionary ideology of mestizaje. They identified themselves mainly as mexicanos and did not seem particularly averse to mingling with or marrying across multiple color lines in cities like El Paso and Los Angeles, where they lived and worked in close proximity with Anglo, Filipino, and African Americans. African American and Mexican workers also belonged to interracial unions, such as the Longshoremen's Union in Texas and California and the International Union of Mine, Mill, and Smelter Workers in New Mexico and Arizona.[30]

While much has been written about interracial cooperation and conflict in the labor movement in the United States, Mexican American and African American civil rights workers during and after World War II only rarely viewed their campaigns as a common struggle for equality and full citizenship rights. Part of the reason can be traced to the immigrant status of many Mexicans, many of them unauthorized immigrants, and the deep concern of African Americans that Mexican immigrants competed with them for jobs. Indeed, middle-class African American and Mexican American civil rights advocates turned mainly to progressive whites as allies rather than to each other. The NAACP worked closely with the American Civil Liberties Union (ACLU) and the American Jewish Congress, among other mostly white organizations. Mexican American civil rights organizations like the League of United Latin American Citizens (LULAC) and the American G.I. Forum sought support from Anglo congressmen and senators, courts, governors, the Texas Good Neighbor Commission, and federal agencies like the Office of the Coordinator of Inter-American Affairs (OCIAA) and the President's Committee on Fair Employment Practices (FEPC).

World War II turned things upside down. The war's manpower needs did more to open up job opportunities for blacks and Mexicans than did the dawning awareness among whites that maintenance of white supremacy at home had begun to look uncomfortably like the Third Reich's master plan for the Master Race.[31] Nevertheless, the war profoundly affected the racial views of white Americans, both as a result of the growing concern over the spread of Nazism and the declining influence of scientific racism—the belief prevalent from the late nineteenth century until World War II that the white race was biologically and culturally superior to others. The tragic consequences of that ideology for millions of Jews lent credence to the saying that Hitler gave racism a bad name. As the editors of *Common Sense* put it, "We have made little effort to wipe out our treatment of the Negro as a step towards the defeat of those who treat the Jews the same way."[32]

Roosevelt's Four Freedoms also renewed interest in universal human rights as well as the meaning of democratic governance at a time when these principles seemed to hang in the balance. Highly motivated by the threat of tens of thousands of African Americans marching on Washington in June 1941 to protest against employment discrimination, President Roosevelt issued Executive Order 8802 establishing the Fair Employment Practices Committee. For the first time since Reconstruction, the federal government took action to protect the constitutional rights of African Americans and other nonwhite Americans to be hired in defense industry jobs without regard to race, color, creed, or national origin. African Americans also waged the highly visible "Double V" campaign for victory at home as well as abroad and joined the NAACP in record numbers. By 1944 approximately 85,000 members belonged to 481 NAACP branches across the nation, including 77 youth councils and 22 college chapters.[33] "As the citizens of the United States become interested in the peoples of all the world," declared one ACLU member in 1943, "they are soon made to realize that their concern about Africa, China, Russia, and India will not be honored unless they are equally concerned about New Mexico and Harlem."[34]

Like other minority groups, African Americans and Mexican Americans returned from the war more militantly "Americanized" than before they left. Even before the war ended, African

Americans were determined to win the war for equality at home and had rioted in cities across the nation against police brutality, employment discrimination, and myriad other humiliations. An extreme but telling example of returning soldiers' growing intolerance of discrimination occurred in St. Louis in 1944 when an African American killed a white man because the white man blew cigarette smoke in his wife's face.[35] When a Texas school superintendent told a reporter that blacks returning from the war would have to "remain humble and look to the white man for help," the reporter wrote: "Somebody had better tell him that . . . these docile negroes have been shot [at] . . . and taught how to kill white men. Some one should tell him that the day for humble Negroes is gone forever."[36] But most African American soldiers and veterans expressed their longing for equality and respect in less hostile ways. In a letter to the governor, a black Texas veteran summed up the feelings of returning black soldiers everywhere: "The things we want are what we deserve, and that is to be able to live any place, go any place, to have equal chances in business, and public schools in which the students have the same opportunities for education. To have State Colleges in which the same is provided. To receive the same salary for the same type of work according to qualifications. To be able to travel and shop with the same privileges and conveniences as other races. And to be given a fair trial in all courts when convicted of a crime. In other words whatever privileges the White race have, the Negro should have the same."[37]

Mexican American veterans also demanded whatever privileges the white race had, but with an important difference. Many Mexican Americans continued to base their claim for equality on belonging to the white race. Richard Garza, a Mexican American veteran returning to Houston, for example, complained to the governor of Texas that "jobs . . . are given to the negro race before they are given to us . . . We belong to the white race, but we are treated worse than negroes."[38] Maciano Zamarripa wrote to Mexican President Manuel Ávila Camacho that Texas authorities treated Mexicans with as much hostility as persons of *la raza negra*, the black race.[39] While the vast majority of Texas whites did not regard Mexicans as racially white, a member of the Texas Good Neighbor Commission, J. Conrad Dunagan, explained that although blacks and Mexicans represented two distinct "ethnic groups . . . their problems, with one or two exceptions, are about as different as they can be. It would be about as sensible to try to lump them together as it would to hitch up a Percheron and a Shetland pony to the same plow with the same harness."[40] Mexicans were different from white Americans, he seemed to imply, but they were not to be confused with Negroes. The idea that Mexicans should be accorded equal rights with whites, if not *as* whites, had gained important momentum in the 1940s as a result of the Good Neighbor policy and the growing need of Texas farmers for Mexican farmworkers.

But even before the war, not all Mexicans had been denied the privileges accorded to whites. Some light-skinned middle-class Mexican Americans had always been able to gain admittance to, if not outright acceptance in, Anglo society. Two well-known Mexican American civil rights activists of the 1940s and 1950s, University of Texas professors George I. Sánchez and Carlos Castañeda, could easily have passed for white, although there was little need to. In 1948, two years before the NAACP won its U.S. Supreme Court case—*Sweatt v. Painter*—to force the University of Texas law school to admit African Americans, more than 100 Mexican Americans were enrolled at the university, including the law school.[41] One of them, James deAnda, the son of Mexican immigrants, was a third-year law student at UT who later became the nation's second Mexican American to be named to the federal bench. Other prominent Mexican American civil rights lawyers had graduated from UT law school in 1938 and 1940.[42] Although Mexican Americans faced enormous barriers, light-skinned Mexicans, particularly of the middle class, did not share the same degree of exclusion as their darker-skinned, working-class compatriots, particularly farmworkers, regardless of citizenship status.

In recent decades scholars of race in the United States have succeeded in broadening the field beyond the traditional, historically predominant black-white paradigm to include numerous studies of Latinos and Asian Americans. Most of this later scholarship has made comparisons to the experiences of other marginalized groups, particularly where segregation and other forms of discrimination are concerned.[43] The principal obstacle to writing comparative ethnic history is that these groups' histories often are more different than they are alike.[44] Nevertheless, during the World War II era and the 1950s, African Americans, Latinos, and other minority groups faced varying degrees of exclusion and marginalization in their efforts to secure their fundamental rights as U.S. citizens. The history of African American and Mexican American civil rights activism in Texas and California during and after World War II reveals, more than anything, the missed opportunities and the failed promise of these groups to work together for economic rights and equal education.[45] In three particular arenas, African Americans and Mexican Americans in these states sought to advance their struggle for equality along separate paths that only occasionally converged. In the first chapter, we examine the complex interplay of regional, national, and international politics that enabled African American and Mexican American civil rights advocates to seek ways to make President Roosevelt's Good Neighbor policy with Latin America apply at home to dark-skinned Americans. Both groups sought to convince the federal government that maintaining a *herrenvolk* democracy that denied constitutional rights to its own non-white citizens threatened the war effort and made a mockery of the Good Neighbor policy.

In the next chapter, we explore the strategies of African American and Mexican American workers and civil right activists in Texas and California to enforce Franklin Roosevelt's Executive Order 8802, issued June 25, 1941, prohibiting discrimination in defense industries. World War II offered opportunities for economic advancement for all Americans, and workers themselves demanded equal employment opportunity in hiring, pay, and promotion. Labor rights formed the basis of their struggles, much as they had during the New Deal era, but with important differences.

In the final chapter, we see how Thurgood Marshall and the NAACP Legal Defense Fund turned their attention from employment discrimination and workers' economic rights to launch a frontal assault on the doctrine of separate-but-equal schools. Mexican American civil rights activists and organizations also sought to end school segregation, but on the ground that they were Caucasians, a strategy that at no time overlapped with either the equalization strategy of the NAACP in the 1920s and 1930s (requiring school districts to fund black schools at the same level as white ones) or their direct challenge to *Plessy v. Ferguson* in the late 1940s to end school segregation. Mexicans and African Americans pursued their struggles for equality, in other words, in largely parallel universes.

Immigration from Mexico and other Latin American countries in the last two decades of the twentieth century has further complicated prospects for black-brown cooperation. Many African Americans and Mexican immigrants find themselves confined to low-wage, low-skill jobs, where opportunities for upward mobility are often as rare for citizens as for noncitizen residents, whether in the United States legally or not. The epilogue reflects on the difficult but evolving relationship between Latinos and African Americans in the closing decades of the twentieth century.

1

Bringing the Good Neighbor Policy Home

Anticommunism and the cold war ideology of the postwar years spurred the federal government, including the Supreme Court, to end Jim Crow segregation of black Americans or risk losing the good will and patronage of African and Asian states that decolonized in the aftermath of World War II.[1] The failure of state and local courts and law enforcement to safeguard the rights of citizens of African descent was not lost on the Soviet Union or the more than thirty African nations that emerged from colonial rule between 1945 and 1963. But the story of "cold war civil rights" obscures an even earlier link between civil rights struggles and American foreign policy in another part of the world— that of President Roosevelt's Good Neighbor policy with Latin America during World War II.[2]

The goal of establishing hemispheric cooperation in wartime afforded African Americans and Mexican Americans an opportunity to make the federal government more responsive to discrimination on the home front by arguing that segregation and other Jim Crow practices were incompatible with the stated aims of the Good Neighbor policy. But the United States rarely paid attention to the Latin American republics in its vast "backyard" south of the Rio Grande, except when investors bought a stake in the rich oil, mineral, and natural resources of the region or when it was deemed necessary to send in the Marines to protect foreign investments. "We know what's going on in Yugoslavia more than we know what's happened in South

America," lamented the chair of the Committee for Inter-American Cooperation.[3] One journalist wrote, "If we value the friendship of our good neighbors to the South, we had better get rid of Jim Crow or else Jim Crow will help get rid of us in all those nations of the Western Hemisphere where the color line has not been drawn."[4] After the United States entered the war, the State Department and Office of War Information worried about how to counter Axis propaganda that the United States denied basic rights to its own citizens of African descent even as it claimed to be in a war to establish freedom and democracy around the world. In a letter to *Time* magazine in 1942, a government professor at Williams College, Frederick L. Schuman, warned: "The colored peoples of the earth . . . will conclude, wrongly no doubt but nonetheless irrevocably, that Western white men offer them only fair words and foul deeds, that the darker peoples have no stake in a war between rival oppressors, and that Axis arrogance may be more tolerable than democratic hypocrisy."[5]

But more than democratic hypocrisy was at stake. Even before the attack on Pearl Harbor, the United States had a strategic need to protect its southern flank, the lightly patrolled 2,000 mile border with Mexico that made the United States vulnerable to Axis penetration from its closest neighbor.[6] Strengthening security along the border and establishing reciprocal economic and military relations with Mexico were deemed vital to U.S. security interests. Brazil also figured prominently in national defense plans, not only for its mineral wealth but also for its strategic location in defending the hemisphere against attack. Military strategists considered the possibility, even the likelihood, that Germany might launch an airborne invasion of the western hemisphere across the Atlantic Ocean at its narrowest point— between French West Africa and the protruding eastern bulge of Brazil, a distance of only about 1,000 miles. In addition to extensive Lend-Lease aid, the United States provided a market for Brazilian exports in return for its military cooperation.[7]

Mexican American and African American civil rights leaders recognized the difficulty of achieving hemispheric unity with nations whose nonwhite majority populations were deeply offended by America's racial order and who might be justifiably reluctant to support a war "between rival oppressors." Walter White, the executive secretary of the NAACP, sought to make the federal government aware of the large Afro-Latino population in Latin America, particularly Brazil, who might be especially receptive to Axis claims that the United States denied basic rights to its Afro-descendant citizens. Mexican American activists, on the other hand, focused almost exclusively on discrimination against Mexicans in the border states from California to Texas as the principle obstacle to maintaining good relations with Mexico.

Shortly after the attack on Pearl Harbor, Walter White immediately sensed an opportunity to leverage the Good Neighbor policy on behalf of African Americans. "The U.S. government," the NAACP announced, "had better wake up to the fact that its 'good neighbor policy' is in danger in South American countries unless the U.S. integrates Negroes more fully into the national picture."[8] White cited a Labor Department report that over two-thirds of the population of Latin America and the Caribbean would be viewed in the United States as belonging to "colored races." Since the principal element of the Brazilian population was "Negroid," White reasoned, Afro-Brazilians would be subject to Jim Crow laws and customs in the United States. The report noted that the majority of Latin Americans represented "crosses between colored and white stocks," and that the ascription of "white" sometimes applied to mixed-race persons of African ancestry. In Mexico, citizens of "exclusively white origin" represented less than 10 percent of the population, while the majority population, as in all Central American countries, with the exception of Costa Rica, was made up mainly of "mixed breed" and Indian populations. A substantial majority of the people of the West Indies, the report continued, comprised "African Negroes of pure blood," and that "Negro blood" would always be a factor among Cubans, Puerto Ricans, and Dominicans. In short, only "an attenuated strain of white blood" could be found in most Latin American countries.[9]

White reminded Nelson Rockefeller, appointed by the Roosevelt administration to improve U.S. relations with Latin America, that dark-skinned diplomats and foreign heads of state on official business in the United States were often barred from hotels, restaurants, swimming pools, and other public areas. The State Department tried to shield diplomats, including Afro-descendant Brazilians and other Latin Americans, from experiencing the humiliation of race-based exclusion under the nation's Jim Crow system.[10] White recalled a "glaring example of this prejudice" when the president of Haiti, Stenio Vincent, was invited to attend a conference in the nation's capital on the need for inter-American cooperation to protect the Panama Canal in the event of war. As President Vincent left Washington to return to Haiti, the U.S. Marine Band was slated to play the Haitian National Anthem; instead, it played the popular song "Bye, Bye, Blackbirds."[11] "Whoever was responsible for the choice of this song," White told Rockefeller, "apparently was ignorant of the fact that Broadway hits are heard over the radio in Central and South America at the same time that they are first heard by residents of the United States." It is not clear why White thought playing this popular jazz song represented a "glaring example of prejudice." Even more puzzling was his concern that Latin Americans would find it offensive. White was on more solid ground when he asked Rockefeller to use his influence to persuade Hollywood studios to refrain from portraying African Americans as "buffoons and menials" and to arrange South American tours for great African

American singers like Marian Anderson, Dorothy Maynor, Paul Robeson, Roland Hayes, Kenneth Spencer, and orchestras like that of Duke Ellington.[12]

On Capitol Hill progressive Rep. John Coffee from Seattle, Washington, argued that the Good Neighbor policy would have to begin at home before exporting it to Latin America. He declared on the floor of the House that "Twenty-six United Nations and many races of men today help the United States fight the Axis Powers, yet American industries and our armed forces continue to discriminate against non-Caucasians, particularly Negroes." West Point, the Naval Academy, and aviation training centers, he said, "must abandon their race prejudice. If they do not, and quickly, the United States may lose the enthusiastic aid which Negroes, Chinese, Filipinos, Hindu and Moslem East India, dark-skinned Latin Americans, and other non-Caucasian peoples now give to the world-wide war against Nazi, Fascist, and Japanese barbarism." Representative Coffee asked how white Americans could "denounce the racial bigotry of Nazi-ism but permit our industrialists . . . to discriminate against 13,000,000 loyal American Negroes who have over 25,000,000 relatives in Latin America."[13]

A successful Good Neighbor policy, nevertheless, required, among other things, that the State Department abandon its custom of hiring bigoted white Southerners to staff U.S. embassies and consular offices in Brazil and other Latin American countries in the mistaken belief that Southerners knew best "how to handle Negroes." The wives and relatives of these diplomats, Walter White charged, expressed an air of "condescension towards the dark-skinned citizens" and often refused to attend social functions where colored persons were likely to be present. "They . . . often do more harm in subtle, feminine ways than their husbands," White opined, because of their "arrogant, domineering, suspicious, quarrelsome, and vulgar" behavior. To remedy the problem, he urged Rockefeller to send only "enlightened" Southerners to Latin American countries and to hire "qualified American Negroes" for diplomatic, consular, and other positions.[14]

White became convinced that the American public might soften its commitment to Jim Crow if it fully understood how damaging racial discrimination was to the Allied war effort and how it sullied America's image in the western hemisphere. He began to conduct research for an article he hoped to publish in the *Saturday Evening Post* or *Atlantic Monthly* and sent letters to scholars and colleagues asking for information on race relations in Brazil and other Latin American countries.[15] He wanted to know more about the effects of "Yanqui imperialism" in Cuba, widespread hostility prompted by our occupation of Haiti, and historically strained relations with Mexico.[16] He circulated an article reproduced in the *Congressional Record* titled "Brazil: The Largest Negro Nation" in which Brazilianist Charles Gauld pointed out that Afro-Brazilians were well represented in the army and navy, rarely faced outright barriers to their rights, and never faced the threat of lynchings.[17] News of lynchings, race riots, and other violent conflict in the United States, on the other hand, was widely circulated in the Latin American press and did more than American movies, White declared, "to form opinions of and prejudices against the U.S."[18]

The federal government worried that Jim Crow at home made it difficult to counter Axis propaganda in Latin America. The director of the Office of Facts and Figures, Archibald MacLeish, reported that the Japanese Embassy in Madrid was "using U.S. anti-Negro bias to create disunity in South America."[19] When Cleo Wright, an African American oil-mill worker, was lynched in Sikeston, Missouri, a few weeks after the bombing of Pearl Harbor, Radio Tokyo reported: "Democracy . . . may be an ideal and noble system of life, but democracy as practiced by the Anglo Americans is stained with the bloody guilt of racial persecution and exploitation."[20] "The only sacred right and equality which the Negro shares with white Americans," announced a German radio broadcast, "is the privilege of shedding his blood in Jim-Crow regiments . . . to die as cannon-fodder for his beloved Roosevelt."[21] Carter Wesley, publisher of the *Informer,* the largest newspaper for blacks in Texas, wrote to President Roosevelt that "the only difference between the practice in America and that of the Nazi . . . is that the Nazis *openly* profess superiority, whereas in America it is practiced by conspiracy and tacit agreement on the ground of white superiority," adding that "this discrimination not only applies to Negroes, but also to Mexicans and other darker peoples."[22]

President Roosevelt had good reason to be concerned over the negative image of the United States in Latin America. Fearing a possible German invasion of Brazil as a launching site for bombing American cities, FDR ordered his military to draw up plans to send 100,000 U.S. troops to Brazil.[23] He also appointed Nelson Rockefeller, a young Republican with financial and cultural interests in Latin America, to head the newly created Office of the Coordinator of Inter-American Affairs (OCIAA). Officially, the OCIAA sought to promote better relations with other American nations and to establish hemispheric solidarity through reciprocal trade agreements and cultural and scientific exchanges.[24] Chandler Owen, former coeditor with A. Philip Randolph of the *Messenger,* urged Rockefeller to establish a "Negro Division" within the agency because American Negroes were "the recognized leaders of all Negroes" in the hemisphere and played an important role in the "maintenance of morale among the large Negro population of Brazil—the biggest of our Good Neighbors."[25] Rockefeller appointed Rayford Logan, a Pan-Africanist, civil rights activist, and Howard University history professor, to the

OCIAA Advisory Committee, which approved funding for Logan to undertake a study of the "Negro Contribution to Hemispheric Solidarity, with Special Reference to Cuba, the Dominican Republic and Haiti."[26] OCIAA official Louis Olom noted that African Americans had for years been interested in "racial conditions" in Latin America and that many looked upon Latin America "as a kind of heaven where the Negro allegedly received more cordial treatment from his immediate neighbors."[27]

In the early years of World War II, the Good Neighbor policy awakened in African American leaders a growing awareness of their hemispheric ties to Afro-Latinos as well as to colonized peoples in Africa and Asia. In 1942 the Rand School of Social Sciences in New York organized a series of lectures on "Negroes in the Western Hemisphere." Lectures included topics such as "What constitutes a 'Negro' in the different regions of the Americas? What is the difference between the 'anthropological Negro' and the 'sociological Negro'?" "To what extent has race mixture taken place . . . in the different countries?" "Is the Negro part of the National Culture?" Is he permitted to become an "integral and wholesome element in the national or regional culture" or is he forced by discrimination to develop a "minority culture" as a "defense mechanism"? "Whither is the Negro going in the Americas?—Is the ultimate future of the Negro in the Western Hemisphere to be decided by amalgamation and absorption, by parallel development along racial lines within the same society, or by establishment of separate Negro communities in distinct geographic areas?"[28]

Latin American scholars, artists, and government officials toured the United States in an effort to introduce Latin American culture and perspectives to a neighbor that had long regarded the southern hemisphere as racially and culturally inferior. The Brazilian poet and diplomat, Ribeiro Couto, who had traveled extensively in the United States, stressed that Afro-Latin Americans and African Americans shared a common history in the hemisphere. In one of his talks, Couto recalled Langston Hughes's poem "I, Too" and noted how Hughes characterized himself as the "Negro brother who eats in the kitchen"—but who also proclaims "I too am America!" Couto told his distinguished white audience at the British Academy of Letters that the Negroes of the United States, like those in Cuba, Venezuela, and other nations of the hemisphere, "are America also." Couto acknowledged that racism existed in Brazil, calling race "the exposed nerve of Brazil," but that "this nerve of ours . . . hurts less than . . . in the United States."[29]

The exposed nerve hurt less because *pretos* (blacks) and *pretos retintos* (dark blacks) could, at least theoretically, achieve a degree of acceptance and respect based on their social and economic status, as well as skin color. Both color *and* class determined one's position in the social hierarchy through a phenomenon that Brazilian anthropologist Charles Wagley called "social race." The historian Carl Degler illustrated the principle by which class mitigates race in Brazil with an anecdote: A light-skinned mulatto in Recife, Brazil, had three daughters. "One of the daughters had a white boyfriend who was a factory worker; because he was white the father accepted him as a son-in-law. The second daughter had a boyfriend who was a Negro, studying to be a lawyer. After the wedding of the two couples, the father told the third daughter: 'A worker only if he is white: a Negro, only if he is a doctor.'"[30]

Another Latin American visitor, Luis Sarmiento, secretary of the Colombian Ministry of National Education, proclaimed that Afro-Colombians enjoyed greater freedom than did American Negroes. In his country, he told an audience of white sociologists in North Carolina, the governor of the state of Bolívar was "a pure Negro." But the fact that blacks and mestizos could be elevated to high positions in South American countries, he said, was "the secret and underlying cause of the disregard you [North Americans] have . . . towards the Latin Americans." North Americans look at South America and think " 'Negroes, Mestizos, Mulattoes, Indians . . . so few authentic white men down there.' " Sarmiento hoped to assure his audience that the racial situation in Colombia was "not so bad as you think." In Colombia, only 3 percent of the population was Negro, 2 percent Indian, 10 percent mulatto, and 50 percent mestizo, while 35 percent of all Colombians, he claimed, were "pure white men and women." "The bad mixture," he further explained, was "the Indian and Negro mixture," called *zambos*, although "there were statistically few of them," while the mixing of whites with mestizos, he boasted, gave Colombia "the most beautiful and enduring women in the South when the Negro begins to fade."[31]

During the numerous cultural exchanges between the United States and Latin America during the war, some African American scholars who visited Latin American countries experienced firsthand the ambivalence of light-skinned Latin Americans toward dark-skinned Afro-Latinos. Dr. Ellen Irene Diggs, an African American anthropologist of Afro-Latin culture who received a State Department grant to conduct research on Afro-Brazilians, was refused admittance at the Serrador Hotel, one of Rio de Janeiro's newest and finest hotels. The Brazilian press called it an "isolated incident" of racial prejudice "confined largely to certain artificial social sets and to owners of hotels catering to Americans." The hotel manager called the incident "a mistake." A newspaper in Brazil declared, "Brazil does not have the tormenting problems of the Republic of the North, with its abysmal separation . . . of the colored . . . We live fraternally— the world's chief melting pot . . . We combat racism, admitting to Brazil men of all continents, types, tongues and religions . . . There is no place in Brazil for those who seek to create a Harlem in this hospitable and Christian land traditionally the home of three races." Dr. Diggs, unimpressed, returned to the United States where she informed the press that she was disillusioned by what she had experienced in Brazil.[32] In fact, however, many hotels in major Latin American cities that catered to white tourists and businessmen from the United States often refused admittance to dark-skinned persons, even their own citizens.

During the war a number of large hotels in Mexico City began to discriminate against African Americans. Richard Pilant, a member of NAACP, reported that Mexico City "appears . . . to be losing its wide open attitude toward American Negroes" because white American tourists refused to patronize hotels that served blacks. "I had thought of that city . . . as the perfect place for American Negro organizations to hold conventions and enjoy themselves," Pilant sadly noted, but the director of a leading travel association told him it was no longer possible for American blacks to hold conventions in four of the finest hotels in Mexico City.[33]

What began as a plausible strategy to persuade the federal government to dismantle Jim Crow to more effectively pursue a Good Neighbor policy with Latin American republics with large Afro-descendant populations never got off the ground. The nation with the largest Afro-descendant population, Brazil, received the lion's share of Lend-Lease aid (almost ten times as much as Mexico) as the most important ally of the United States in the western hemisphere and was the only Latin American country to send troops into battle. Discrimination against African Americans in the United States did not appear to jeopardize the growing military and economic relationship with Brazil.[34]

Walter White had been warned that his single-minded emphasis on the mistreatment of African Americans in the United States would not resonate with the majority of Latin American republics, whose principal racial Other was the Indian, not

Afro-Latinos, most of whom were largely ignored and marginalized in countries like Colombia, Brazil, and Mexico. Henry Allen Moe, philanthropist and later president of the John Simon Guggenheim Foundation, reminded White that, like the title of Lesley Byrd Simpson's book *Many Mexicos* (1941), "there are likewise many Latin Americas, each country . . . as distinctive as our own country is distinctive." The racial situation in Latin American countries varied, he told White, "from no color-line to color-lines more rigidly drawn than in the United States."[35] W. G. Warnock, a journalist knowledgeable about race relations in South America, pointed out that White's focus on black-white relations in the western hemisphere to the exclusion of mestizos and Indians would fail to arouse Latin Americans to the cause of American Negroes. "Certainly you cannot hope to interest a pure-blood Indian in the problems resulting from discrimination against the Negro," Warnock explained, "for in most instances, the Indian feels superior to the Negro." Most Latin American nations, with the possible exception of Brazil, "have not been called upon to consider the Negro problem." The NAACP's efforts to demonstrate how Jim Crow in America could imperil the Good Neighbor policy might have proved effective, Warnock noted, if White could convince the American people that "South America is black and never will be friendly with us unless we treat our own Negroes as equals."[36]

White and the NAACP would have had no need to convince most Americans that Latin Americans, regardless of their ancestry, were mostly mixed-race, dark-skinned peoples who often received the same treatment in the United States as that of black Americans. It was precisely this strategy that Mexican American civil rights activists pursued in their attempt to influence the federal government to end discrimination against Mexican-origin people in the United States, regardless of citizenship. The Mexican diaspora had been confined largely to the southwestern region of the United States and hardly approached the global scale or historical significance of the African diaspora in North, South, and Central America, as well as the Caribbean. But Mexico and the United States shared a long and complicated history, as well as a 2,000-mile border. More important, the Mexican government, through its many consuls, had a long-established tradition of defending the rights of resident Mexican nationals in the United States, often including the rights of Mexican Americans. African Americans, on the other hand, could not count on any foreign government to champion their interests.

Mexican American civil rights activists were confined mostly to California and Texas, where the majority of Mexicans resided in the 1940s. In Texas, second and later-generation middle-class Mexican Americans founded the League of United Latin American Citizens (LULAC) in 1929 and the American G.I. Forum in 1948, organizations that sought to end discrimination mainly by insisting on their loyalty and patriotism as American citizens and their Caucasian racial status in the United States. When many middle-class Mexican Americans identified themselves as "Latin Americans" rather than "Mexicans," they did so less in solidarity with other Latin Americans than to avoid the label "Mexican," which in the Southwest was a moniker for racial inferiority. For these Mexican Americans, the identity markers "Latin American" and "Anglo American" suggested a harmonious symmetry between whites of "Latin extraction" and whites of European or Anglo-Saxon ancestry, in contradistinction to Negroes, Chinese, Japanese, Indians, and other nonwhite citizens who had yet to achieve the status of hyphenated Americans, much less their constitutional rights as U.S. citizens.

Texas civil rights advocates, such as LULAC leaders Manuel Gonzales and Alfonso Perales, University of Texas professors George I. Sánchez and Carlos E. Castañeda, and American G.I.

Forum founder Dr. Hector García, all sought to enlist the federal government during the war years, particularly the OCIAA and the Fair Employment Practices Committee (FEPC), in ending discrimination and inequality for Mexican Americans. The federal government initially regarded racial discrimination as a problem affecting mainly African Americans. For that reason Sánchez had frequently called Mexican Americans the "orphans" and "forgotten people" of America. Like Sánchez and other Mexican American advocates, Rockefeller believed that relations between Mexico and the United States could not be separated from the problem of Anglo American prejudice against Mexicans. To learn more about the problems they faced, he dispatched field representatives to Texas and California to investigate discriminatory practices aimed at Mexican Americans.[37]

One of the OCIAA field representatives, Thomas Sutherland, a native Texan, described the Latin American minority in Texas as the "salt of the earth" who were "ignored by the Anglo-American society except at election time." The attitude of most Anglos toward Mexicans, he reported, was "not so much one of fear as of contempt," as expressed by their conviction that Mexicans, or "meskins" as they were often called, "carry long knifes and stab you with them—always in the back."[38] David Saposs, another experienced labor investigator, reported that any federal agency concerned with "rehabilitating the Spanish Americans and Mexicans" must also concern itself with the important task of reeducating Anglos. To take the racist attitude of Southern Anglos toward Mexicans for granted, he wrote, "is to encourage the perpetuation of poverty and discrimination and their increasingly debilitating effects on both Anglos and Mexicans." Saposs opposed a merely informational campaign among Spanish Americans without simultaneously seeking ways to rehabilitate the racial views of Anglos. "No constructive work of rehabilitation can be performed among Spanish-Americans," he wrote, "until the world in which they live accepts them as persons rather than as members of a separate racial category. Anglos must learn that the American way of life does not tolerate the creation of a submerged racial group."[39] Millions of Mexicans, blacks, and Asian Americans knew better, as did Japan and Germany. German propaganda attempted to persuade black and Mexican domestic workers that when Hitler wins, "they will be the masters and own the houses where they work, and that their present employers will work for them."[40]

The Office of Facts and Figures of the Office of War Information, the agency responsible for managing war propaganda, conducted its own study of "Spanish-Americans" in Texas, New Mexico, southern Colorado, Arizona, and southern California. The report noted that Mexican Americans were "educationally and economically submerged, linguistically and culturally isolated" and were subject to intense economic, social, and educational discrimination as well as political exploitation. "As a group," the report noted, "they present perhaps the most striking need of economic rehabilitation and cultural assimilation in the entire United States."[41] The report also noted that there were nearly as many Mexicans in Texas (738,000) as African Americans (900,000). "The attitude of Texans toward race questions is the Southern one," the author observed, "a circumstance profoundly affecting Mexicans, to whom . . . has been transferred the Southern attitude toward Negroes. The result is that discrimination against Mexicans follows much the same pattern as Jim Crowism."[42]

Mexican consular officials from Los Angeles to New York and from Chicago to Houston continued to pressure the State Department to take action to eliminate discrimination against Mexican nationals as well as U.S. citizens of Mexican origin. The Mexican consul in Houston, Adolfo G. Domínguez, informed the Mexican ambassador and the minister of Foreign Affairs that "there is a lack of faith in the great cause of the democracies among even the citizens of the United States of Mexican origin, because the Anglo-Saxon population of the state—including the local authorities . . . take for granted that there is a definite differential place in society for 'whites, Negroes, and Mexicans,' regardless of citizenship."[43] He wanted the foreign minister to ask the War Production Board to establish a "minorities group branch" in Houston to address the problem of discrimination in defense industries. In California, Ernesto Galarza, head of the Office of Labor and Welfare Information of the Pan-American Union, reported in a confidential memo to the Mexican ambassador that even when Mexican nationals were not discriminated against on the basis of race, they soon became "keenly aware of the practice of discrimination against Negroes in certain parts of the United States . . . a type of negative education which . . . is making a deep impression on them."[44]

What made a deep impression on Mexicans in the United States was the arresting ubiquity of the color line that placed whites on one side where they enjoyed the privileges, rights, and opportunities that capitalism and democracy afforded, and on the other side, African Americans, Chinese, Japanese, and more often than not, Mexican Americans, whose race and skin color excluded them from exercising their constitutional rights as citizens. While social distinctions were not unfamiliar to them in Mexico, in their own country Mexicans rarely experienced the harsh reality of color segregation that was sanctioned by law and custom in the United States. Rarely did Anglos distinguish between Mexican Americans and resident Mexican nationals, and often they did not distinguish between Mexican farmworkers and Mexican diplomats, particularly in rural West Texas. When the Mexican senator, Eugenio Prado, and the former mayor of Ciudad Juárez, Teófilo Borunda (at the time a representative in the Mexican House of Deputies), visited Texas on official business, they were refused service in a local café and advised to eat at the "Negro restaurant" across the street. The incident was widely reported in the Mexican press. One Mexico City newspaper editorialized that the congressional representatives of the Mexican people were "rightfully irritated" for having to eat in a restaurant "reserved for the 'Untermensch'" of American society.[45]

Nevertheless, Mexicans in the Southwest had important allies not available to African Americans—the Mexican Foreign Ministry and its numerous Mexican consuls. The foreign minister of Mexico, Ezequiel Padilla, banned Texas in 1943 from receiving Mexican contract workers under the Bracero Program because of the state's history of extreme and intolerable racial discrimination against Mexicans. The ban was announced a month after the Texas State Legislature passed a nonbinding resolution, often called the Equal Accommodations Resolution (or the Caucasian Race Resolution). The resolution stated that since "our neighbors to the South" were cooperating in the effort to "stamp out Nazism and preserve democracy" and to "assist the national policy of hemispherical solidarity," the state of Texas resolved that "all persons of the Caucasian Race . . . are entitled to the full and equal accommodations, advantages, facilities, and privileges of all public places of business or amusement."[46] By framing the problem of discrimination in terms of respecting the rights of all Caucasians, including Mexicans, the resolution avoided the delicate problem of calling for an end to discrimination against black citizens. Clarence Mitchell, associate director of Field Operations for the FEPC and labor secretary of the NAACP from 1946 to 1949, called the resolution "a very unfortunate piece of legislation" that would fail utterly to end discrimination against Latin Americans in Texas.[47] Its sole emphasis on eliminating discrimination for members of the Caucasian race (including Mexicans) was contrary to the goals of the FEPC as well as the NAACP. "Needless to say," he told his FEPC colleague Marjorie Lawson, "we do not regard it as a monumental achievement in the betterment of race relations."[48]

Texas legislators failed to pass an antidiscrimination law for Mexican Americans in 1941, 1943, and again in 1945, mainly because legislators worried that any attempt to enact laws to end discrimination against Mexicans might also strike a blow against Jim Crow laws and customs segregating black Texans. The authors of the bills made it clear that their passage would in no way attenuate strict segregation between whites and African Americans. A section of the 1941 antidiscrimination bill, for example, affirmed that "this Act shall not apply to persons, corporations, or associations owning or operating public places of business or amusement exclusively for the benefit of persons of the Negro Race, and persons of the Caucasian Race may be lawfully excluded from all such places."[49] In less disingenuous terms, African Americans would continue to be "lawfully excluded" from white-only public places.

Repeated attempts to pass an antidiscrimination bill raised questions about the constitutionality of a bill granting rights only to visiting citizens of Latin American countries and U.S. citizens of Mexican descent—but not to African Americans. Robert C. Eckhardt, a field representative for the OCIAA, posed the problem this way: "If a Haitian [or Brazilian] Negro were to seek the protection of the law, the provision clearly includes him . . . On the other hand, if a Mississippi Negro were to seek its protection, he would clearly be excluded."[50] How, Eckhardt wanted to know, could a state law bestow rights on an Afro-Brazilian or Haitian citizen while denying the same rights to a Texas Negro? It likely could not, but by making the attempt anyway legislators and the governor hoped the Mexican government would lift its ban on allowing desperately needed Mexican farmworkers into Texas.

Eckhardt was not the only one concerned about the delicate matter of passing a law to end discrimination against one group but not another. The American consul in Ciudad Juárez, William Blocker, told a meeting of the Mexican consuls at a Conference on Inter-American Relations in Austin in 1943 that Texans needed to be schooled through a program of education and propaganda "to distinguish between other racial problems existing in the state" because, he emphasized, "the Negro problem was delicate and any legislation involving penalties might raise a serious and delicate situation from that angle." The reluctance on the part of the Good Neighbor Commission or the University of Texas Committee on Inter-American Relations to sponsor or support such legislation was due, he explained, "to the fear of raising an issue that might involve other racial problems entirely separate from the Latin-American situation."[51]

For four years Mexican consuls, Mexican civil rights activists, the Mexican press, Mexican senators and deputies, and the foreign minister himself had urged the Texas legislature to pass an antidiscrimination bill as a condition for receiving bracero contract laborers, but Texas legislators worried that passing a law making it a punishable offense to discriminate against Mexicans might presage attempts by African Americans to have a similar law passed to protect them against discrimination. When the antidiscrimination bill came before the legislature in 1945, only Carlos Castañeda among the Mexican American activists opposed its passage. Although he supported the antidiscrimination bills in 1941 and 1943, Castañeda hoped the bill would die a "peaceful death" in committee, as had a similar bill in 1941. But pressure from the Mexican government and Mexican American activists resulted in its being placed on the calendar one final time.[52]

Appointed special assistant to the chairman of the FEPC on the problems of Latin Americans in 1943 and named regional director for the states of Texas, Louisiana, and New Mexico in 1945, Castañeda became deeply acquainted with the stubborn resistance of war industries and unions to hire or promote African Americans. Born in Mexico and raised in Brownsville on the U.S.-Mexico border, Castañeda likely had little contact with or knowledge of African Americans. But after two years of defending the rights of African American as well as Mexican workers in three states, Castañeda could no longer support an antidiscrimination bill that excluded African Americans.[53] When an amendment calling for equal employment opportunities was stricken from the bill, he called the bill "practically worthless."[54] Even more disturbing to Castañeda was an amendment, suggested by the Texas Good Neighbor Commission, that would exclude from the law's protection all Latin American visitors from Cuba, Haiti, Santo Domingo, Puerto Rico, and other countries where Afro-Latinos constituted a large percentage of the population. The final argument that killed the bill, according to Castañeda, was the testimony of a member of the Texas Good Neighbor Commission that many Mexicans lived with or were married to blacks and that under the terms of the bill these Mexicans would also have to be accorded equal rights with whites. Although Mexicans were officially white, rarely were any charged with violating the state's antimiscegenation law for marrying African Americans.[55]

Many progressive Texans nevertheless supported the bill because they hoped it would eventually end Jim Crow practices for African Americans as well as Mexicans. Shortly after the defeat of the bill in May 1945, an Anglo private in the U.S. Army and graduate of the University of Texas, PFC Robert Jones, wrote to Governor Stevenson that he attended high school with many Mexicans, some of whom "obviously had traces of Negro ancestry," and that at the University of Texas he saw "boys and girls with kinky hair and Negroid features from Cuba, Puerto Rico, Brazil, Panama, Nicaragua, Venezuela and other countries." "I am familiar," he told the governor, "with what you didn't do for the Mexicans with your Good Neighbor Commission. I know from almost a whole lifetime in contact with Mexicans that they deserve more. I think the same can be said for the Negro."[56]

The Texas governor did not share the expansive civil rights perspective of this white soldier and alumnus of the University of Texas. Like all governors in the South at the time, Governor Stevenson was committed to enforcing segregation of African Americans, but his view of Mexicans was less harsh, even if his motivation for ending discrimination against them had as much to do with placating Texas farmers, who had become addicted to cheap Mexican labor, as with establishing good relations with the government of Mexico in time of war. When Thomas Sutherland, a field representative for the OCIAA, asked Stevenson to create a good neighbor commission, the governor, according to Sutherland, "puffed on his pipe, agreed on the necessity of some such gesture, and declared, 'Meskins is pretty good folks. It if was niggers, it'd be different.'"[57]

LULAC leader Alfonso Perales also believed that Mexicans ought to be entitled to rights and privileges routinely denied to African Americans. He proposed that Anglo Americans conduct a "vigorous campaign" in Texas "to end all racial prejudices in so far as members of the Caucasian race are concerned."[58] The Mexican foreign minister and Mexican consuls continued to insist that Texas and California end all discrimination against Mexicans with little concern for discrimination against African Americans or Asian Americans. Mexico's postrevolutionary nationalist embrace of the mestizo character of its people—la raza cósmica—excluded its own citizens of African or Asian origin.

As historian Gary Gerstle correctly notes, "If the leaders of post-revolutionary Mexico had found a way to celebrate the brown character of their country's peoplehood, they remained uncomfortable with the black and yellow hues in the Mexican population."[59]

Examples abound in Mexican history of laws and circulars designed to prevent the immigration or settlement of Africans in Mexico. In 1833 the Mexican consul Franciso Pizarro Martínez refused to grant immigration rights to free-blacks from Texas because in his view " 'people of color' were immoral and lazy."[60] In the 1920s, the Mexican ministry of the interior (gobernación) issued a circular prohibiting African Americans in the United States from crossing the international border for even a brief visit to Mexico: "The measure prohibiting persons of the black race from immigrating to Mexico applies to the entire border in such a way that no American citizen of this race can spend even a few hours of recreation in any of the Mexican border towns." The Mexican consul in San Antonio, perhaps in response to pressure from the NAACP, recommended to the foreign minister that citizens of la raza negra, the black race, be allowed to visit Mexico within a zone of thirteen miles along the border for a period of three days. The Foreign Ministry relented and agreed to allow black Americans to visit Mexican border cities, but reduced the time of their cross-border visits from the proposed three days to fourteen hours and stressed that they be allowed only "occasional visits."[61]

In the summer of 1943, three white female college students from the United States objected to sitting in the same classroom with five African American female students enrolled in summer classes in sociology at the National Autonomous University of Mexico in Mexico City. Mexican students and organizations protested the attempted segregation of the black female students, and the rector of the university conducted an investigation. He reported that the source of the problem was a U.S. tourist agency whose policy was to separate white and black students on excursions to foreign countries. When a Mexico City newspaper reported the incident in an article headlined, "Incredible: Mexico City Treats [American] Blacks Disgracefully," the rector decided to honor the African American students at an official event sponsored by the university. The Mexican sociology professor apparently sided with the white female students and refused to teach the class. One girl enrolled in the class believed that the Mexican professor had spent time as a visiting professor at the University of Texas where he likely "had been . . . contaminated."[62]

Discrimination was particularly acute along the border where the War Department had a long history of stationing African American soldiers to protect citizens against cross-border Indian raids as well as violence spilling over from the Mexican Revolution, such as Francisco "Pancho" Villa's 1916 attack on Columbus, New Mexico. The mayor of Ciudad Juárez, Antonio M. Bermudez, opposed the U.S. Army decision to increase the number of black soldiers stationed at Fort Bliss in El Paso from 4,000 to 10,000. He worried that an increase would lead to "serious trouble" in Ciudad Juárez between black soldiers and Mexican residents, which would adversely affect the tourist trade. He also warned that the police force "could not cope with such a large number of negro soldiers" on leave in the city and that stationing black soldiers so close to the border "could develop into a race riot, and other disturbances of a serious nature."[63] U.S. Ambassador George Messersmith agreed to recommend their withdrawal but was put off by the mayor's hypocrisy. "Although the Mexican people object very strongly to . . . any discrimination of any kind against themselves," he told Secretary of State Cordell Hull, they nevertheless ". . . are inclined to discriminate against Negroes."[64]

At Fort Huachuca in Arizona where 17,000 African American soldiers were stationed, hundreds visited the border town of Nogales on weekend passes and crossed the border into its twin-city, also named Nogales, in Sonora, Mexico. Restaurants on both sides of the border refused to serve black soldiers, as did restaurants and dance halls in Sonora that catered to white American tourists and the "better class of Mexicans." Some restaurants in Sonora also refused to serve dark-skinned Mexicans fearing the loss of trade from white Americans. Black soldiers were welcome in the cantinas (bars) and the "red-light" district, however, where they represented its principal source of income. The American consul general in Nogales suggested that the War Department replace the black soldiers at Fort Huachuca with white troops or deny them weekend passes.[65]

The Arizona governor, Sidney Osborn, had a better idea. He suggested that Fort Huachuca's 17,000 black soldiers be exempted from their military training in order to pick cotton. Arizona was the only state that grew large quantities of long-staple cotton, a type of cotton used for weaving parachutes, which the governor claimed was "vitally necessary in the war effort." The idea of putting black soldiers in the cotton fields where presumably they could be more useful prompted an angry response from Walter White: "It is characteristic of uninformed white people," he told Osborn, "to think that the mentality of the majority of Negroes is such that prior to enlistment in the Army they could do nothing but pick cotton." White was further offended that Osborn conspicuously neglected to include in his request that white soldiers stationed in Arizona be assigned as cotton pickers. "You will find at Huachuca Negro officers and soldiers who were doctors, dentists, artisans and skilled mechanics, many of them from the North, who never saw a cotton boll until they went South," adding that Osborn would probably find "among white troops in Arizona those who have done nothing but raise and pick cotton all their lives." White was gratified when the War Department denied Governor Osborn's request for Negro-soldier cotton pickers.[66]

In the same year Anglo Texans protested the War Department's decision to station 800 black soldiers in Eagle Pass on the U.S.-Mexico border for field operations and training. The NAACP urged the War Department "to resist any attempt on the part of prejudiced Texans to try to run the War Department." The War Department agreed: "In this and many other cases[,] military considerations outweigh the convenience either of the civilian population or the soldiers who will be immediately affected." Anglos pointed out that there was only one Negro family in Eagle Pass, which had no school for educating Negro children nor any cafés, theaters, or other public places that could serve Negro soldiers and that across the border in Piedras Negras, they would encounter Mexican hostility as they had in other border towns and cities.[67]

Mexicans in the northern border states of Chihuahua and Sonora tended to be hostile not only to African Americans but also the Chinese. While the United States enacted a law in 1882 to prohibit immigration from China and interned its own citizens of Japanese descent in World War II, the Mexican government launched a campaign in the 1930s to deport the Chinese, many of them Mexican citizens, reducing their numbers from 40,000 to 5,000 by 1940.[68] Congressional Deputy Bernabé A. Soto, with the support of the Comité Anti-Chino, introduced a bill in the Sonoran legislature to cancel a favored-nation trade agreement (Amistad Comercio) between China and Mexico because *la raza amarilla*, the yellow race, according to Marcelo Tadeo Pérez, president of the Liga Nacional Anti-China y Anti-Judía (National Anti-Chinese and Anti-Jewish League) was destroying "our race, our trade, and our homes."[69] And while Mexico's indigenous population was at the center of the nationalist ideology of mestizaje, in actuality they occupied the lowest social and economic level in society as a result of centuries of exclusion and discrimination. In a rare admission, a Mexican Army officer in World War II said he was disgusted by the hypocrisy of the Mexican press in blaming American racism for the zoot suit riots in Los Angeles while completely ignoring "discrimination against ten million Indians in Mexico."[70] Given Mexico's history of paying homage to mestizaje while fetishizing white skin and *ojos claros* (light eyes), it is not surprising that Mexican consuls, the foreign minister, and the Mexican press demanded that Mexicans in Texas be given the same rights as whites.

Mexico was not the only Latin American country that did not welcome black soldiers during World War II. When the U.S. Navy assigned 250 African American enlisted personnel to the Panama Canal Zone, the U.S. ambassador to Panama urged the secretary of state to cancel the assignment because of the risk of protest from the Panamanian government, which denied entry to "persons of the colored race."[71] In 1941 the Panamanian president, Arnulfo Arias, an admirer of Hitler and Mussolini while ambassador to Italy in the 1930s, amended the constitution to deny entry of all immigrants of the "black race whose native language is not Spanish, of the yellow race, and the races originating in India, Asia Minor, and North Africa." Article 23 of the new constitution also revoked the citizenship, retroactively, of children of Panamanians whose parents were of African or Asian descent.[72]

President Arias spoke of the necessity of "improving the biological conditions" of Panamanians and was especially critical of the U.S. policy of having imported thousands of "colored aliens" from the West Indies and Asia to construct the Panama Canal. The foreign minister defended Article 23, declaring that Panamanians were "anxious to guard against the danger that

Panama, situated at the crossroads of the world, should degenerate from a Spanish-speaking, white nation into . . . a Babel of tongues, and an utterly bastardized race."[73] The NAACP asked the State Department to issue a formal protest over Panama's discriminatory immigration policy but the State Department refused on the ground that the United States could not interfere in the laws of another country, especially when the United States also placed racial restrictions on the entry of nationals from other countries. Panama was not the only country to prohibit or restrict the immigration of Afro-descendants: Uruguay, Paraguay, Honduras, and Costa Rica prohibited the immigration of persons of African origin, while Venezuela and the Dominican Republic placed restrictions on their numbers.[74]

Walter White and the NAACP had begun to learn that Latin American countries were not always what they seemed or claimed to be with respect to racial harmony and equality. White was astonished to learn that immigration authorities in Venezuela had issued instructions to all ship captains arriving in Venezuelan ports that "Any member of the crew belonging to a belligerent nation; Any person of the Negro race; [and] Any person of the Yellow race (Chinaman)" was not permitted ashore in any Venezuelan port. Robert Haskins, an African American member of the crew who was denied shore leave, said that hundreds of American Negroes sailing aboard merchant ships deeply resented the racist and humiliating policy of the Venezuelan government and hoped the NAACP would take the necessary steps to have "this degrading and humiliating order revoked."[75]

White turned the matter over to Thurgood Marshall, who sent a copy of the order to Secretary of State Cordell Hull and to FDR as evidence of the Venezuelan government's "clear discrimination against Americans of both the Negro and Oriental races." Marshall told Secretary Hull that the State Department's failure to take firm action against Mexico and Panama for discrimination against Negro citizens of the United States had given rise to a spread of discrimination in Venezuela and other countries. Marshall referred to the practice of many Mexican consuls of denying tourist visas to African Americans and opposing the presence of black soldiers near the border. He further reminded Hull that the United States had protested discrimination "against other races by foreign countries in Europe even to the extent of protesting discrimination against people who are not citizens of the United States." Marshall of course was alluding to European Jews under Nazi persecution. He concluded: "It is difficult to understand how unity is to be built up in this hemisphere if other nations are permitted to discriminate against American citizens because of their race or color." The same of course could be said for the treatment of dark-skinned Latin Americans in the United States.[76]

If Latin American republics were not the Mecca of racial democracy the NAACP had originally believed them to be, many African Americans nevertheless viewed Mexico as a country that offered them far more opportunities than the United States and certainly more than they could hope for in the U.S. South. Afro-Latinos in Mexico and other Latin American republics were not denied fundamental rights, such as the right to vote, to marry whomever they wished, to choose to live wherever they could afford, to travel with whites on public transportation, and to send their children to nonsegregated schools—and they were not subject to the daily threat of violence and lynching.[77] Mexico had served as a beacon of hope for many African Americans since before the Civil War when slaves from Texas escaped to freedom in Mexico. During the Mexican Revolution, the U.S. government, fearing that U.S. citizens of Mexican descent could not be relied on to defend American interests, stationed African American soldiers on the border where they often enjoyed close relations with Mexicans and had come to admire the courage

Roy Wilkins, Walter White, Thurgood Marshall (between 1940 and 1950). Library of Congress, Prints and Photographs Division, Visual Materials from the NAACP Records, LC-USZ62-84466.

and daring of Mexican revolutionary leader Pancho Villa. Some married Mexican women in open violation of the state's miscegenation law, which held that Mexicans were white. As the population of African Americans increased in El Paso in the mid-1920s, they formed the El Paso branch of the NAACP and organized the first of three U.S. Supreme Court challenges to the "white primary" in Texas.[78]

Black artists Richard Wright and Langston Hughes traveled extensively in Mexico and said the only time they experienced racism was when they encountered white American tourists. Hughes often visited his father, who owned a ranch in Toluca, near Mexico City. He traveled in Jim Crow cars from Chicago to the border, but once in Mexico, he declared, "nothing is barred from me. I am among my own people for . . . Mexico is a brown man's country."[79] Another well-known African American, heavyweight-boxing champion Jack Johnson, a personal friend of President Carranza, was refused service in a Mexico City café owned by Walter Sanborn, a white American businessman. Hours later Johnson returned with three or four of Carranza's generals, who demanded, with pistols drawn, that Sanborn apologize to Johnson, shake his hand, and serve his family. Mexico was not, the commanding general informed Sanborn, a "white man's country."[80]

Like most Latin American countries, Mexico continued to see itself as morally superior to the United States. A year after the war, the Mexican press carried the story of the lynching of two African American couples in Monroe, Georgia, alongside the news of African American opera singer Ellabelle Davis, who sang the part of Aïda, Verdi's Ethiopian princess, in Mexico City's Palacio de Bellas Artes. It was an operatic part that in the United States, the journalist noted, continued to be played by white women "smeared . . . with cocoa-colored grease paint." The journalist applauded her talent and the ovations she received, calling her success in Mexico a "triumph . . . over the intransigence of racism in North America" that forced its best black artists to perform in other countries.[81] During the war the Embassy of Peru in Mexico City distributed an article to other American countries, including the United States, in which the author, Alfonso Junco, declared that "never is race the motive for hatred nor exclusiveness" in Latin America and asked, "Does anyone see the possibility of a Negro or Indian being the President of the United States?"[82]

With the exception of border cities, African Americans did enjoy far greater liberty in Mexico—or virtually any other Latin American republic—than anywhere in the United States, particularly the South. Sadly, however, America's long history of oppression of African Americans rarely aroused diplomatic opposition or protest from Brazil, Mexico, or any other Latin American country. Brazil, with the largest Afro-Latino population, became America's most valued military ally and trade partner. The Mexican foreign minister, Ezequiel Padilla, mollified anti-American sentiment in Mexico by banning bracero workers to Texas but otherwise was an outspoken proponent of closer economic and cultural ties to the United States and was virtually silent on the issue of equality for African Americans. The reluctance of Mexico and other Latin American governments to criticize the United States for its violation of the civil and human rights of African Americans and other nonwhite citizens stems in part from the Latin American doctrine of noninterference in the affairs of neighbor states, a doctrine created largely in response to the persistent intervention of the United States in the domestic affairs of its Latin American neighbors. The long-standing presence of American corporate interests in Latin America and Latin American dependency on American aid also served to constrain condemnation of human rights abuses in the United States.[83]

The efforts of Mexican Americans and African Americans to enlist the federal government in ending racial discrimination for the sake of hemispheric solidarity in time of war also yielded few returns. The War Department, the State Department, the Office of the Coordinator of Inter-American Affairs, and other federal agencies, including the FEPC, were careful not to disturb the time-honored tradition of Jim Crow for fear of angering white conservative Southern congressmen and governors who felt it their sacred duty to safeguard the nation from the threat of social equality. Even FDR's executive order to create the FEPC was the direct result of A. Philip Randolph's threat to lead a march of 100,000 blacks on Washington rather than any concern for America's moral standing in the world, much less in the western hemisphere. The federal government still had not committed itself to the cause of civil rights.

Many Latin American countries still maintain that racism does not exist south of the Río Grande and that north of it white Americans only begrudgingly extend constitutional rights to blacks, Latinos, and Asians. While the United States has by no means laid to rest the shameful legacy of state-sanctioned racial discrimination, nothing confounded Mexicans in Mexico more than the possibility, sixty years later, that the United States might elect its first black president. I spent eight months in Mexico City in 2008 and spoke with many Mexicans, the majority of whom thought it impossible for an African American to be elected president on account of pervasive and intractable racism in the United States. Many were surprised when Senator Obama won the Democratic nomination. Could a nation that had long oppressed its black citizens possibly elect a black man to become the president of the United States? It would be perhaps no less improbable, I suggested, than Mexicans electing as their own president *un mexicano negro*.[84]

2

The Politics of Race in the Fight for Fair Employment Practices

Nothing embittered African Americans more during the war years than the blatant hypocrisy of fighting and dying abroad for the very freedoms denied them at home. A black cafeteria worker in Kansas, James G. Thompson, suggested in a letter to the *Pittsburg Courier* that black Americans adopt a "Double V" sign for victory over Nazism abroad and racism at home. Double Victory quickly became a popular slogan among African Americans in what W. E. B. Du Bois aptly called the "War for Racial Equality."[1] Yet many African Americans were more optimistic about defeating Hitler than Jim Crow, or as the Afro-Trinidadian intellectual C. L. R. James succinctly put it, "the democracy I want to fight for, Hitler is not depriving me of."[2] Jim Crow represented not only a grave injustice and deep humiliation to all black Americans but also an insurmountable barrier to economic advancement. Despite increased employment opportunities and manpower shortages, fewer blacks worked in manufacturing jobs in 1940 than in 1910.[3] All across America white employers in defense industries refused to hire black workers except as menial laborers, claiming that white workers would strike if forced to accept blacks as their equals on the job. In June 1943, 25,000 white workers struck Packard Motors in Detroit to protest the upgrading of three black workers, halting over 90 percent of the plant's production of bomber engines. One of the striking workers expressed the sentiments of many white workers across the nation when he declared, "I'd rather see Hitler and Hirohito win than work next to a nigger."[4]

During the war years, resident German nationals often enjoyed opportunities denied to black Americans. When a patriotic white woman fired her German-born gardener, he was hired the following day at a local airplane plant that refused to hire African Americans.[5] Even German prisoners of war received better treatment in the United States than black soldiers in uniform. Capt. Charles Thomas, an African American soldier from Detroit stationed in Texas, remembered being unable to eat in an off-base restaurant where white soldiers and German POWs shared an easy camaraderie, laughing and making friends with each other and the waitresses. "Nothing infuriated me as much," Thomas wrote, "as seeing those German prisoners of war receiving the warm hospitality of Texas" when Military Police would have "busted my skull, a citizen-soldier of the United States, . . . had [I] tried to enter that dining room."[6] Yet many soldiers risked violence by refusing to move to the back of the bus, often meeting violence with violence rather than submit to second-class citizenship. Axis propagandists daily carried the news of America's racial violence all over the world, "proving to the colored allies," a black worker wrote the secretary of state, "that America, the land of the free, in reality is an armed camp in which Negro is pitted against white and white against Negro."[7]

African Americans were not the only group denied full citizenship rights. Many Jews, Jehovah Witnesses, and Catholics were denied employment in defense industries because of their creed, just as were Italian and German Americans because of their national origin.[8] Race and national origin often combined to keep many Mexican, Chinese, and Japanese workers from being hired. When the undersecretary of the War Department, Robert P. Patterson, received complaints from the Mexican government that defense industries refused to hire "aliens" from Mexico and other Latin American countries allied with the United States, he confessed that he "had never before appreciated the extent to which such discrimination existed in the case of persons coming from the other Americas."[9]

Minority workers suffered from inadequate work, low wages, unacceptable working conditions, and segregated accommodations on the job. But African American workers were by far the nation's most visible minority group with a long history of struggle against the worst abuses of Jim Crow, including mob violence, vigilantism, and lynching. They were also the most organized and aggressive minority group in the struggle for equality. When labor leader A. Philip Randolph threatened to lead a march on Washington of thousands of African American workers in the summer of 1941 to protest racial discrimination in the military and war industries, President Roosevelt issued Executive Order 8802, establishing the President's Committee on Fair Employment Practice (FEPC) to address employment discrimination on the basis of race, creed, color, or national origin.[10] In a total war involving the mobilization of women as well as men, workers as well as soldiers, the labor needs of the nation became a paramount concern of various federal agencies, including the War Manpower Commission and the FEPC. In one of its first reports, the FEPC declared: "The negro is a very important part of the Nation's manpower, whether that duty is to grip a rifle or a welding tool or a plough handle."[11]

To ensure the most efficient use of manpower during the war, the FEPC held hearings across the nation to investigate charges of discrimination in Gulf shipyards and refineries, West Coast aircraft and shipbuilding industries, railroads and their brotherhoods, Midwestern defense contractors, Southwest mining companies, the International Brotherhood of Boilermakers, and public transportation companies and their unions, including those in the nation's capital. Union leaders and the rank and file of many locals of the American Federation of Labor (AFL) and Congress of Industrial Organizations (CIO) either denied membership to blacks or opposed training them for skilled positions on the production lines.[12] Complaints from African American workers—routinely denied skilled jobs, training, and membership in all-white unions—poured into the offices of the FEPC and NAACP.[13] In addition to litigation to end school segregation and residential covenants that forbade white homeowners from selling to blacks, the NAACP filed numerous suits against unions that denied membership to African American workers as well as shipyards and railroad and transit companies that limited the kinds of jobs blacks could hold. With the support of the NAACP, the Urban League, locally based church and civic groups, labor leaders like A. Philip Randolph, and civil rights litigators like Thurgood Marshall, African American men and women succeeded in bringing to national consciousness the economic, political, and moral consequences of discrimination.

Mexican Americans, on the other hand, had a long history of organizing in the Southwest and the upper Midwest as industrial and agricultural workers, middle-class professionals, and immigrants, but never as a single, cohesive ethnic group that prevailed over regional and class differences, much less citizenship status. Stark differences separated Mexican Americans from Mexican immigrants, even as language, culture, and ancestral history bound them together. In New Mexico, for example, many Mexicans claimed to be of "pure" Spanish ancestry to distinguish themselves from Mexican immigrants and assert their status as American citizens of European descent.[14] Mexican immigrants, however, defined themselves in nationalistic rather than ethnic terms, and more broadly as transnational workers with ties to both Mexico and the United States. In short,

Mexicans lacked the national visibility of African Americans, whose organizations, such as the NAACP and Urban League, had been advocating for them on a national scale since the early twentieth century.

FEPC officials were the first to admit that they knew next to nothing about the Mexican population of the Southwest (or women workers of any race). While knowledgeable government officials, like Nelson Rockefeller, followed the practice of referring to Mexican Americans as Latin Americans or Americans of Mexican origin, Lawrence Cramer, executive secretary of the FEPC, often referred to them as "Mexicans of American citizenry," which had about as much currency as calling black Americans "Africans of American citizenry."[15] Ernesto Galarza, chief of the Division of Labor and Social Information of the Pan American Union, explained that the importance of Mexican workers to the economy of the Southwest was "so obvious that the establishment of fair and just practices in employment for this large national minority . . . [was] an important part of the national defense program."[16] Preliminary FEPC investigations revealed that oil-refining and shipbuilding industries in Texas and copper-mining in New Mexico and Arizona, obviously key components of the war industry, were the worst offenders of Executive Order 8802. Mexican immigrant workers were often reluctant to lodge complaints with the authorities because many entered the United States unlawfully and were afraid of losing their jobs if they complained. When they did complain, it was often to Mexican consular officials rather than city, state, and federal agencies.[17] Many hoped to return to Mexico and were loath to relinquish their Mexican citizenship. In their segregated neighborhoods in cities like Los Angeles and San Antonio, they sought to re-create the patriotic and nostalgic sentiment of México Lindo, or beautiful Mexico. The Office of War Information observed that for alienated young Mexicans, sometimes called *pachucos* and *pachucas*, "The American Dream does not enter their fantasies any more than the American way of life enters their reality."[18]

The power of African Americans to dominate the agenda of the FEPC was made evident to Mexicans in the first public hearings held in Los Angeles in 1941 to investigate discriminatory hiring practices in the aircraft and shipbuilding industries. Despite the fact that Mexicans outnumbered blacks in Los Angeles County five to one, the hearings centered almost exclusively on the grievances of black workers.[19] Two Mexican American representatives, Manuel Ruiz and Dr. Victor Egas, were asked to give statements. Neither Ruiz nor Egas was given sufficient time before the hearings to investigate individual cases of discrimination, which is probably why the committee allotted them a total of six minutes over a period of two days of testimony. More crucially, however, neither of them had ties to Mexican workers or the problems they faced. Ruiz was an attorney who cofounded the Coordinating Council of Latin American Youth. He and Egas also cofounded Cultura Panamericana, a group whose main goal was to promote cultural exchange with Latin American countries. Ruiz noted that although over 250,000 Mexicans constituted the single largest minority group in Los Angeles, they had not established an organized presence, unlike African Americans and Japanese Americans. Egas's and Ruiz's informative but somewhat diffuse testimony on the Mexican workers left some committee members with the impression that Mexicans did not face the same intensity of discrimination as black workers.[20]

Bert Corona, a well-known Mexican labor activist and member of Local 26 of the International Longshoremen and Warehousemen's Union, was also called before the committee. The committee's field investigator, Eugene Davidson, asked Corona only about relations between black and white workers in the union to prove his point that blacks and whites could work together. Not once did he ask about the problems faced by Mexican or Latin American workers, and Corona limited his responses to explaining the union's openness to membership regardless of race.[21] While the longshoremen's union admitted blacks to segregated locals, Mexicans, regardless of citizenship, were sometimes denied membership or faced discrimination within the union. In a letter to President Roosevelt, California resident Gregorio Narvaez complained, "They even have negroes . . . and . . . Italians" in the Longshoremen's Union, but "they don't want us [Mexicans] to join their union."[22]

It is not clear why Dr. Ernesto Galarza, an economist and labor historian with a deep understanding of Mexican agricultural and industrial workers, was not asked to testify.[23] Even more surprising was the failure of the FEPC to invite Los Angeles labor activist Josefina Fierro de Bright, general secretary of El Congreso Nacional de Pueblos de Habla Española (National Congress of Spanish-Speaking People), to testify at the hearing. Fierro de Bright, well known for her strong record of defending worker rights in agriculture as well as industry, had written numerous letters to Nelson Rockefeller, the Coordinator of Inter-American Affairs (OCIAA), Vice President Henry Wallace, and Mexican President Manuel Ávila Camacho to acquaint them with the hardships Mexican workers faced because of discriminatory employment practices.[24] Labor organizer and cofounder of El Congreso, Luisa Moreno, criticized Mexican leaders in Los Angeles for their reluctance to advance the cause of the Mexican worker. These middle-class leaders, Moreno speculated, were concerned that Mexicans might develop a "minority complex" similar to that of African Americans if they complained too much.[25] The activist, author, and director of the Division of Immigration and Housing for the state of California, Carey McWilliams, offered another explanation. Liberal-minded Anglo field agents investigating discrimination in the Southwest, he surmised, were "actually afraid of Mexican-Americans" and "insisted on working with the least representative elements in the various Spanish-speaking communities."[26]

Vicente Peralta, the Mexican consul in Los Angeles and the person most responsible for the welfare of Mexican nationals (and often Mexican Americans), did not help the situation when he announced a few months after the zoot suit riots that "the last vestiges" of racism against Mexicans had been "wiped out in Los Angeles." Peralta's successor, Manuel Aguilar, told the FEPC that "the Mexican employment situation had reached the point where a few Mexicans were discriminated against in their attempts to secure employment." Peralta's and Aquilar's cheerful pronouncements stood in stark contrast to the aggressive advocacy of Mexican consuls in San Antonio, Austin, and Houston, whose efforts to document employment discrimination and foment support for antidiscrimination bills resulted in their being recalled by the Mexican foreign minister. Aguilar and Peralta believed, like many high-ranking officials in the State Department and the Mexican Foreign Ministry, that publicizing discrimination against Mexican workers might awaken anti-U.S. sentiments in Mexico, which were never far beneath the surface. The Los Angeles representative of the OCIAA, Maurice Hazan, blamed Peralta's public pronouncement for making it more difficult for Mexican workers to come forward with complaints, while an FEPC official urged the Mexican ambassador to have Peralta's statement "retracted or to determine whether or not he was misquoted."[27]

The hearings left the Mexican community of Los Angeles with the impression that the FEPC had been created to address employment discrimination against African Americans but not Mexicans. Indeed the Los Angeles office of the FEPC handled more complaints from the NAACP and various Jewish groups than it did from El Congreso, LULAC, and other Mexican and Mexican American organizations, despite having publicized the Los Angeles investigations in the Spanish-language newspaper *La Opinion* and the bilingual newspaper the *Aristo News*.[28] Manuel Gonzales, a Texas attorney and the executive secretary of the League of United Latin American Citizens, regretted that the FEPC exerted a great effort "to create jobs for the colored people" but not for Latin Americans, especially in Texas.[29] As a result of the lopsided attention given to black workers in the Los Angeles hearing, the FEPC, under pressure from Mexican American civil rights activists and labor leaders, promptly dispatched field investigators to California, Arizona, New Mexico, and Texas.[30]

Sen. Dennis Chávez of New Mexico (the first Latino ever elected to the U.S. Senate) and the multiracial Union of Mine, Mill, and Smelter Workers urged the FEPC to hold hearings in El Paso to air grievances of Mexican workers in the mining industry. About 40 to 50 percent of all workers employed in the mines, mills, and smelters in New Mexico, Arizona, and southwest Texas were Mexicans, although mainly in departments in which unskilled or semiskilled labor was required. A large number of Native Americans (Apache, Navajo, Hopi) worked in unskilled positions, while African Americans constituted less than 1 percent, mainly because of the low population of blacks in New Mexico and Arizona.[31] Mexican workers complained that mining companies paid higher wages to Anglo workers for the same work and with the same level of experience and skills. Trinidad Garcia, an employee of American Smelting and Refining Company in El Paso, complained to the FEPC that "not one Anglo is employed at the common labor rate in the entire plant," and that Mexicans, despite many years of seniority and experience, were rarely upgraded to skilled or semiskilled jobs because of their "dark skin."[32] Some companies refused to hire any Mexicans for skilled jobs, whether U.S. citizens or not. When one Mexican American explained to a mining foreman that he was born in the United States, the foreman replied, "I don't care if you were born in China, you're still a Mexican."[33] Another Mexican American, Gilbert Lujan, gave his race as "French Italian" in order to be hired by the Phelps Dodge Copper Corporation as a relatively high-paid furnace helper and slag brakeman, but the foreman demoted him to a common laborer after it was discovered that he was of Mexican ancestry.[34]

Another cause of tension and conflict among the various groups of mine workers was the strong rivalry between the CIO and the AFL. In their efforts to secure larger membership and obtain control as the bargaining agency in the mining region, these rival unions appealed to different classes and races of workers. In general, the CIO sought to enlist Mexicans and Indians, claiming that membership in its ranks would result in wage increases and job upgrades. The AFL appealed mainly to the Anglo newcomers' prejudice against Mexicans and Indians by promising that membership in its ranks would keep them from having to compete with nonwhites and "alien" Mexicans. In Silver City, New Mexico, for example, Anglos from Texas and Oklahoma positively refused to work with Indians, Negroes, or Latin Americans, while Anglos native to New Mexico objected mainly to Negroes and Indians. Carlos Castañeda, an FEPC regional administrator, noted that "violent campaigns for membership in the two rival organizations have intensified the feeling between Anglos and Latin-Americans, and has tended to polarize prejudice."[35]

The State Department opposed the El Paso hearings from the start. It repeatedly warned that public hearings on discrimination against Mexican workers would give rise to racial agitation and embarrass the Mexican government.[36] William Blocker, U.S. consul general in Ciudad Juárez, argued that the hearings would be used in Mexico as a "weapon to arouse anti-Americanism" and characterized the FEPC's insistence on public hearings as "an attempt to willfully and deliberately kick a sleeping dog who should . . . be permitted to slumber in peace."[37] Texas civil rights activist George Sánchez worried that "subversive elements" were responsible for "fomenting . . . acts of discrimination and stirring up the 'Mexicans' to acts of resistance and retaliation."[38] George Messersmith, the U.S. ambassador to Mexico, claimed that Mexican Foreign Minister Ezequiel Padilla and Undersecretary of Foreign Affairs Jaime Torres Bodet unequivocally opposed public hearings because they could be used in Mexico "as a means of attack against the [Mexican] Government in its program of collaboration in the political, economic and military field with the United States."[39]

The Mexican government, however, disputed Messersmith's claim. Mexican ambassador Francisco Castillo Nájera informed FEPC chairman Malcolm Ross that the Mexican government would indeed welcome the holding of a public hearing, and that Secretary of Foreign Affairs Ezequiel Padilla "not only never has opposed the holding of the public hearings in question but, on the contrary, highly welcomes all steps taken . . . toward the elimination of unjust practices affecting Mexican workers . . . [and] hopes that similar means shall be found to put an end to discriminating practices suffered by Mexican workers in the oil section of Houston, Texas."[40]

The El Paso hearings might have complicated the Good Neighbor policy with Mexico and caused domestic political problems for the Mexican government, but the FEPC aggravated the situation locally when it assigned an African American, James Fleming, to head its team of investigators to the El Paso area. FEPC chairman Lawrence Cramer hired Fleming to conduct interviews with Mexicans in advance of the hearing because he thought Fleming might be in a better position than a white or

Latino investigator to mediate between black workers, white-only union locals, and management. Fleming held a degree from the University of Wisconsin and, according to an OCIAA labor investigator, was a "very level-headed individual." But in a strictly confidential memo to Secretary of State Cordell Hull, Blocker expressed his astonishment that Cramer would assign an African American to head its team of investigators. "This is still Texas," Blocker fulminated, "and while [Anglo] Texans have come a long way since 1865," they had not come nearly far enough to accept being questioned by a Negro investigator. Mexicans would also resent the presence of a Negro investigator, he claimed, because it was "contrary to their way of thinking" and gave the impression that a federal agency regarded Mexicans "on an equality with the negroes." He explained that Mexicans held views of the Negro not unlike those of Anglos in the United States and reminded the secretary that "México itself prohibits, under its immigration laws, the migration into Mexico of persons of negro blood."[41] To avoid the possibility of offending the Mexican government, the FEPC immediately replaced Fleming with a white investigator. The committee's frequent concern for the sentiments of reactionary Southern whites and the sensitivities of the Mexican government served to erode its credibility among African American, Mexican, and other minority workers.

Despite State Department objections, the FEPC scheduled and publicly announced the hearings. In a last-ditch effort to convince the State Department of the importance of holding the hearings, Cramer wrote President Roosevelt that "our enemies can assert . . . that the hearing was canceled because so much that was unsavory was discovered in the course of preliminary investigation that our Government found it necessary to suppress the evidence."[42] What concerned Roosevelt most, however, was not the potential embarrassment to his Good Neighbor policy, but the political fallout the hearings would cause on both sides of the border in connection with delicate negotiations then underway with the Mexican government. For months the United States and Mexico had been negotiating a wartime emergency measure to import temporary Mexican contract laborers, or braceros, to work in agriculture and the railroads to offset the loss of U.S. workers to the armed services and defense industries.[43] Holding the hearings would have made it difficult, if not impossible, for the Mexican government to sign a temporary labor agreement with the United States—popularly called the Bracero Program—since the Mexican people would (and did) accuse Mexican President Manuel Ávila Camacho of ignoring the mistreatment of Mexican citizens throughout the Southwest. The Mexican government faced sustained opposition to the agreement from its own labor unions, congressional representatives, governors, chambers of commerce, and farm owners, who feared that a labor exodus would harm agricultural production in Mexico.[44]

Public hearings thus had international as well as domestic ramifications that FDR could not ignore: powerful Southern conservatives viewed FEPC hearings—indeed the very existence of the FEPC—as unwarranted federal meddling and a thinly veiled effort to establish "social equality" in the South, while the State Department and Mexican government worried that the El Paso hearings could threaten the vitally important Bracero Program for temporary farmworkers. With the wartime agricultural labor needs of the United States at stake, Roosevelt authorized Secretary of State Cordell Hull to cancel the hearings.[45]

The cancellation of the El Paso hearings angered Mexican American activists and FEPC officials, but hardly made national news, as did FDR's postponement of hearings on the railroad industry and its unions for their blatantly discriminatory practices against black workers. FDR's decision to postpone the railway hearings was influenced less by the potential harm of the hearings to international or hemispheric relations than by the possible disruption of transportation networks so vital to the production of war materials. The reaction of the FEPC and the African American community was highly public and harshly critical. FEPC chairman Malcolm McLean resigned, as did numerous committee members, including prominent attorney and civil rights activist Charles Houston (who over a decade earlier mentored Thurgood Marshall at Howard University law school). In his letter of resignation, Houston characterized the cancellation as a flagrant "surrender of principle" that followed "the traditional pattern of sacrificing the Negro whenever an attempt to do him justice antagonizes powerful reactionary forces in industry and labor." He was especially fed up with decisions handed down by government officials without the slightest effort to consult with African Americans or their representatives on the committee. "Negroes are citizens," Houston declared, "not wards."[46]

Despite the cancellation of the El Paso hearings, FEPC field agents continued to investigate and resolve complaints without the only weapon the FEPC had at its disposal—the threat of public hearings. With mounting pressure to extend protection to Mexican workers, Chairman Cramer appointed Carlos E. Castañeda to investigate complaints in Texas, New Mexico, and Arizona. Castañeda grew up in Brownsville on the border with Mexico, and as a professor of Latin American history at the University of Texas, was well known throughout the state for his scholarship on Mexican Americans.[47] Cramer no doubt believed that appointing an educated, Spanish-speaking investigator to his staff would help the FEPC in dealing with the delicate task of mediating among industry and union officials, Mexican consuls, and the Mexican workers themselves.[48]

Like Texas Gov. Coke Stevenson, State Department officials, the Texas Good Neighbor Commission, and the OCIAA,

Castañeda believed that the time had come to end racial distinctions between Latin Americans and Anglo Americans, particularly in view of the farm labor shortage created by the war and the Mexican ban on braceros to Texas. But like most liberal-minded Texans, he also believed that the color line between blacks and whites could not be breached anywhere in the South without serious, even lethal consequences. Despite its long border with Mexico, Texas was still very much a Southern state on the western border of the Deep South.[49] In a conference with Castañeda and Mexican consuls, Governor Stevenson reminded Castañeda that the "Negro problem . . . should be distinguished from any connection whatever with Anglos and Latins." And the FEPC, he warned, should "proceed slowly in so far as the color line is concerned, because it might raise an issue dangerous to the communities, the state, and the nation."[50]

With the support of LULAC members and Adolfo Domínguez, the Mexican consul in Houston, Castañeda immediately began investigating complaints against oil refineries in Texas, particularly Humble Oil, Shell Oil, and Sinclair Oil.[51] Over sixty Mexican and Mexican American members of the Oil Workers International Union (OWIU) complained to Consul Domínguez that, in addition to being paid less than Anglos for the same work and denied opportunities for upgrading, they were forced to use the same time clocks as black workers, ride in the same trucks with them, eat with them in segregated mess halls, and use segregated changing and shower rooms.[52] The superintendent of the refinery, D. A. Young, blamed the union local for refusing to permit "the commingling of the different races employed at this plant."[53] One Mexican worker, Mr. Sánchez, representing numerous complainants, asked the OWIU local representative, W. R. Lee, to have the company provide separate accommodations for Mexicans rather than require them to use the same facilities as black workers. When Castañeda told the refinery superintendent that the FEPC would likely pursue a case against the union local for its discriminatory practices, Superintendent Young replied, "Do you realize what part of the country you are in?"[54] Castañeda's response to the union's discriminatory policy is worth quoting in full:

> Mexican employees should use the same facilities as *other* white employees; under Texas law they are white, and have a legal right to insist on not being classified as colored. Furthermore, let me state at this point also that they did not ask for separate transportation, pay windows, and time clocks, but that they protested against being classed as colored . . . Regrettable as the fact is that the law in Texas establishes separate facilities for Whites and Colored in public conveyances and other public facilities, it is nevertheless the law, and if your union has been tolerating the use of facilities intended for Colored employees by Mexicans, who under the laws are White, you have not only been violating the provisions of Executive Order 9346, but also the laws of the State of Texas.[55]

Castañeda explicitly called for ending not only the practice of race-based job classifications but also requiring Mexican workers to share accommodations with blacks on the job.

In what became a controversial issue within the FEPC as well as in the oil industry, Castañeda sought to redraw the color line with Mexicans on the same side as Anglos. In a meeting with Sinclair Oil officials, the Mexican consul, and union representatives, he declared: "We have no objection to segregation . . . of Negroes in one . . . [facility], and Anglos and Latin-Americans in another. We do not expect a complete change at this time, we merely request that positive action be started to . . . [educate Anglo workers] that Mexicans are not Negroes."[56] Castañeda reassured union and company officials that physical segregation for African American workers was not the concern of the FEPC.

The management agreed in principle that Mexicans should be able to use the same time clocks, pay windows, and transportation trucks as the "other white employees" and would make every effort to integrate Mexican and Anglo workers.[57]

Castañeda then asked Consul Domínguez to inform Mexican workers at the Sinclair Refinery to put the matter to a test by riding in the trucks for whites, lining up at the same pay window, and punching the same time clocks.[58] As with so many informal agreements among management, union representatives, and FEPC officials, little actually changed. One of the Mexican workers at the refinery protested: "We're still in the same circumstances, we are still transported in trucks with Negroes, we punch the time clock with Negroes, and receive our pay at the window for Negroes."[59] Frustrated by the refusal of the oil company to force the integration of Mexicans with Anglo workers, LULAC member Robert Meza complained to Rep. Richard M. Kleberg that the oil companies ignored the Texas attorney general's statement that "all person of Mexican extraction shall be treated as '*white*.'"[60]

Castañeda clearly understood that the law sanctioned the segregation of blacks and whites at all levels of Southern society, but he also knew that the segregation of Mexicans—whether in schools, parks, restaurants, or the workplace—was often arbitrary and nowhere in the United States sanctioned by law. Castañeda was a living example of the differential treatment sometimes accorded Mexican Americans: some light-skinned Mexican Americans could pursue Ph.D.'s and law degrees at our nation's finest universities, while others, usually dark-skinned Mexicans, regardless of citizenship, were segregated in "Mexican schools" and later forced to accept meager wages for menial jobs. This betwixt and between nature of Mexicans in the Southwest—neither Anglo nor Negro—became even more confusing because the ascription of "Latin American" signified not only American

Carlos E. Castañeda, FEPC regional director and professor of Latin American history at the University of Texas. Nettie Lee Benson Latin American Collection, University of Texas Libraries, University of Texas at Austin.

citizens of Mexican descent but also citizens of nineteen Latin American republics, including Mexico.[61]

In practice, appearances often mattered more than ethnic identity, surname, or even citizenship. One airplane plant manager stated that his company would employ Mexicans "if they were not 'too racial'—'too dark.'"[62] Another plant manager, C. N. Waterman, told Castañeda that he was not sure he could tell who was and who was not Latin American: "we have men working in this plant that I know to be of Latin American extraction who have American names, blue eyes and light brown hair." One worker with a Latin American surname, Waterman observed, "doesn't admit he's a Latin American." Another worker, William Budd, "is blond as anybody could be, who claims to be a Latin American, born in Mexico," while others with Latin American names deny being Latin Americans. "They say that are American citizens" and refuse to discuss their ethnic origins.[63]

But whether light-skinned or not, U.S. citizen or not, Mexican members of the OWIU informed the union representative "that they did not intend to continue to be closely associated on the job with the negro employees."[64] The president of the OWIU, O. A. Knight, worried that Mr. Sánchez's request for separate facilities for Mexicans countered union policy to combat any form of discrimination against any member of the union. Although the union's policy of segregating black workers from white workers did not seem to trouble Knight, the request for separate accommodations on the job for Mexican workers, he told a union representative, could be "distorted and used as evidence of discriminatory attitude on the part of the Anglo-American employees toward Mexican employees, or as evidence of a discriminatory attitude on the part of the Mexican employees towards Negro employees."[65] Knight urged union locals to allow Mexicans to share the same facilities as whites but stopped short of calling for an end to segregation for black workers.

In another case involving segregated facilities, the Humble Oil and Refinery Company in Baytown, Texas, segregated restrooms three ways—"'Colored,' 'White,' and 'Spanish-American.'" Of the company's 5,300 employees, women constituted about 9 percent, African Americans 9 percent, and Mexicans 2 percent. About 1,700 were classed as skilled, 1,800 as semiskilled, and about 1,700 as unskilled. Some of the Mexican workers complained that management did not provide a sufficient number of restrooms for them, forcing them to use those set aside for blacks since they were not permitted to use white-only restrooms. Castañeda attempted to persuade management to solve the problem by eliminating "Spanish Only" restrooms altogether and allowing Mexican workers to use those reserved for "Whites Only." The superintendent of Humble Oil, G. L. Farned, blamed white workers and their union policies for segregated facilities at the refinery: "Our company is not responsible for any race prejudice which might exist and unless and until there is a change in public feeling and sentiment about the matter, we do not feel that we can force . . . employees of both Anglo and Mexican extraction to use the same rest room facilities when there is such an opposition on the part of Anglos to . . . racial equality."[66] When these same workers complained of wage differentials based solely on race and the refusal of the company to reclassify skilled Mexican employees for promotion, Farned lectured the FEPC: "Unless and until there is a change in public feeling and sentiment, . . . it is an undeniable fact that Anglo American workmen and the public generally . . . do set themselves apart and do consider themselves to be superior mentally, physically and socially to Mexicans . . . Without going into the factors that motivate the sentiment towards the absolute equality of races . . . it is inescapable that all theories and philosophies of racial equality will amount to very little as long as those conditions exist and as long as the public at large has a viewpoint and conviction that is so pronounced and different from the ends sought by your Committee."[67] The Baytown Employees Federation, an independent union at Humble Oil, adamantly opposed any changes in segregated facilities or promotions to skilled positions for Mexicans and blacks, and blamed the CIO for stirring up Mexican and African American workers. The Employees Federation distributed a bulletin to its white workers alleging that the aim of the CIO was "to put the white, colored, and Mexican employees on an absolute social

and economic equality" and "to make white men's jobs immediately available to negroes."[68] Castañeda opposed the reactionary stance of the Employees Federation, but only insofar as it
gave company managers the excuse that they could not upgrade
Mexican workers because no separate restrooms and other accommodations had been provided in certain sections of the
plant.[69]

"Segregation by location" as opposed to "segregation by
job" was also a subject of debate within the FEPC. Presidential
Executive Order 9346, like 8802, which it replaced, reiterated
the policy of forbidding discrimination in hiring and promotions in defense industries on the basis of race, color, creed, or
national origin. To comply with the executive order, companies
were required to abolish all references to race in job classifications and upgrade charts. All jobs were to be open to all workers on the basis of ability, training, and experience. However,
segregation of bathrooms, eating areas, pay windows, and so
forth did not fall within the jurisdiction of the FEPC. Regional
director W. Don Ellinger maintained that segregation of facilities could not be allowed when it interfered with job opportunities of workers. Refusing to upgrade a Mexican or African
American worker on the ground that no segregated restrooms
existed for a particular job classification would thus be in violation of the executive order. "The only segregation we have accepted," Ellinger stressed, "is segregation by location, and, of
course, the statutory requirements as to rest rooms, etc." Securing promotions for Mexican and black workers was more important than attempting to force companies to end segregation
of mess halls and bathrooms. "We have insisted that even if
segregated, Negroes must have the same wage rates, the same
upgrading privileges and the same maximum wage." By maintaining these standards, Ellinger believed, segregation by loca-

tion would become unprofitable to the employer and its elimination would be "much easier than a direct attack upon it."[70]

"Segregation by location" became a heated issue on the tenth floor of the Mercantile Bank building in Dallas where two federal agencies, the FEPC regional office and the Office of Defense Transportation (ODT), shared the floor and the same restrooms. The executive secretary of the ODT, John A. Lubbe, told FEPC regional director, Leonard Brin, that Virgil Williams, an African American FEPC agent, was required to use the "colored toilets" in the building basement. Brin refused to comply with his fellow bureaucrat's wish, whereupon the regional director for ODT, John C. Massenburg, told the building management that "if he ever caught Williams in the toilet he would throw him out." The building management responded to the interagency altercation by locking the tenth-floor bathroom and providing keys to the white employees, whereupon Brin gave a copy of his key to agent Williams. Infuriated by Brin's stubborn refusal to observe racial protocol, Lubbe told Brin that "this was the South and 'Negroes ought to know their place.'" Brin stood his ground and told Lubbe: "I have sworn to an oath . . . to uphold the Constitution and to defend the nation against enemies foreign and domestic . . . [an] oath broad enough to include defense against anyone who might harm one of our employees." He threatened to have a U.S. marshal assigned to protect Williams and promised to have constituted authorities investigate the case should any harm come to him.[71]

Resistance to upgrades for Mexican and black workers was fiercest at the Shell Oil and Refinery Company in Dear Park near Houston. Ellinger called the Shell Company "FEPC Enemy #1" and noted in an office memo that "the shell crowd are rats."[72] As in other refineries, blacks and Mexicans were limited to the most menial jobs. African American workers made it clear that what concerned them most was gaining the right to work in any job for which they were qualified, even if it meant working in segregated spaces.[73] Carter Wesley, publisher of the *Informer*, a Houston newspaper for African Americans, stressed the importance of job opportunities over physical segregation. Mexicans, on the other hand, objected to any form of physical segregation from Anglos, claiming, erroneously, that they were not segregated in schools, restaurants, parks, or public swimming pools. The OWIU Conciliation Committee, charged with finding a solution that would be acceptable to white workers and the FEPC, expressed greater hostility toward Mexican workers than black workers because the latter group did not demand integration with whites as long as they received equal job opportunities. White workers also objected to upgrading Mexicans who were not U.S. citizens or did not speak English. When the FEPC pointed out that the U.S. and Mexican governments would object to any effort to discriminate against resident nationals of Mexico, the Conciliation Committee agreed to consider upgrading some Mexican workers, but only if provisions for segregation were included.[74]

Although Shell Oil admitted that it paid Mexican and African American workers a lower wage than white workers for the same jobs, the company superintendent, P. E. Foster, believed that Shell had been made a "guinea pig" for the FEPC's not-so-secret agenda to integrate the workforce.[75] Castañeda accused the company and the OWIU local of maintaining an upgrade system that "dead-ends all Latin-Americans at the level of janitor and gardener." The union defiantly informed Castañeda that it did not propose to change any of its policies on job classification and upgrades and demanded that the FEPC hold hearings because, the union frankly acknowledged, "we consider ourselves and the company both in violation of the Executive

Order."[76] The threat of public hearings was supposed to motivate companies to comply with Executive Order 9346, not be used as a tactic to forestall and obstruct compliance. But Shell executives feared that compliance would give its competitors an unfair advantage and that its skilled white workers would strike rather than work alongside Mexicans and African Americans.[77]

The FEPC scheduled a public hearing to be held in December 1944. Regional Director W. Don Ellinger suggested that the hearing be designed "primarily to emphasize the Latin-American question" since most of the complaints came from Mexican workers through the office of Consul Domínguez. LULAC organized a group of Mexican American servicemen, some decorated for gallantry in action, to speak at local meetings in support of workers' demands. As a result over 100 Mexican Americans from San Antonio wired the federal government requesting that "the interests of Latin-Americans be protected in Texas." The public hearing, however, was never held. Shell management and union officials agreed to take "affirmative action" to end discriminatory practices within a ninety-day period.[78] But the agreement met considerable opposition from the union rank and file, forcing the company to delay upgrading its minority workers.[79]

Under sustained pressure from the FEPC, Shell managers agreed to upgrade two Mexican and seven African American workers, all of whom held seniority for promotion and passed language and arithmetic tests. R. Flores, a Mexican American, was promoted from laborer to car repairman's helper, and J. Casas, a Mexican citizen, was upgraded from laborer to truck driver. Seven black workers were also upgraded. Anglo workers in the maintenance departments unanimously refused to accept the upgrades and threatened a work stoppage.[80]

Faced with the threat of a strike, Shell immediately rescinded the upgrades for all but one of the African American workers, who was transferred to the automotive department as a truck driver. The workers in the automotive department then presented the company with an ultimatum to remove the black and Mexican truck drivers from their department under threat of a strike. The company immediately removed the black truck driver but refused to remove the two Mexicans. The next day, without informing the FEPC official at the plant, who was attempting to get the company and the union to comply with the upgrade order, Shell abruptly removed the Mexicans from the automotive department.[81]

The FEPC was powerless to compel the union local to change its discriminatory policies, and the OWIU claimed it could not dictate policy to its locals. If Shell obeyed the directive, Anglo workers would strike; if it sided with the union, it would be in open violation of an executive order of the president. Faced with what seemed an impossible dilemma, the Shell president lashed out at the leadership of the OWIU and the FEPC, accusing them of behaving like "dictators." Nevertheless, after a series of meetings between Shell management and union officials, the Shell company manager told union workers that he had orders to place two Mexican workers on the job. The company again upgraded the two Mexican workers, and again the automotive department refused to return to work. It was a familiar pattern. The company would agree with the FEPC directive, the workers would walk off, and the company would rescind its policy. After months of meetings and delays, the pattern would repeat itself. As Castañeda observed, "The company blames the unions, and the unions blame the company, but the fact remains that Latin-Americans, regardless of their ability or seniority, are never promoted to certain jobs."[82]

In a final round of meetings, this time with a mediator from the War Labor Board, Anglo workers insisted on their right to strike rather than comply with the directive. The president of the OWIU flew to Houston and explained to the white workers the proper procedure under the Smith-Connally Act for striking in wartime. The workers agreed to petition the National Labor Relations Board (NLRB) for a strike ballot and to return to work without demanding the removal of the two Mexican truck drivers. In granting the union the ballot to strike, however, the NLRB in effect sent the message that compliance with the president's Executive Order 9346 was subject to the will of white workers.[83]

On the eve of the strike vote, Anglo workers attempted to sow discord between Mexican and black workers. They told Mexicans that if black workers had not been included in the desegregation order, a satisfactory adjustment of their complaints could have been reached. They told African American workers not to support Mexican "pretensions" that they were superior to colored workers.[84] The company, however, clearly hoped that Anglo workers would allow two Mexicans to retain their jobs as truck drivers. Two days before the vote, a Shell company official offered to solicit a statement from Gov. Coke Stevenson urging tolerance toward Latin Americans.[85] A vote not to strike might buy the company more time, which was something the FEPC did not have. The vote took place in June 1945, only two months before the war ended and less than a year before the U.S. Senate let the FEPC die. Nevertheless, the wording of the ballot carefully avoided mentioning the FEPC and the executive order. The strike ballot read: "The major issue involved in the dispute is the protest of certain employees at the Shell Oil Company . . . to the upgrading of two Latin-American employees. Do you wish to permit interruption of production in wartime?"[86] Not surprisingly, a majority of the workers voted to strike, and the FEPC was forced to stand down. A Texas employer, who blamed racist unions as the real source of the problem, compared the FEPC to a cowboy who is "bold, aggressive, insistent, relentless and determined to allow no contractual document to escape being branded, like a Maverick, with the FEPC clause, but cowers from any attempt to lasso the Champion of the herd—organized labor."[87]

Mexican Consul Adolfo Domínguez had earlier predicted, incorrectly, that it would be easier to end job segregation for Mexicans than for African Americans at the Shell Oil Company. "Once the line of resistance has been broken for the Mexican group," he told FEPC officials and Shell managers, Negro workers "would expect the same considerations, and while it is doubtful whether the Anglos would quit because of equality with the Mexicans, it is certain that something short of mutiny would occur in the case of [equality with] Negroes." Domínguez clearly underestimated Anglo workers' resistance to shared facilities and job upgrades for Mexicans. Any upgrades for Mexicans, Anglo workers reasoned, would presage upgrades for black workers as well. Although Domínguez said he was "not unsympathetic to the Colored question," he preferred that Shell and the OWIU concentrate their efforts on ending segregation of Mexicans "in accordance with the Constitution [of the United States], which does not recognize but two races—White and Colored."[88] Publisher Carter Wesley, on the other hand, believed that the full integration of Latin Americans would represent "a step ahead for Negroes" and urged black workers to support upgrades for Mexicans.[89] Perhaps if Domínguez had encouraged Mexican oil workers to support upgrades for African American workers, both groups could have combined forces to strike all three major refineries unless management and union locals agreed to comply with FEPC directives.

In contrast to the reactionary OWIU local in Texas, the OWIU won its case against the Southport Petroleum Company in Delaware before the National War Labor Board (NWLB) in 1943 to abolish classifications of "colored laborer" and "white laborer" and reclassify both simply as "laborers" with the same rates of pay. It is not clear if the suit was brought by the OWIU national office in defiance of the wishes of its local, but it raises questions about the refusal of the national office to force its Texas local to end discrimination within its ranks. In ruling against the Delaware oil company, the NWLB unanimously declared: "This equalization of economic opportunity is not a violation of the sound American provision of differentials in pay for different skills. It is rather a bit of realization of the no less sound American principle of equal pay for equal work as one of those equal rights in the promise of American democracy regardless of color, race, sex, religion, or national origin . . . America, in the days of its infant weakness the haven of heretics and the oppressed of all races, must not in the days of its power become the stronghold of bigots . . . The Negro . . . is a test of our sincerity in the cause for which we are fighting."[90]

Noticeably absent from the executive orders charging the FEPC with eliminating discrimination was any reference to gender-based discrimination. While white women found employment in many war industries, race and gender combined to keep African American and Mexican women from being hired, except in positions as janitors and other menial jobs. Cleo Garcia, who turned down an offer to work as a janitor, wrote to the War Production Board: "There are over a quarter of a million Latin-American boys in the front lines now, we feel that we are pretty well represented as far as the fight for this country is concerned, so why is it that we cannot help in war plants and get the same rights as all of the others . . . ?" A company official told her that "Latin American people weren't capable of doing war work in that particular plant."[91]

While many FEPC officials in the Southwest took the complaints of discrimination against women seriously, the FEPC could require only that companies not exclude women on the basis of race, color, creed, or national origin; it could not require that they hire women. This legal loophole allowed many companies to deny employment to all women, while enabling some companies, like the Phelps Dodge Copper Corporation, to hold different policies toward women in the different states where it operated. In El Paso, for example, it hired only Mexican women because they worked for less than white or black women.[92] When told that she could not be hired by mining companies because of the lack of facilities for African American women, Ida Wren complained directly to President Roosevelt that "these mines hire every nationality but colored, but . . . color was not thought of when it came to sending the boys overseas . . . We colored women should have the same right to work in any defense or government plant as any other nationality. We are American born citizens," she reminded FDR.[93] Another African American woman, Helen Phillips, complained that the person taking applications at a mining company was a Mexican woman who told her that the company did not hire "colored women" except as laundresses and window washers on an hourly basis.[94] The Phelps Dodge Copper Corporation in Morenci, Arizona, on the other hand, hired only white women. The company manager claimed that there was only one dressing room and one shower room available to women mill workers and that "frankly, there existed a strong prejudice on the part of the Anglo women" against hiring Mexican and black women, although the company did hire Mexican women for some jobs in the company's store, hospital, and hotel.[95]

A cement company in New Orleans hired white women and African American men, but not black women. The company president admitted that this was discriminatory and in violation of Executive Order 9346, but defended his actions on the ground that there were no "sanitary facilities for Negro women" and that "white women would quit rather than work with Negro women." The FEPC regional director Don Ellinger explained that "As citizens we cannot agree that the protection of rights of one group of people justifies the removal of rights from others . . . To deny a chance to work to Negroes because of a segregation policy which is imposed by the white community is not fair. If segregation is to be maintained, it must be separation with equal rights—not exclusion." He stated that at least a dozen plants in New Orleans have "proven that white and colored workers can work together in harmony," and added, "If you can work Negro men and white women without trouble, you should have no fear of white and Negro women [working together]."[96] Ellinger told the company it could not refuse to hire black women workers even if it meant integrating the restrooms or providing them with separate restroom and locker facilities.

White women not only refused to work with Mexican and African American women workers, but in one case they refused to work under the supervision of a Mexican American male. At Kelly Air Force Base in San Antonio, the white women workers, known as "Kelly Katies," threatened to resign rather than work under Ernest Herrera, a Mexican American unit chief of the Supply Division. The military command promptly informed the women that it was their privilege to resign if they so desired, that their resignation would be accepted, but that "they would have to state as the reason [for their resignation] their refusal to work under a Mexican foreman." None of the Kelly Katies resigned.[97] Shortly afterwards, Castañeda visited Kelly Field to review progress made toward ending discrimination at the base. The head of the civilian personnel section, Maj. Alex Chesser, showed Castañeda the records of the discharge of a white woman chauffeur for refusal to transport civilian and military "colored personnel." She appealed her discharge to Texas Sen.

Tom Connally, but the commanding general refused to back down and reiterated that he would discharge any employee "who fostered and abetted discrimination."[98]

African American and Mexican American women complained that job ads for women often specified race, such as ads for waitresses. As one employer explained, "only white girls were suitable for jobs as waitresses," although he also ran ads for "colored girls" for other positions.[99] At first it seemed a simple matter of informing employers that specifying race in job ads was a violation of Executive Order 9346, even though eliminating reference to race in ads for waitresses would not change the fact that African American and Mexican women would not be hired in white restaurants.

FEPC Regional Director Leonard Brin's aggressive approach to eliminating racial reference in want ads not related to the war industry began to meet resistance even from other federal agencies, such as the U.S. Employment Service (USES) and the War Manpower Commission (WMC), which claimed that African Americans often would not respond to ads unless they specifically stated that "colored labor" was needed. On the other hand, when reference to race was omitted, African Americans who applied for the jobs were often told that "the company was not hiring colored people." The Texas state director of WMC, C. W. Belk, declared that the reference to race or color in advertising for workers should be determined "on the basis of local conditions." "As a matter of fact," Belk wrote, "in a State the size of Texas where there is predominance of Mexicans and Negroes in the potential labor supply . . . , an advertisement referring to race is not considered discriminatory."[100]

When the regional director of USES in San Antonio, Irving Wood, complained that the majority of its offices in Texas, New Mexico, and Louisiana failed to report cases of employers specifying race in their employment requests, the state director of the USES, T. H. Bond, told him that manpower allocation in wartime was a "large and complex task, one not to be performed by the meticulous completion of a form designed to reflect temporary employment inequities between various segments of our population. Rather than creating a state or national 'bogey-man' regarding the employment of Negroes," Bond advised, "more rational emphasis should be placed upon the fact that Negroes are being assimilated into industrial employment at a more rapid rate than at any time in our national history, and that this rate is steadily accelerating." USES personnel saw the problem clearly and shaped their policies accordingly, Bond reminded Wood, without "attempting sharply to contravene social and economic patterns which have grown up over many decades." As a parting shot aimed at FEPC officials like Leonard Brin, he added: "Under ordinary conditions the Employment Service in Texas as well as Texas management and labor have exceptional respect for the 'ivory-towered' experts who wish to solve our problems by remote control. Unfortunately, however, we are at war and the practical application of established fact and flexible judgment appear to us essential at this time."[101]

As far as the War Manpower Commission and the U.S. Employment Service were concerned, segregation in the South was a fact of life. Job ads simply reflected that fact. When Brin explained that running ads for "colored men" barred white people from applying and therefore were discriminatory, he was of course correct, but eliminating the reference to race would in no way end Jim Crow protocols in nonwar industries from drawing upon different racial groups to fill different jobs.[102] White men and women were not likely to be employed in segregated barber shops and restaurants, any more than African Americans could be employed in supervisory positions over white workers. WMC and USES continued to ignore the reference to race in job ads for black workers in nonwar industries, in conformance with long-standing social practice in the South.

Job ads for "whites only" in war industries or union membership drives were almost always contested. When the International Longshoremen's Association (ILA) ran an ad for "200 White Men . . . for Longshore Work for the War Effort," the FEPC and the executive secretary of the Houston branch of the NAACP, Lulu B. White, contacted the union for an explanation. The president of ILA Local 872 promptly replied that the interracial union tried to maintain equal numbers of white and black longshoremen in its segregated locals. The black local, however, greatly outnumbered the white local, which was short 200 men. "We work together, we meet in joint meetings and discuss our problems, and in these meetings," he assured Lulu White, "the word Negro isn't used but we always address one another as Bro."[103]

Castañeda and other FEPC officials puzzled over what to do about a want ad that read, "War Workers Wanted, White or Colored," which was intended to be nondiscriminatory. The regional director worried that in Texas the ad might possibly be construed to exclude Mexicans. On the other hand, asking the company to rerun the ad with the word "Mexican" included along with "white" and "colored" might suggest that Mexicans were neither white nor colored. After much consultation, the regional director and special assistant Castañeda advised FEPC headquarters in Washington that the ad should be allowed to stand because "we both consider Mexicans to be white."[104] In California, the U.S. Employment Service, which mainly oversaw the placement of agricultural laborers, continued to include Mexican farmworkers in the "non-white bracket."[105]

The FEPC's persistence in eliminating all references to race in want ads, whether for jobs in war industries or not, raised a storm of protest from Texas senators W. Lee (Pappy) O'Daniel and Tom Connally, as well as Gov. Coke Stevenson. When Leonard Brin informed the American Beauty Cover Company that its ad for "white women" in the *Dallas Morning News* was in violation of the executive order and informed the *News* that its own want ad for a "Colored Man . . . to Work as Paper Handler" was also discriminatory, the *News* refused to remove the ads: "The position of the *News* is that if a mother wants a white girl to take care of her children that is exactly what she wants, not a Negro, or if she wants a Negro girl, that also is what she wants, and this rule holds true in all . . . want ad columns."[106] On the same day the *News* editorialized: "If white and colored people can be segregated in schools, on streetcars and elsewhere on the basis of our state laws, sustained by a United States Supreme Court decision, it is absurd for a federal agency, having no more authority than a presidential ukase, to transcend the theory held by the Supreme Court, in its directives to employers in their private business . . . It would be easily possible for the President's fair employment practice committee to perform its legitimate function of seeing that Negroes get a fair deal in war industry employment, yet without attempting to break down the time-honored southern tradition of segregation."[107] The state Democratic chairman, E. B. Germany, declared that the FEPC's challenge to the South was as "clear as was the challenge of the carpetbagger and scalawag fourscore years ago."[108] An angry reader wrote that if the federal government could tell a newspaper how to word its want ads, it could tell a theater manager that "his female ushers must wear slacks." "What in the name of democracy," he asked, "does Washington think we are fighting a war for?"[109] Another reader tellingly asked, "Would it violate any regulation if we advertised to buy or sell a Hereford bull? Or could we only say 'cattle' without specifying breed or sex?"[110]

Sen. Tom Connally declared that the FEPC had no legal authority in Texas and that companies should ignore FEPC directives. Senator O'Daniel opposed continued funding of the agency and demanded Brin's resignation, but FEPC Chairman Malcolm Ross, who was far more conservative than many of his regional directors, sought to appease the segregationist Democrats.[111] He explained that the dividing line between a war industry and nonwar industry was sometimes difficult to draw and admitted that a beauty supply company and newspapers were not essential war industries and thus fell outside the scope of FEPC jurisdiction. "I am not unaware," he further explained, "of a prevailing supposition that the FEPC somehow concerns itself with social relationships between Negro Americans, Mexican Americans, and those other Americans among whom they live. This is not so. The committee was established to act against employment discrimination in war industries and it has stuck to that job."[112]

Gov. Coke Stevenson was not so easily mollified. He challenged the authority of the FEPC in Texas and publicly accused Leonard Brin and the FEPC of "an open violation and defiance" of at least fifteen Texas laws providing for the segregation of the races. Stevenson asked Brin if the FEPC intended to pursue policies in Texas that were in violation of state laws.[113] Texans across the state supported Stevenson's open defiance of the FEPC. "Good for you," one Texan wrote, ". . . all Texans with any guts will back you on your letter to the Harvard Jew Leonard Brin. You hit the right spot and right Jew."[114] A Baptist minister praised Stevenson for his "courage . . . and backbone against federal blackness."[115] Another rhapsodized that "this free government was established by white men who gave their blood and lives in order that we might have a free government for white folks. These white folks are not going to surrender their government to the alien or colored peoples."[116]

A resident of New Mexico seethed: "This bunch in Washington . . . would marry the Negro bucks to our white girls if they thought the off-spring of this kind of a union would perpetuate the New Deal in power."[117] The FEPC backed down and Texas newspapers continued to run ads for "colored boys" and "white girls" for employers who sought black workers for black work and white workers for white work, just as they had since the Civil War.[118]

Resistance to Executive Order 9346 outside the South was often just as fierce, but in a few places compliance led to an end to segregated facilities as well as job classifications. When African American workers objected to segregated tables in the mess hall of the Kaiser Corporation in Portland, Oregon, the president, Edgar F. Kaiser, set up tables for mixed groups so that each person "could make his own choice as to how he wished to eat at the mess hall."[119] When San Quentin warden Clinton Duffy ended segregation at meal times, 1,100 white prisoners refused to eat in the mess hall. Duffy told the white prisoners: "You are not required to sit with Negroes, nor are the Negroes required to sit with you, but the privilege to do so is no longer denied you." Faced with lock-up without any meals, most of the white prisoners reconsidered and for the first time in its history, all San Quentin prisoners ate at the same time in the same mess hall with the option of sitting at the same tables.[120] Texas civil rights activist George Sánchez noted that the largest prison in Texas was no longer segregated by race and claimed that "anti-gringo" and anti-Mexican sentiments were not as pronounced in Texas as those between "blue stocking" and "hillbilly" or "normal men v. homosexuals."[121] Augustus F. Hawkins, an African American and Democratic member of the California State Assembly, introduced a bill in 1945 to end segregation in all public and private establishments that were not essential to the war effort, including prisons.[122]

Virtually all Southern Democrats believed that the FEPC sought as its goal the transformation of the entire labor structure of the South and not merely the efficient use of manpower without regard to race, color, creed, or national origin. Across the South and Southwest, unprecedented numbers of African Americans and Mexican Americans demanded upgrades to jobs for which they were qualified, while company and union officials advised them to remember which side of the Mason-Dixon Line they were on.[123] With the exception of LULAC and the NAACP, few organizations in Texas rallied to the cause of Mexican and black workers. As Castañeda explained at a meeting of Mexican workers in Chicago hosted by Hull House, the interracial Steel Workers Union, and the American Council on Race Relations, "liberal groups in our area are as rare as hen's teeth."[124] Even if that had not been the case, Southerners had little to fear from the FEPC, which could not force compliance with the president's executive order and whose mission was often undermined by other federal agencies, especially the U.S. Employment Service. Moreover, 90 percent of all FEPC cases arose outside of the South. FEPC Chairman Malcolm Ross boasted that his agency's intervention in employment practices across the country "has never resulted in the cancellation of any war contract, the seizure of any war plant, or the infliction of any penalty whatsoever."[125] Ross's predecessor, Mark Etheridge, emphasized that FDR's executive order was not intended as a "social document" on "the question of segregation," but he nevertheless came to believe that "The destinies of the white people and the Negro people are inextricably linked; there can be no prosperity for one if the other must live in poverty; there can be no happiness for one unless there is happiness for both."[126]

It was not a sudden interest in the welfare of African American workers that opened up job opportunities for African Americans, Mexicans, and other minorities; it was the growing shortage of labor as a result of the draft, which reduced the number of skilled and semiskilled workers at precisely the moment when industries were expanding their operations. One white company manager met the shortage by taking the progressive step of replacing men with black as well as white women: "Anyone handling personnel problems will realize that it is revolutionary to introduce women into a tool room, but . . . I thought I might just as well go the whole way and take colored women."[127] Labor shortages rather than FEPC directives did more to increase the percentage of nonwhites employed in war industries from less than 3 percent in early 1942 to 8 percent by the end of the war. Wartime necessity thus trumped the saying among white union machinists that " 'a Negro must never be allowed to pick up a tool."[128] By the war's end, more blacks and whites and Mexicans—women and men—wielded tools together on assembly lines in aircraft and shipbuilding industries, as well as other defense industries, than at any other time in our nation's history. Joseph James, chairman of the Negro Shipyard Workers Committee, observed: "White workers for the first time have found themselves working side by side on the same jobs with Negroes and other non-white peoples . . . White workers thus learned, to their own good, and to the good of the Nation, that their darker and otherwise different fellow citizens are intelligent, friendly and were competent workers. Antagonism and blind prejudice are minimized and sometimes entirely eliminated by the mere reality of working together for a common victory. It has been an experience in practical education."[129]

Although Mexican and black workers faced many of the same barriers on and off the job, they nevertheless pursued their economic goals along separate civil rights trajectories. Many African American workers viewed Mexicans as immigrants and foreigners and, like many Anglo employers, often made no distinction between citizens and noncitizens, or predominantly

English-speaking Mexican Americans and Spanish-speaking resident nationals. Mexicans, on the other hand, learned early on that close association with African Americans would undermine their claim to a white racial status and limit their opportunities for economic advancement. Perhaps they might have found common ground for cooperation and collective action had there been more interracial unionism in defense industries or had the two groups been able to bridge the cultural distance that often separated and prevented them from effectively resisting white workers' racism and "gentlemen's agreements" with company managers.

After the war the NAACP and numerous other organizations lobbied Congress to make the FEPC permanent, but Southern white conservatives ended any hope of the agency's resurrection and the hope it gave to African American and Mexican workers for equal employment opportunities regardless of race. In 1948 South Carolina Gov. Strom Thurmond called bills to establish a permanent FEPC "an anti-American invasion of the fundamental conception of free enterprise . . ." and added that arguments in favor of such bills were wholly based on "the economic and political philosophy of the Communist party."[130] Increasingly, the NAACP focused its resources on ending segregation in schools rather than fighting for economic rights of workers.[131] LULAC and other Mexican American organizations also began to file suits against school segregation in California, Arizona, and Texas. Both groups hoped that educational equality would be the key to ending residential segregation, employment inequality, segregation in public spaces, and other forms of discrimination. But even in states like California and Texas where African Americans and Mexicans shared long histories of discrimination, they mainly lived in segregated communities that limited opportunities to come together and know each other as more than just members of another "minority group" or rivals for low-wage, low-skill jobs in often grim working conditions with few or no benefits. Although Mexican and African American lawyers and activists began to cautiously cooperate after the war in an effort to end school segregation, the legal strategies they adopted and the assumptions on which they rested reveal fundamental differences about what it meant to be black or Mexican in the post-World War II era.

3

Black v. Brown and
Brown v. Board of Education

Segregation of African Americans in Texas followed the pattern of other Southern states, which meant that the color line was rigidly observed with serious, often lethal, consequences for black Texans. Mexican Americans, by contrast, occupied a complicated middle ground, sometimes white, sometimes not, depending on local custom, proximity to the border, class position, and skin color. Each state had its own laws and customs for educating its Indian, black, Asian, and Mexican populations. Thus, while Mexican children were segregated by custom in California, Asian and Native American children were segregated by law. Texas, with few Native Americans or Asian Americans, adopted a tripartite system of segregation with separate schools for Mexicans, blacks, and whites. When it was not possible to segregate Mexicans in separate schools, Anglo school officials put Mexican-descent children, whether citizens or noncitizens, Spanish dominant or English dominant, in separate classrooms in all-white schools. Mexicans thus attended segregated schools throughout the Southwest by custom rather than by law. African American children, of course, never attended white schools in Texas or any other Southern state.[1]

After World War II, Thurgood Marshall and the Legal Defense Fund filed numerous lawsuits to end school segregation in elementary and high schools as well as in professional schools at state universities. But one California segregation case, brought by Mexicans and Mexican Americans, succeeded not only in ending segregation, but in obtaining a federal district court ruling that directly challenged *Plessy v. Fergusson* (1896). Between 1946 and 1950, Mexicans won two school segregation cases in California and Texas, *Mendez v. Westminster* (1947) and *Delgado v. Bastrop* (1948), respectively, while the NAACP submitted a "friend of the court" brief in *Mendez* and prepared its own case against segregation at the University of Texas law school (*Sweatt v. Painter*, 1950). In these two states with large populations of African Americans and Mexican Americans in segregated schools, Thurgood Marshall and Mexican American civil rights advocate George Sánchez briefly exchanged letters to see how they might share affidavits and legal strategy. In the end, however, Sánchez (and Gus García, the lead lawyer in *Delgado*) cleaved to a narrow reading of the law that allowed segregation for blacks but not Mexicans, while Marshall and the Legal Defense Fund abandoned the equalization strategy in favor of a direct and uncompromising assault on the *Plessy* doctrine. Marshall used the *Mendez* case to test the developing argument, based in part on social science research, that equal protection of the laws could not be achieved under a system of segregation.[2]

Thurgood Marshall and George Sánchez were born two years apart, 1908 and 1906 respectively, and grew up in regions of the country more dissimilar than alike—Baltimore, Maryland, and Albuquerque, New Mexico—but the racial order of the mid-Atlantic South and the Southwest affected them profoundly. Marshall considered himself "born and brought up" a Southerner in what he called, with only slight exaggeration, the "most segregated city in the United States." The great-grandson of slaves, Marshall was raised in a middle-class African American community in a "respectable" neighborhood. His mother taught kindergarten in a segregated school. His father, a dining-car waiter on the Baltimore and Ohio Railroad, was fair-skinned and blue-eyed and could have passed for white. After graduating from historically black Howard Law School (he was denied admission to the University of Maryland law school because of his race), Marshall became active in the Baltimore branch of the NAACP in the mid-1930s, where he honed his legal skills in requiring school districts to pay black teachers the same salaries as whites. One of his first goals, he later recalled, "was to get even with Maryland for not letting me go to its law school." With the help of his mentor and Howard University law professor Charles Houston, Marshal filed suit against the University of Maryland. The appeals court judge, C. J. Bond, ruled that the Maryland law school could no longer offer "scholarships" to blacks to attend integrated law schools in other states. A few years later, in 1940, he was appointed chief council for the NAACP at the national headquarters in New York.[3] Having spent most of his life on the East Coast, Marshall had little knowledge of the problems Mexicans faced in states like California, Arizona, New Mexico, and Texas, particularly in the education of Spanish-speaking children. The person most responsible for addressing that issue was himself a Spanish-speaking denizen of the Southwest.

George Isidore Sánchez, a native New Mexican and descendant of settlers from the Spanish colonial era, had been drawn early on to teaching and researching the problems of Native Americans and mostly poor Spanish-speaking children in rural schools. He was only sixteen when he obtained his first job as a teacher in a rural school in Bernalillo County. Years later he graduated from the University of New Mexico with a bachelor's degree in education and Spanish. With the aid of a scholarship, Sánchez pursued graduate studies at the University of Texas in Austin, where he received an M.S. in educational psychology and Spanish. In 1934 he received his Ph.D. in educational administration from the University of California, Berkeley. After completing his doctoral studies, he conducted field research on rural

Thurgood Marshall, director of the NAACP Legal Defense Fund.
Library of Congress, Prints and Photographs Division, Visual Materials
from the NAACP Records, LC-USZ62-118214.

education in Mexico and published his first book, *Mexico: A Revolution by Education.* Sánchez undertook to understand revolutionary Mexico's rural reform movement, which, according to historian Ruben Flores, shed light on "social conflict in the American West." He also conducted fieldwork on rural education and blacks in the South as well as a survey of Taos County, New Mexico, that later resulted in the publication of his best-known work, *Forgotten People: A Study of New Mexicans.* In 1940 he accepted a position at the University of Texas in the Department of History and Philosophy of Education where he and his scholar-activist colleague, Carlos E. Castañeda, often worked together to promote the civil rights of Mexican Americans.[4]

George I. Sánchez, University of Texas professor and civil rights activist. Nettie Lee Benson Latin American Collection, University of Texas Libraries, University of Texas at Austin.

Shortly after World War II, George Sánchez and Thurgood Marshall, as well as other civil rights activists and organizations, paid close attention to a Mexican school segregation case in Orange County, California, as a result of a surprising ruling by the district court judge, John Paul McCormick. On March 2, 1945, in the final months of the war, Gonzalo Mendez, a native of Mexico and a moderately prosperous vegetable farmer, filed suit against four school districts in Orange County, California, on behalf of his children—Sylvia, Gerónimo, and Gonzalo, Jr.—and 5,000 other students of Mexican descent who had been arbitrarily assigned to attend segregated schools. He claimed that their children were required to attend schools "reserved for and attended solely and exclusively by children . . . of Mexican and Latin descent" while other schools in the same system were reserved "solely and exclusively" for children "known as white or Anglo-Saxon children." The plaintiff argued that segregating persons of Mexican ancestry, in the absence of state law mandating their segregation, was a violation of their Fourteenth Amendment right to equal protection of the laws.[5]

School officials argued that Mexican children suffered from language deficiencies that prevented them from keeping up with Anglo students, a pretext used in segregation cases in Texas and California fifteen years earlier.[6] The Orange County superintendent of schools admitted under questioning that language deficiency was not the only criterion for separation: "If they look Mexican, they are sent to the segregated schools. If they look white, they are sent to the white schools."[7] Joel Ogle, attorney for the school board, argued that no constitutional issues were at stake in the case since the establishment of separate-but-equal schools was supported by *Plessy v. Ferguson* and that the Mexican schools were equal to, and sometimes superior to, those reserved for Anglo students. The Mexican parents, however, filed the suit to end segregation—not to force the school districts to provide equal facilities. California law made it legal for school boards to segregate Indians, Japanese, Chinese, and other "Asiatics," but no law existed mandating the segregation of Mexicans or even African Americans. There was no need for such a law, since Mexicans and African Americans were segregated by custom in states outside the South where segregation laws had not been formally adopted.

Almost a year after Gonzalo Mendez and other parents filed the suit, District Court Judge Paul McCormick issued a ruling in language that went well beyond a narrow reading of the law that maintaining a segregated school system in the absence of a

Felicitas and Gonzalo Mendez, plaintiffs in *Mendez v. Westminster* (1946). Courtesy of Sylvia Mendez, daughter of Felicitas and Gonzalo Mendez.

state law was a violation of the Fourteenth Amendment. Instead, McCormick attacked the very premise that separate educational facilities could be made equal: "The equal protection of the laws pertaining to the public school system in California is not provided by furnishing in separate schools the same technical facilities, text books and courses of instruction to children of Mexican ancestry that are available to the other public school children regardless of their ancestry. A paramount requisite in the American system of public education is social equality. It must be open to all children . . . regardless of lineage." In other words, a federal district court judge had ruled, in essence, that the *Plessy* doctrine was unconstitutional. The Fourteenth Amendment required that schools provide "social equality"—not equal facilities. McCormick further declared that "methods of segregation . . . foster antagonisms in the children and suggest inferiority among them were none exists.[8] Exactly eight years later, Chief Justice Earl Warren ruled in *Brown v. Board of Education* that "separate educational facilities are inherently unequal" and, echoing the words of Judge McCormick, that to separate some pupils from others "solely because of their race generates a feeling of inferiority as to their status in the community that may affect their hearts and minds in a way unlikely ever to be undone."[9]

Judge Paul John McCormick was born in New York in 1879 but was raised in southern California, the son of an immigrant father from England. In 1910 McCormick was appointed judge of the California Superior Court for Los Angeles County, where he served for fourteen years. Although he never earned an academic degree from any college or university, McCormick taught Law and Procedure at the University of Southern California Law School from 1912 to 1924. In 1924, Pres. Calvin Coolidge nominated McCormick as Judge, U.S. District Court, Southern District of California, in part because of his lifelong political affiliation with the Republican Party in California. He was one of the few progressive Catholics in Los Angeles who, according to historian Michael Engh, S.J., "believed it was possible to be Catholic, American, and supporters of the Wilsonian approach to Progressivism."[10] Another progressive Republican,

Earl Warren, served as governor of California from 1943 until President Eisenhower appointed him in 1953 as Chief Justice of the Supreme Court.

McCormick's ruling represented a radical departure from court rulings that until 1954 required state universities to admit black students to graduate and professional schools or build separate and equal schools for them.[11] McCormick's ruling left no constitutional room for segregation: public education must be open "to all children regardless of lineage." The Orange County school districts immediately appealed the ruling to the Ninth Circuit Court of Appeals, while news of McCormick's insurgent ruling caught the attention of the American Civil Liberties Union (ACLU), the American Jewish Congress (AJC), the Japanese American Citizenship League (JACL), the National Lawyer's Guild (NLG), and the NAACP, all of whom submitted amicus briefs in the case. A. L. Wirin, an ALCU attorney with ties to Thurgood Marshall, and Loren Miller, a longtime civil rights attorney for the West Coast region of the NAACP, brought the *Mendez* case to the attention of Marshall and his assistant Robert Carter, who sought permission from the Ninth Circuit Court to file a brief in the case. Carter also asked David Marcus, the lead attorney in the *Mendez* case, if he had any objection to the NAACP's filing an amicus brief.[12] David Marcus, who had successfully represented Puerto Ricans and Mexican Americans in a class action suit to desegregate San Bernardino public parks and pools, welcomed the submission of so many amicus briefs, including one from Robert W. Kenney, the attorney general of California during Governor Warren's administration.[13]

McCormick's frontal attack on the "separate but equal" doctrine was exactly the kind of ruling that Marshall and the Legal Defense Fund hoped to obtain from the U.S. Supreme Court. Marshall and Carter had grown impatient with the slow progress of forcing school districts to provide the same educational facilities, teacher salaries, and per student expenditures for blacks as they did for whites. After the war, however, Marshall and his team of lawyers sought to develop arguments that directly challenged the constitutionality of *Plessy* by stressing the harmful psychological consequences of segregation. Curiously, however, Marshall's brief did not take advantage of the testimony by social scientists in the *Mendez* case indicating the harmful psychological effects of segregation on Mexican children. This, even though his assistant, Robert Carter (largely credited with having written the brief), was not only convinced that the time was ripe for attacking *Plessy* with social science rather than merely legal arguments but also that "the social science approach would be the only way to overturn segregation in the United States."[14] The attorney, civil rights activist, and *Nation* editor, Carey McWilliams, nevertheless expressed the hope that if the *Mendez* case reached the U.S. Supreme Court, "the decision may sound the death knell of Jim Crow in education."[15] Marshall, however, was not so optimistic. He told Carl Murphy, president of Afro-American Newspapers, "frankly and confidentially . . . there is serious doubt in the minds of most of us as to the timing for an all-out attack on segregation per se in the present United States Supreme Court." Marshall authorized the NAACP Legal Defense Fund to undertake a complete study of the "evil of segregation to demonstrate that there is no such thing as 'separate but equal' in . . . schools, health, recreation, transportation, etc. When this is completed, it might then be possible to make an all-out attack."[16]

In his brief Marshall adopted the language of McCormick's ruling to argue that "separation itself [is] violative of the equal protection of the laws . . . on the grounds that equality cannot be effected under a dual system of education."[17] Marshall also skillfully combined the goals of both African Americans and

Latinos, namely, "equality at home" as well as the "equality which we profess to accord Mexico and Latin American nationals in our international relations." He invoked the Good Neighbor policy with Latin America and the recent wartime effort to "forge an iron ring of solidarity among the nations in this hemisphere by means of peaceful association on the basis of equality . . . We cannot preach equality abroad successfully unless, in actuality, we effect such equality at home."[18] For added measure, Marshall reminded the Court that the United States ratified and adopted the Charter of the United Nations in 1945, obligating its signatories to promote "uniform respect for . . . human rights and fundamental freedoms for all without distinction as to race."[19] In the final section of the brief, Marshall argued that *Plessy* had never specifically decided the question of whether a state could maintain separate schools for members of various races, and urged the Court to reject the "separate but equal" doctrine.

Marshall understood what he was up against: school segregation had been the subject of litigation in 113 cases in twenty-nine states and the District of Columbia. In forty-four of the cases, the question of whether segregated schools were constitutional was directly raised, and forty-four times the answer was yes.[20] In spite of the odds, Marshall hoped to persuade the Court that "separate equality" was a judicial myth—a "legal fiction"—and that a dual school system implied social and racial inferiority even when it provided equal facilities.[21]

In contrast to Marshall's brief, the brief submitted by the American Jewish Congress went much farther by demonstrating the "crippling psychological effects" of segregation on segregated children. The AJC brief also deployed language far more critical of the courts for upholding the *Plessy* doctrine: "When a more or less inarticulate social feeling of racial superiority is clothed with the dignity of an official law, that feeling

Students from Lincoln Elementary School for Mexican children in Orange County, California, c. 1930. Courtesy of Yolanda Alvarez from the "Fire in the Morning" Collection.

acquires a concreteness and assertiveness which it did not possess before . . . Where prejudice is legalized, where bigotry is given official sanction, where prestige of law is lent to bias, there ignorance, narrow-mindedness, and hatred assert themselves openly and operate *as a right.* An official action based on a discriminatory classification breeds in turn more inequality and more prejudice."[22] Carey McWilliams called the AJC brief a "brilliant and devastating analysis of the social effects and the unconstitutionality of segregation."[23]

The Ninth Circuit Court of Appeals did not take the bait. In upholding the lower court's ruling, Judge Albert Lee Stevens refused to rule on the broader constitutional question of the legality of separate but equal. Instead, he upheld the narrow

interpretation that California law authorized only the segregation of children belonging to "one or another of the great
races of mankind," which Stevens identified as Caucasoid,
Mongoloid, and Negro, but that no state law authorized the
segregation of children "*within* one of the great races." Since
the census regarded Mexicans as "within" the white race, in
the eyes of the law Mexican Americans were Caucasians who
consequently could not be segregated from "other whites."[24]
In other words, Judge Stevens ruled in favor of the Mexican
American children not on the ground that the "separate but
equal" provision of *Plessy* was invalid, but rather on the ground
that Mexicans were members of the white race and that there
was no California statute mandating the segregation of Mexicans from other whites.

Judge Stevens pointedly dismissed Marshall's argument and
that of the American Jewish Congress that segregation per se was
unconstitutional. These briefs, Stevens noted, asked the court
"to strike out independently on the whole question of segregation, on the ground that recent world stirring events have set
men to the reexamination of concepts considered fixed." While
he acknowledged the importance for judges of "keeping abreast
of the times," alluding to the recent war against Nazism and fascism, he warned that judges must never exercise their power to
"rationalize outright legislation." "We are not tempted," he insisted, "by the siren who calls to us that the sometimes slow and
tedious ways of democratic legislation . . . [are] no longer re-
spected in a progressive society."[25]

Contrary to Judge Steven's faith in the "tedious ways of
democratic legislation," it was not likely that state houses
throughout the South would repeal Jim Crow laws in anybody's lifetime. The remedy to racial segregation would have to
come from the courts, if it was to come at all—or from a state

legislature outside the Deep South. California pointed the way, in part because of its sensitivity to national and international criticism in the wake of Japanese internment and the zoot suit riots in 1943. Gov. Earl Warren had cultivated friendly relations with Mexico from his first year in office (only six months before the zoot suit riots) and worried about a backlash from Mexico that could jeopardize the Bracero Program. Ending segregation for Mexicans and other racial minorities would ensure California's continued good relationship with Mexico and its growing postwar need for agricultural laborers. Shortly before the Ninth Circuit ruling in the *Mendez* case, Warren signed a California State Assembly bill to repeal sections of the Education Code that allowed school boards to establish separate schools for Indians and Asians, thereby ending all school segregation in the state based on race.[26]

In the spring of 1947, some African American parents decided to test the new education code by enrolling six of their daughters in Fremont High School in Los Angeles, an all-white school. On their first day of school, 500 white students walked out and hanged a "Negro in effigy" on a nearby street corner. The principal, Herbert Woods, snatched racist placards from the students and promptly ended the strike.[27] Although the majority of African American and Mexican children continued to attend segregated schools in California, where patterns of residential segregation had been established many decades earlier, it is nevertheless significant that California ended de jure segregation seven years before *Brown v. Board of Education*. California was no racial paradise, but geographically and culturally it was a long way from the Deep South and Texas, where it would have been inconceivable that Jim Crow could be struck down by a legislative amendment to the educational code and the courage, at least in one case, of a high school principal.

Marshall and the Fund were disappointed, but not surprised, that the Ninth Circuit ruling evaded the central argument of the NAACP brief, that race-based segregation violated
a citizen's right to equal protection of the law. In ruling that
the school districts had violated the constitutional rights of
the Mexican children, it neither adopted nor rejected the social science arguments that segregation did irreparable psychological harm to segregated children. NAACP attorney
Robert Carter nevertheless regarded the brief as a "dry run"
for testing the "temper of the court" with respect to social science arguments without running the risk of a reversal.[28] "The
Circuit Court in affirming the decision did not go as far as
requested in the brief of the NAACP," wrote Carter, but he
felt nevertheless that "This case brings the American courts
closer to a decision on the whole question of segregation."[29]
The response of the southern California branch of the ACLU
was less charitable: it described Judge Stevens's opinion as
"devoid of social imagination."[30]

The *Mendez* case galvanized Mexican civil right activists to file
suits in Texas where separate schools for Mexicans were maintained in 122 school districts in 59 counties across the state.[31]
LULAC leaders, the Mexican American attorney Gus García,
and University of Texas Professor George I. Sánchez, began preparing the first school segregation case in Texas since the 1930
Salvatierra case, in which an appeals court judge ruled that
"school authorities have no power to arbitrarily segregate Mexican children, assign them to separate schools, and exclude them
from schools maintained for children of other white races, merely
or solely because they are Mexicans." The arbitrary exclusion
of Mexican American children from "other whites," the court
ruled, constituted "unlawful racial discrimination."[32] Nevertheless, the court allowed for the segregation of Mexicans in the first

three grades for those students whose English fluency was minimal, but only if separate schooling was applied with equal force to both white and "Mexican race" students. Sánchez recalled how "the whole issue" was lost in the *Salvatierra* case when "a stupid judge was permitted by [our] unprepared lawyers to comment to the effect that separation for instructional purposes was quite all right."[33] As a result, many Texas school districts continued to use the "language handicap" excuse as a pretext to segregate Mexican children in the lower grades.

In 1948, three years after Gonzalo Mendez filed suit in California, Minerva Delgado and twenty parents of Mexican American children from five segregated school districts in Texas filed a complaint alleging that the school districts had "prohibited, barred and excluded" Mexican children from attending school with "other white school children" and that segregation denied them the equal protection of the law "as guaranteed by the Fourteenth Amendment."[34] The parents received financial support from LULAC and the legal assistance of attorney Gus García, who used the "other white/no state law" strategy that had succeeded in previous segregation suits.[35] School officials claimed that Mexican parents exercised "free choice" in sending their children to the "Latin American School" and argued that language deficiency made it necessary to place Mexican students in separate schools and classes.[36] "A language is not learned in isolation," Sánchez pointed out in one case challenging the pedagogical logic of segregation. "These children are put in a separate grade because they don't know English, and they don't learn English because they're in a separate grade. Children don't learn English from a teacher—they learn it from each other." The "language handicap," he maintained, was a "subterfuge to keep these 'dirty little Mexicans' away from the 'lily white' children." If there were no state law mandating the segregation of blacks,

Sánchez claimed, school officials would use the language handicap to justify *their* segregation: "The Negroes have 'a language handicap' too, you see."[37]

Judge Ben H. Rice, citing *Mendez*, ruled that the five school districts named in the *Delgado* suit and the state superintendent of public instruction were "permanently restrained and enjoined from . . . segregating pupils of Mexican or other Latin American descent in separate schools or classes."[38] Immediately following the ruling, the superintendent of public instruction, L. A. Woods, issued an order forbidding the segregation of Mexican-descent children on the grounds that only "colored children" could be legally segregated. The phrase "colored children," Woods pointed out, "has been interpreted by the Texas courts and the Texas legislature as including only members of the Negro race or persons of Negro ancestry. The courts have held that it does not apply to members of any other race."[39]

If "colored" in Texas meant having "Negro ancestry," in Mississippi "colored" took on a broader, more inclusive meaning. In 1927 the U.S. Supreme Court upheld a Mississippi court ruling that allowed school officials to classify Chinese American school children as "colored" to prevent them from enrolling in white schools.[40] In their brief the lawyers for Gong Lum and his daughter, Martha Lum (who was denied admittance to a white school), argued that since white people did not want to have their children exposed to the "danger" of black people, "the White race may not legally expose the Yellow race to a danger that the dominant race recognizes and, by the same laws, guards itself against." Chinese Americans in Mississippi, like Mexican Americans in Texas, mainly objected to being denied the right to attend white schools.[41]

The *Delgado* case did little to end segregation because it was still legal to separate Mexicans from Anglos for language deficiency, even when Mexican children spoke English better than the children from whom they were segregated. In one case, school officials had placed Linda Pérez in the "Mexican" school, although the only language she could speak was English.[42] Sánchez had grown tired of "begging and cajoling" school officials "to do as a favor what they should do as a matter of compliance with the law . . . [Segregation] is either legal or it isn't," he declared. "If it is illegal, we can stop it, whether the politicos like it or not."[43] In an angry letter to the assistant attorney general of Texas, Sánchez wrote that if students could be segregated in separate buildings for language deficiencies, "why can't they be segregated on the basis of deficiencies in arithmetic, or ability to draw, or muscular reaction speed . . . ?" Calling the practice "pedagogically unsound," he reminded the assistant attorney general that the laws of Texas "do not authorize the maintenance of separate school buildings for any race or class except the Negro. The organization of schools for all other children . . . and the facilities and programs of such schools," Sánchez insisted, must "be equally open to all . . . [non-Negro] children."[44] Cristóbal Aldrete, a war veteran and student at the University of Texas, informed Attorney General Price Daniel that continuing to allow segregation for language deficiency "gave aid, comfort, and a cloak of authority" to school boards wishing to maintain segregated schools.[45] When a bill was introduced in the state legislature to grant greater discretionary power to school boards, Sánchez warned that any "sly attempt to place Mexican children at the mercy of school boards in much the same manner as the Negroes" must be "attacked vigorously."[46] State Superintendent Woods blamed the cost of maintaining segregated schooling for African American and Mexican students for Texas ranking twenty-sixth among all the states in ability to provide quality public education to its citizens.[47]

Thurgood Marshall and the Fund were also busy preparing desegregation cases in Texas—one against the University of

Texas law school in 1946 and one in Hearne, Texas, where C. G. Jennings, a prominent businessman, sought to enroll his thirteen-year-old daughter, Doris Fay, in the town's white high school rather than the ramshackle school for "coloreds."[48] Marshall asked the court "to enjoin the Hearne Independent School District from further discriminating against the Negroes of Hearne." In a dramatic break from the equalization strategy, he did not request that the school district provide material equality between the black and white schools; instead, he told the judge: "We insist upon taking no cognizance of the segregation laws of the state [of Texas] since we consider them to be unconstitutional."[49] Marshall and the Fund intended to launch a direct assault on *Plessy* in the case against the University of Texas law school (*Sweatt v. Painter*), and informed the Houston branch of the NAACP that it was no longer prudent to pursue equalization suits in Texas or anywhere else. Marshall declared that equalization had always been a tactical means to achieve a strategic objective—"to destroy segregation."[50]

Lulu White, president of the Houston branch of the NAACP, spearheaded the Hearne segregation case. White agreed that the time had come to end, once and for all, the idea that separate schooling could be made equal. She was particularly encouraged by the activism of Mexican parents in southern California, whom she likely learned about from the NAACP branch in California, which had become interested in the *Mendez* case. "These Mexican Americans suing for damages" in southern California, she told Marshall, also opposed separate facilities and suggested that Marshall meet with the Mexican consul in Houston to discuss the case the next time he came to Texas.[51]

With Marshall joining other civil rights groups in submitting amicus briefs in the *Mendez* case, and both Mexican Americans and the NAACP filing suits in Texas, it seemed only a matter of time before formal contact was established between the two groups. The breakthrough occurred two weeks after the ruling in the *Delgado* case when Thurgood Marshall, on the advice of Los Angeles attorney A. L. Wirin, wrote to George Sánchez requesting the affidavits in the *Delgado* case in preparation for the NAACP's segregation case in Hearne. Sánchez told Marshall that the affidavits would likely not be useful to him because they challenged the "pedagogical soundness of segregation . . . based on the 'language handicap' excuse." In other words, the *Delgado* case did not challenge the doctrine of separate-but-equal facilities for African Americans as mandated by law.[52] Instead, he offered to share with Marshall "the plan of attack" used to win segregation suits before actually appearing in court. The plan consisted of two main arguments: inform the superintendent that it was illegal to segregate Mexicans from "other whites," and join the state superintendent of instruction in all lawsuits. (Marshall had tried joining state superintendents in 1939 to little avail.)[53] Sánchez alluded to "certain procedures" that might have "some value to you in your field," but failed to explain to Marshall how an objection to segregation on pedagogical grounds and the absence of state law could possibly be of use to the NAACP's frontal assault on the *Plessy* doctrine. Marshall quickly lost interest in the Hearne case as the case to desegregate the University of Texas law school began to take shape.[54]

Texas had become a major player in the Legal Defense Fund's school cases in part because the NAACP branches in Dallas and Houston had been instrumental in bringing the case against the "white primary" that resulted in the 1944 U.S. Supreme Court decision in *Smith v. Allwright*, which ended the power of the Democratic Party to deny African Americans the ballot in primary elections.[55] Two years later Heman Marion Sweatt, a Houston mailman with a college degree, applied to the University of Texas law school and was flatly rejected on the ground of his race rather than qualifications. In a letter to the state attorney general, the president of the University of Texas (UT), Theophilus Painter, wrote that Sweatt was "duly qualified" to be admitted to the law school, "except for the fact that he is a Negro."[56] When the case was heard in the county court, the trial judge acknowledged the constitutional requirement to maintain a separate law school for blacks, but gave the state six months to establish one at the Negro Prairie View University in Houston, "an academic hovel that offered college credit," according to one historian, "for mattress-making, broom-making, and other minimal vocational skills." Six months later the Travis County District Court found that the shotgun law school set up in a few rented rooms forty miles from the Prairie View campus had achieved substantial parity with the University of Texas law school, despite a few deficiencies, such as the absence of a student body, a full-time faculty, and a commensurate library.[57]

Soon after Sweatt filed suit in 1946, seventeen University of Texas student organizations signed a petition endorsing Heman Sweatt's right to attend the university's law school, while over 200 white students set up the only all-white chapter of the NAACP in its history. Thurgood Marshall personally helped the students obtain the charter, explaining that the only way for African Americans in Texas to get "full and complete legal training" was in an integrated law school.[58] One UT student and NAACP member, John Stanford, led a drive to raise funds for the Sweatt case, while fifty students at a campus meeting hosted by the NAACP voted unanimously to support the drive.[59] "Those of us who are not Negro are working for the advancement of the race," wrote one white student and charter member of the campus NAACP, "because they are denied democracy, and we know that as long as they are, we are none of us safe."[60] Donald Logan, another UT student, blasted Texas Gov. Beauford

Jester for supporting segregated schooling and opposing President Truman's civil rights stand: "It is most disheartening to see our name among those governors who would like to remain in the dark ages. Texas has risen above her backward and stagnant sister states, but you, Governor Jester, have tied the millstone around her neck. Give the negro a break—if not because he's human, then because he pays taxes."[61]

After the war, Americans were deeply divided by the growing domestic and international pressure to move the country out of the dark ages of racial prejudice. The Southern states and their Democratic leaders were just as determined to defend segregation and the "Southern way of life." In the fall of 1947, the President's Committee on Civil Rights issued its blue-ribbon report, *To Secure These Rights,* calling for the elimination of school segregation, the poll tax, housing and employment discrimination, segregation in the armed services, and many other reforms, including federal protection from lynching.[62] The Committee on Civil Rights also emphasized that "not even the most mathematically precise equality of segregated institutions can properly be considered equality under the law."[63] The following year President Truman issued executive orders to desegregate the armed services and the federal work force. In response, Dixiecrat Southerners laid plans to bolt the Democratic Party and man the barricades of white supremacy, blaming Truman's "communistic philosophy" for advancing the cause of civil rights. Conservative Democrat and former Texas governor, Sen. W. Lee O'Daniel, charged that Truman's civil rights agenda was concocted on the "orders of Joe Stalin . . . through his stooges . . . [in] our White House."[64]

At the University of Texas, students and professors became targets of anticommunist offensives even before the war ended. In his second term as governor in 1941, W. Lee O'Daniel told his political advisors that he had appointed six of the nine-member

UT Board of Regents with the goal of taking control of education at the University of Texas because UT was the source of all "radicalism" in the state. Shortly afterwards, University of Texas President Homer Rainey was forced to resign for defending academic freedom and refusing to carry out witch hunts for subversive professors, which included those whose views were pro-labor or showed "any friendliness . . . to Negroes."[65] Ernest Patterson, an economics professor opposed to banning the Communist Party on or off campus, and J. Frank Dobie, a literature professor and scathing critic of the state legislature's resistance to dismantling Jim Crow, were denounced in the legislature and the press for perverting "the American way of life." The Texas legislature, concerned that pro-civil rights students and faculty were not sufficiently anticommunist, passed H.C.R. 50, a joint resolution instructing the presidents of all Texas colleges and universities to conduct investigations of students and faculty and expel any deemed to be "disloyal to this nation."[66] (After Professor Dobie resigned from UT, he wrote: "When I get ready to explain homemade fascism in America, I can take my example from the state capitol of Texas.")[67] The resolution was prompted by the activities of a UT student, Wendell Addington, who as youth director of the Texas Communist Party, called for support for anti-lynching legislation, repeal of the poll tax, abolition of Jim Crow practices, and land reform for the legions of sharecroppers and day laborers who had created the agricultural wealth of Texas for generations.[68] Although the legislative resolution did not have the force of law, UT President T. S. Painter declared that the university "will, of course, comply with the letter and spirit of the legislation." Addington, however, was defiant: "I shall resist any attempt to expel me, both in the courts of law and in the higher courts of public opinion."[69]

Changes were taking place in universities in other parts of the South in the waning years of the 1940s. When the University of

Virginia football team played Harvard in the fall of 1948 in Charlottesville, 24,000 Virginia students rose to applaud Chester Pierce, Harvard's African American tackle and the first black player to appear on a Southern gridiron against an all-white team. The roar of applause, according to one journalist, reflected the "evolution . . . in attitude" of a new generation of Southern whites who believed in a "spirit of fair play" and the struggle of blacks "for progress and due recognition of their merits."[70] Virginia Gov. William Tuck did not share the students' enthusiasm for civil rights. In a speech before the General Assembly, he declared that the enactment Truman's civil rights program would be "an unwarranted assault upon the established customs and traditions of the entire Southland."[71]

A different scenario unfolded in Texas during the same football season. Lafayette College in Pennsylvania was invited to play in the Texas Sun Bowl at UT El Paso (then called the Texas College of Mines). The UT Board of Regents did not permit blacks to play on its teams and prohibited athletic competition with college teams that did. When the UT Board of Regents informed Lafayette College that their African American halfback could not play in the bowl game, the Lafayette football team unanimously agreed to cancel the game. UT student Donald Smith fired off an angry letter to Gov. Beauford Jester that the university's athletic policy was a "disgrace to America" and added, unselfconsciously, that he failed to understand why the university could be so offended by the idea of a Negro football player in a state "largely populated by half breed Mexicans."[72]

Some of those Mexicans attended the University of Texas. In 1946, the same year as the campaign to admit Sweatt to the law school, 114 Mexican American students ("Spanish-name, Texas-born") attended UT, and the faculty included two well-known professors of Mexican ancestry—Carlos Casteñeda, a professor of Latin American history, who served as FEPC regional director during the war, and George Sánchez, a professor of education specializing in the Spanish-speaking peoples of the Southwest.[73] In addition to Mexican American students, a sizable number of students attended UT from Mexico, Cuba, Puerto Rico, Brazil, Panama, Nicaragua, Venezuela, and other Latin American countries, many of whom, one student observed, "obviously had traces of Negro ancestry."[74] Latin American students belonging to the Latin-American Union student group wavered between supporting the Sweatt campaign and remaining neutral. After a heated meeting, they passed a resolution condemning "discrimination at any place or time" but refused to support the Sweatt campaign. It would be "against our conception of international courtesy," they resolved, "to state our opinion concerning any concrete case [of segregation] in any country in which we are visitors."[75] Their desire to remain neutral in a contentious local and national debate over the rights of America's black citizens was understandable, perhaps even prudent; however, dark-skinned Latin American students, many of them members of the elite classes in their home countries, were sometimes mistaken for blacks and barred from Austin's shops and restaurants. By insisting they were Latin Americans, they may have been reluctant to be too closely identified with the cause of African Americans.[76]

The presence at UT of Mexican American students and faculty, as well as international students from Latin America, many of them manifestly dark-skinned, was not lost on black Texans and the larger African American community. Charles Thompson, Howard University professor and founder of the journal *The Negro in Higher Education,* used the term "non-Negroes" advisedly rather than "whites" to specify UT students because, he said, "there are non-white students regularly enrolled in the University of Texas."[77] Heman Sweatt himself remarked at a press conference that Mexicans had been admitted to the University of Texas for many years, and Thurgood Marshall made a point of challenging the notion that UT was an all-white school. "As a matter of fact," Marshall told the editor of the *New York Times,* "the student body of the University of Texas includes all racial and ethnic groups *except* Negroes."[78]

One black Texan, George Allen, managed to slip past the guardians of Jim Crow in the University of Texas's Division of Extension. Allen registered by phone to attend a business psychology class, but the division dean, T. H. Shelby, determined that the "negro man misrepresented his race." In an article titled "Negro Discovered in Class at U.T.," the *Austin [American] Statesman* reported that the "dark-complexioned Austin youth" told the professor he was of French-Jewish ancestry. When an investigation revealed Allen was "of the Negro race," the dean returned his admission fee and barred Allen from attending the class.[79]

University segregation policy also extended to nonacademic areas: it required segregated audience seating for any public entertainment held on campus in which black Texans might be in attendance. When African American pianist and singer Hazel Scott learned that UT segregated public audiences on campus, she refused to play before a sell-out crowd of 7,000 people at the University of Texas Gregory Gymnasium. Scott, married to Rep. Adam Clayton Powell, the first African American elected to Congress from New York, said she would have played had the audience been only students, since there were no black students enrolled at the university. She refused, however, to perform before segregated audiences anywhere in the world, adding, "If I were a citizen of Austin, I wouldn't want to attend a concert and be segregated."[80]

When Thurgood Marshall traveled to Texas to try the Heman Sweatt case in 1946, only months after having submitted his amicus brief in the *Mendez* case, he was encouraged that the Travis County courtroom was "jammed with people, about one-half Negro and one-half white." The whites in the courtroom consisted mainly of UT students opposed to the exclusion of African Americans from the University of Texas.[81] By the time the case went to the Texas Court of Civil Appeals the following year, the state legislature decided to abandon the Prairie View law school for Negroes and create a "first class" law school in the basement of a two-story building near the state capitol occupied by a firm of petroleum engineers.[82] The makeshift Jim Crow law school consisted of three professors from the UT law school and offered students access to the law library at the state capitol. Sweatt refused to enroll. Although the temporary UT Negro law school offered a better student-teacher ratio than the UT law school, few Texas blacks would freely choose to attend a mock law school designed for ten students over the University of Texas law school. Henry Doyle became the sole black student in what Thurgood Marshall called the UT "Uncle Tom's Cabin" law school. "It's just like having a steaming plate of chicken on a box in the backyard," Doyle told a reporter for the UT student newspaper. "I'd rather have it in the house, but chicken is chicken and it's better in the backyard than not at all."[83]

As the Sweatt case wound its way to the U.S. Supreme Court, Governor Jester stepped up efforts to end discrimination against Mexicans in Texas, mainly to persuade the Mexican government to lift its ban on braceros, but also because he believed that Mexico and Texas shared a common future based on trade and mutual cooperation. Shortly after his inauguration, Governor Jester visited Mexican President Miguel Alemán in Mexico City to assure him that he fully supported efforts to end discrimination against Mexicans in Texas.[84] In another meeting with Alemán in the border city of Matamoros, Jester publicly

apologized for "several unfortunate incidents of discrimination" in Texas and expressed the hope that Texas might soon be
removed from the blacklist forbidding the importation of
Mexican braceros.[85] As a measure of his concern to have the
ban lifted, Jester asked Secretary of State George C. Marshall to
encourage the Mexican government to consider Texas's "progress in ridding ourselves of our regrettable, but not exclusive,
imperfections and ask itself, if this progress warrants . . . [Mex-
ico's] continued application of economic and moral sanctions
against this State." Texas had made steady progress, he told
Marshall, in "harmonizing the living together of two dynamic
cultures."[86] In an address to the Texas Good Neighbor Commission, Jester expressed the belief that "the continents of
America should be bilingual continents," and that "we in Texas
should be able to speak, read and understand the language of
our Latin American neighbors." He even recommended that
teaching Spanish be made compulsory in Texas public schools.[87]

Many black Texans questioned how Governor Jester and State
Atty. Gen. Price Daniel could commit themselves and state
agencies to eliminating discrimination against Mexicans but not
blacks. In 1947 Attorney General Daniel issued an opinion that
Texas law "clearly prohibits discrimination against or segregation
of Latin-Americans on account of race or descent, and that the
law permits no subterfuge to accomplish such discrimination."[88]
When Jester reiterated his commitment to the Good Neighbor
policy with Mexico, J. E. Palmer, the president of the largest
fraternal organization for African Americans in Texas, wrote
Jester: "We have noticed . . . that you are very much concerned
about discrimination and segregation as practiced against our
Latin American Citizens and Non-Citizens, but . . . your every
act as governor has been in the direction of strengthening the
present segregation laws against the Negro Citizens of this
State . . . Must we accept the White man as our friend, if the

Chief among them behaves as you do?"[89] Lulu White of the NAACP Houston branch put the matter a little more delicately: "We are glad to know that you are trying to end prejudice against the Mexican Americans. We know you cannot very well stop prejudice against one minority group without stopping it for all . . . Americans, be they Mexican, Negro or white."[90] Leon Guitry, a black soldier stationed in Illinois, wrote Jester: "I am a native of Houston and a Negro soldier . . . Some day I am planning on returning home . . . When will the day come that I don't have to sit on the back seat of the buses because of my color . . . ? I would like to have some of the freedom your people have."[91] And some of the freedom the governor hoped to win, at least in his official pronouncements, for Mexicans in the state.

As Marshall and the Legal Defense Fund had predicted, the Texas courts, including the Texas Supreme Court, upheld the University of Texas's contention that the establishment of a basement law school for black students met the constitutional requirements of *Plessy*. The Sweatt case finally came before the U.S. Supreme Court in 1949, three years after the suit was first filed in Travis County Court. Numerous civil rights organizations had joined the suit as "friends of the court," including the Federal Council of Churches, the CIO and AFL, the American Veterans Committee, the American Jewish Committee, the American Federation of Teachers, and 187 leading law professors (Committee of Law Teachers against Segregation in Legal Education).[92] The solicitor general of the United States, Philip Perlman, also submitted an amicus brief arguing that the *Plessy* doctrine could no longer be defended. Texas Atty. Gen. Price Daniel called on eleven Southern states to submit amicus briefs to counter those submitted by the federal government and numerous civil rights organizations. If Texas loses the case, Daniel said, "my office will be deluged with law suits for entry of Negroes into white colleges, high schools and grades schools."[93]

On June 5, 1950, in a unanimous decision, the U.S. Supreme Court ordered that Heman Sweatt be admitted to the UT law school, the first time the Court had ordered a black student admitted to a segregated school on the ground that the state had failed to establish a separate school that offered equal educational opportunity to blacks. However, like other cases involving higher education, Chief Justice Fred Vinson refused to address the larger constitutional questions raised by Thurgood Marshall's brief and the brief of the 187 law professors who roundly criticized the Court for failing to end race-based injustice committed under the cloak of *Plessy*. In his narrowly tailored ruling, Vinson wrote: "the University of Texas Law School possesses to a far greater degree those qualities which are incapable of objective measurement but which make for greatness in a law school. Such qualities, to name but a few, include reputation of the faculty, experience of the administration, position and influence of the alumni, standing in the community, traditions and prestige. It is difficult to believe that one who had a free choice between these law schools would consider the question close."[94] Although Marshall did not get the expansive ruling he had hoped for, he declared that "segregation no longer has the stamp of legality in any public education."[95] "Of course it would have been good for the court to have overruled *Plessy v. Ferguson*," he told black feminist attorney Pauli Murray, "but a careful reading of the opinions will show that for all intents and purposes, *Plessy v. Ferguson* has been gutted."[96]

Although the Sweatt case took place in a state that was at the time home to more Mexican-origin citizens than any other state, as well as to LULAC and the G.I. Forum, there is little evidence that George Sánchez or other LULAC leaders, such as Manuel Gonzales and Alfonso Perales, showed any interest in the case, much less offered their support. When ACLU attorney A. L. Wirin, who had submitted an amicus brief in *Mendez* and

Heman Sweatt in registration line at the University of Texas School of
Law. Prints and Photographs Collection, di_01127, Dolph Briscoe
Center for American History, University of Texas at Austin.

served as counsel with Gus García in *Delgado,* suggested that LULAC file an amicus brief in the Sweatt case, Sánchez demurred, stating that he "would like to see an amicus brief developed along somewhat different lines from those forwarded by Thurgood Marshall." In fact, however, Sánchez fully endorsed the logic of Marshall's brief that separate was inherently unequal. It is worth citing Sánchez at length on this point:

> In the first place, 'equal protection' should go far beyond mere comparison of professors-books-buildings in law school. The comparison should be one which involves the *whole* of education that has been made available to the white law-school graduate and the *whole* of education available to the Negro. This would involve comparison of the entire common school program, the preparation of teachers, general college libraries, the pre-law programs, cultural entertainment and lecture programs, etc. Such a comparison would lead to the conclusion that equality would call for duplication all the way along the line—an impossibility since experts (not only in law but in the sciences and arts) cannot be duplicated. Furthermore, the whole idea of dichotomous education implies ostracism—and its whole spirit is based on the concept of inequality.[97]

Marshall would have wholeheartedly concurred that dichotomous education did indeed imply ostracism—the "badge of inferiority" that the majority of justices in *Plessy* fraudulently claimed was a figment of the African American imagination. "The whole spirit" of *Plessy* was indeed "based on the concept of inequality." So what exactly did Sánchez mean when he told Wirin he would be inclined to develop an amicus brief "along different lines" than that of Thurgood Marshall?

Whatever Sánchez had in mind, he was not inclined to submit a brief in the Sweatt case, in part because the "language handicap" pretext rather than state law was the central issue in

Mexican segregation cases, but also in part because of the difficulty of raising the funds necessary to pay Wirin, who offered to write the brief. LULAC did not have an impressive fundraising record, and Sánchez had become increasingly critical of the organization. He called LULAC and "amateurish operation" that failed to establish a program of action at the national, state, or even local level, focusing instead on establishing new councils that accomplished little and faded away after a few years. "The Lulac mountain labors mightily," he told LULAC president John Herrera in 1953, "and, except on very rare occasions, gives birth to a mouse."[98] Gus García, the lead attorney in the *Delgado* case, called LULAC and other Mexican American organizations "mere skeletons" with no national leadership, no national newsletter, and no national consensus.[99] LULAC was no NAACP.

The American G.I. Forum, the Mexican American civil rights organization for veterans, promised to be more effective. Established shortly after the war, the Forum's founder, Dr. Hector García, a Corpus Christi physician and World War II veteran, organized a statewide protest when T. W. Kennedy, the manager of the Three Rivers funeral home near San Antonio, refused to allow a wake for the remains of PFC Feliz Longoria because, he told the Longoria family, "other white people object to the use of the funeral home by people of Mexican origin."[100] The incident received national attention, including front-page coverage in the *New York Times,* whereupon Sen. Lyndon Baines Johnson offered to have Private Longoria's remains buried with full military honors in Arlington National Cemetery.[101] The incident established the G.I. Forum as a promising civil rights organization for Mexican Americans, even though García insisted that the G.I. Forum was a "charitable organization" and that "we are not and have never been a civil rights organization." "Personally," he confessed, "I hate the word."[102]

García's reluctance to have the G.I. Forum identified with civil rights is instructive. The phrase "civil rights" was so firmly linked in the post–World War II era to the struggle of African Americans that García perhaps thought it best not to suggest any solidarity with blacks. Although the G.I. Forum was committed to ending school segregation, employment discrimination, and residential segregation—traditional civil rights concerns—García and the Mexican consuls with whom he often worked were also deeply committed to the idea that Mexicans were white and called any suggestion that they were not a "slur" and an affront to all Americans of Latin descent.[103] He wrote to the census supervisor in Dallas to complain of the state's practice of designating the race of Mexican Americans as "Latin" or "Mexican" instead of "white."[104] He complained to the Texas Department of Public Safety that police officers issuing traffic citations to Mexican Americans used the notation "Mex" or "Latin" in the space for "race" instead of "white"—a practice, he told the Public Safety director, that "continues to perpetuate our humiliation, suffering, and embarrassment."[105] When PFC Efrain Vela informed him that U.S. Army officials at Fort Hood listed his race as "Mexican," García wrote to the commanding officer: "we are sorry to see that the U.S. Army is taking to Texas customs of discrimination and implantation of feelings of inferiority in a group that has been so faithful and brave in fighting for our country. I can assure you that we are of American Nationality and members of the white race."[106] The Mexican consul in Austin, Efraín Domínguez, Jr., demanded a public apology from the president of the Chamber of Commerce in Mission, Texas, for repeatedly referring to Anglos as "members of the white race" and to Mexicans as "Latin Americans." The consul objected to the implication that Mexicans were not members of the white race and called the president's comment "grossly insulting and untactful." The "sadly uneducated, uncultured, and tactless" main speaker "openly gave us a slap in our face."[107]

Middle-class activists like Hector García and George Sánchez, as well as LULAC members and Mexican consuls generally, appeared at times more concerned about the stigma and humiliation of being regarded as nonwhite than they did about fighting for the economic rights of impoverished Mexican American and immigrant farmworkers, many of whom were illiterate, poor, and dark-skinned, and would not have troubled themselves over whether their Anglo employers considered them white.[108] As lawyers, doctors, professors, and businessmen, these activists, like the Mexican consuls with whom they often worked, occupied positions of privilege compared with the overwhelming majority of Mexican Americans, to say nothing of Mexican immigrants. That the "badge of inferiority" attached even more strongly to African Americans as a result of de jure segregation, economic oppression, lynching, and other Jim Crow realities hardly seemed to enter their consciousness.

Working-class Mexican immigrants and Mexican Americans did not share many of the cultural, class, and racial assumptions of some activists. When the G.I. Forum *News Bulletin,* for example, published a survey in 1955 titled "Mexican Americans Favor Negro School Integration," Manuel Avila, a member of the G.I. Forum and close personal friend of Hector García, complained bitterly that "Anybody reading it can only come to the conclusion [that] we are ready to fight the Negroes' battles . . . for sooner or later we are going to have to say which side of the fence we're on, are we white or not. If we are white, why do we ally with the Negro? To go to bat for the Negro is suicide."[109] In Arizona some Mexican restaurant owners were being treated like white people, he claimed, because they discontinued the practice of serving African Americans and had placed White Only signs in their windows. If Mexican restaurants would refuse to serve Negroes, Avila suggested, Anglo restaurants might begin serving Mexicans. Mexican Americans must say to Negroes, "I'm White and you can't come into my restaurant."[110]

The president of LULAC and well-known Mexican American civil rights activist Felix Tijerina owned a chain of restaurants in Houston that refused service to African Americans, even as many Houston restaurants refused service to Mexicans. He issued instructions to his employees on what to do if an African American were to enter his restaurants: "The proper thing to say is, 'I'm sorry, we cannot serve you.'" Tijerina cautioned employees that "if the Negro refuses to leave . . . and becomes noisy or demonstrative, it would be alright to call the police and have the Negro evicted or arrested."[111] Tijerina maintained his discriminatory policy until the passage of the Civil Rights Act in 1964. Not surprisingly, then, finding common cause with African Americans in the Sweatt case generated little interest among middle-class Mexican American leaders (and Mexican consuls) whose main concern was placing Mexicans on the white side of the color line rather than eliminating it or the structures of Jim Crow erected to keep out those on the wrong side of it.

A year after *Sweatt v. Painter,* the U.S. District Court for the District of Kansas heard Oliver Brown's suit against the Topeka School District for refusing to allow his third-grade daughter, Linda, to attend the white elementary school, which was nearer to her house than the segregated grade school on the other side of a railroad switchyard.[112] When Wirin suggested in 1953 that the *Mendez* and *Delgado* segregation cases in California and Texas would likely influence the outcome of the *Brown* cases, Sánchez exclaimed: "There is no connection! Our cases really were on the 'due process' clause [that segregation was] ('arbitrary, capricious') much more than on the equality . . . clause—whereas the present [*Brown*] cases attack the right of the states to legislate segregation (something which has never been done for Mexicans). Does one of the present cases attack Negro segregation where there is no law decreeing such segregation? Only in such a case would we be concerned."[113] For Sánchez the overriding issue was not the constitutional right of states to legislate segregation, but rather the illegality of segregating Mexicans from other whites in the absence of state law. While Thurgood Marshall sought to overturn a half-century-old Supreme Court decision, Sánchez challenged local school districts that arbitrarily segregated Mexicans for their alleged language handicap. But Sánchez's narrow focus on "due process" for Mexicans rather than "equal protection" for blacks missed the point that Sánchez himself made years earlier that the "whole spirit" of segregation was based "on the concept of inequality." No one knew better than Sánchez that the language handicap excuse was little more than a bureaucratic ruse to segregate Mexican children, but he seemed little concerned that no ruse was necessary to segregate African American children.

In the years after *Brown* and *Brown II,* attention shifted to the efforts of school boards to desegregate schools "with all deliberate speed" and the tactics of conservative white Southerners to circumvent the rulings by invoking interposition, or the nullification of federal laws that violate "states' rights." Sánchez meanwhile urged Roger Baldwin, the national director of the ACLU, to continue funding Mexican segregation cases because, he implausibly argued, Mexicans' status as whites could put them in the vanguard of civil rights struggles: "Let us keep in mind that the Mexican-American can easily become *the front-line defense* of the civil liberties of ethnic minorities. The racial, cultural, and historical involvements in his case embrace those of *all . . . other minority groups.* Yet, God bless the law, he is 'white'! So, the Mexican-American can be the wedge for broadening of civil liberties for others (who are not so fortunate as to be 'white' and 'Christian'!)." He concluded, "I am sorry that Thurgood Marshall and the NAACP have not seen fit to consult with us in these matters."[114] Marshall had, in fact, good reason not to. Marshall, after all, could not bless the law that granted white privilege to Mexican Americans but denied it to blacks. Nor could he bless a strategy against segregation on the narrow legal ground that school districts could not segregate Mexicans from "other whites." Far from being a wedge to broaden civil liberties for others, the Mexican litigation strategy had driven a wedge even more deeply between blacks and Mexicans.

Sánchez's almost exclusive focus on court cases also made it difficult to work with grassroots Mexican American organizations, such as the Allianza Hispano-Americana (Allianza) in Arizona and the Community Service Organization (CSO) in California, that did not always share his priorities or strategies for promoting the welfare of mexicanos. With funding from the Robert Marshall Civil Liberties Trust (aka the Marshall Fund), Sánchez and other activists founded the American Council of Spanish-Speaking People (ACSSP) in 1951 to serve as a "national clearing house" for Mexican American organizations throughout the Southwest through which Sánchez and other board members would "give them expert advice and assistance in the pursuit of their patriotic aims."[115] Roger Baldwin, who helped manage the Marshall Fund, hoped that the ACSSP might develop into a national organization similar to the NAACP, but Sánchez had a different model in mind.[116] He believed that the ACSSP should offer local organizations advice and financial support when possible, but that local organizations should set their own agendas and raise their own funds.[117] Sánchez wanted ACSSP to function more as a think tank consisting of political leaders of local groups and "the expert type . . . who know[s] the people and understand[s] their problems." But he disliked some local leaders, like muckraking newspaper publisher Ignacio López and Los Angeles CSO organizer Antonio Ríos. Ríos and the CSO organized voter registration drives to empower barrio residents of East Los Angeles to demand that the city provide better schools and more city services. Sánchez dismissed them as "trouble makers" and told a colleague that the CSO was "no more representative of the local people than those Jewish-Negro-Anglo-Asiatic groups we had lunch with!"[118]

It may have been impossible to establish a national organization along the lines of the NAACP in which local branches paid dues. On behalf of the Marshall Fund, Baldwin told Sánchez that to build a strong organization, the ACSSP needed to to build confidence in the organization's leadership by publishing a regular newsletter on law cases against discrimination.[119] But a year after its founding, Baldwin expressed his disappointment that the ACSSP functioned mainly as a local, Texas organization and had not made any progress in building a national organization.[120] Unlike the NAACP, the ACSSP lacked a national program, while groups like the CSO, Allianza, LULAC, and G.I. Forum often pursued objectives that did not always meet the approval of ACSSP. Furthermore, James Marshall, whose family established the Marshall Fund, became deeply concerned that the ACSSP strategy of pursuing court cases to end school segregation using the "other white, no state law" strategy "upheld the rights of Mexicans at the expense of other ethnic groups." ACLU attorney A. L. Wirin conceded the point in a letter to Roger Baldwin: "Any way, the point . . . is not that we do not make the point that Mexicans are of the same race as Anglos, but that we are not content in merely making that point."[121] But how was the other point they made—that no state law mandated segregation of Mexicans—supposed to resonate with African Americans who faced de jure segregation since the *Plessy* ruling over a half century earlier? or with the Chinese in Mississippi or the Native Americans and Asian Americans in California? James Marshall was right, which is why Thurgood Marshall found little to be gained by joining forces with Sánchez in litigating segregation cases. Lacking grassroots support or outside funding, the ACSSP folded seven years after its founding, while the grassroots interracial CSO, still active decades after its founding, helped launch the United Farm Workers Union and elect Edward Roybal in 1949 to the Los Angeles City Council, the first Spanish-surnamed person elected to that body since 1888. With CSO backing, Roybal was elected to the U.S. Congress in 1963, the first Latino from California to serve in Congress since 1879.[122]

In the years after *Brown*, divisions began to appear more openly between the cautious, conservative leadership of LULAC (which worried that siding with African Americans in desegregating schools might result in a white backlash) and other middle-class activists, like Houston attorney John Herrera, who had become increasingly impatient with LULAC President Felix Tijerina's political conservatism. Herrera, the past national president of LULAC, called Tijerina "a White Man's Mexican" for defending Richard Nixon's record on civil rights and publicly declaring his support for the Eisenhower-Nixon ticket in 1956.[123] A more serious issue arose in 1957 when the Texas legislature attempted to pass H.B. 231, a measure that would grant a "free choice" option to school superintendents to place students in whatever schools they deemed appropriate. The NAACP and state senators Henry B. González and Abraham Kazen, Jr., opposed the bill for its obvious intent to subvert the *Brown* decision and mounted a record-breaking filibuster to defeat it. But the legal advisor of LULAC, Phil Montalbo, advised Tijerina that to link arms with the NAACP would "tend to admit to our anglo-american friends that we considered ourselves separate

and apart from the majority of American citizens" and therefore
Mexican Americans should resolve segregation issues on a local
level "with the help of our anglo-american friends and not with
the help of the NAACP." Montalbo thought it best to remain
neutral unless Mexican children were "unjustly transferred to
colored schools."[124] LULAC regional director for West Texas,
A. G. Ramirez, told Tijerina, "We don't never want to be affiliated with the Negroes."[125] "We are white," he insisted in an
open letter to one LULAC council.[126] Felix Tijerina hardly
needed to be convinced. He told the *Houston Chronicle*, "Let the
Negro fight his own battles. His problems are not mine."[127] The
LULAC regional governor for Texas, Pete Tijerina (no relation
to Felix), emphatically condemned H.B. 231 and ridiculed LU-
LAC for refusing to work with the NAACP to defeat the bill.
"There were times," Pete Tijerina observed, "when our conven-
tion seemed more like a White Citizens' Council meeting than a
LULAC convention."[128]

The problem of the color line surfaced the following year in
a newly established LULAC council in Wisconsin when some
Puerto Ricans in Milwaukee applied for membership. The regional director advised that the applicants should not be permitted to join because they were "dark-skinned . . . members of
the colored race."[129] But another LULAC member and former
vice-president, Luciano Santoscoy, said that the Puerto Ricans
in question were "mostly white . . . with only 23.5% negro" and
that, as Christians and Spanish speakers, Puerto Ricans shared
many affinities with Mexican Americans. He advised against
barring any applicant because of color, since the league was
"supposed to have been championing this cause for the past
29 years."[130]

Gus García, the lead attorney in the *Delgado* school segregation case in 1948 and longtime member of the San Antonio
school board, LULAC, and the G.I. Forum, could not ignore

the long history of discrimination against African Americans in Texas and throughout the nation. In 1952 he was invited by the United Nations Economic, Social and Cultural Organization (UNESCO) to deliver an address on the educational problems of the Southwest. At the time García and another San Antonio attorney, Carlos Cadena, represented Pete Hernandez in a jury discrimination case that went before the U. S. Supreme Court. Two weeks before the Court issued its historic ruling in *Brown v. Board of Education*, it ruled in *Hernandez v. Texas* that Mexican Americans represented a "distinct class" that had been systematically excluded from jury duty. García's experience in these cases, and his deep concern that no American be denied the equal protection of the law on account of race, led him to reflect on the treatment of African Americans at a testimonial dinner in his honor in San Antonio:

> It is not sufficient to say, 'I know Negroes are not getting their full share of democracy, but—', and then proceed to voice a long series of apologies and explanations. It would be an indication at least of honesty to say, 'Frankly, I am prejudiced against Negroes and I do not believe that they are entitled to everything that we get' . . . The truth of the matter is: our conduct toward our Negro minority has been reprehensible and regardless of how some people may feel about it, if our form of government is to survive, sooner or later American Negroes will occupy the position to which all citizens are entitled in a truly democratic society.[131]

The problems faced by Mexicans, the overwhelming majority of whom were working class, were in actuality quite similar to those facing African Americans. They attended run-down schools with poorly paid and undertrained teachers, lived in segregated neighborhoods, and were denied equal employment opportunities even after the passage of the Civil Rights Act. In

California, less than a decade after *Mendez* (1947), Mexican Americans and African Americans worked together to desegregate schools in southern California. Loren Miller, chairman of the West Coast NAACP Legal Committee, ACLU attorney A. L. Wirin, and Ralph Estrada, president of the Arizona-based civil rights organization Allianza Hispano-Americana, filed simultaneous suits against the El Centro School District for segregating African American and Mexican American children in Washington Elementary and Douglass Junior High schools since 1934, when Mexicans and African Americans first began to move into the Imperial Valley school districts to work in agriculture.[132]

A decade after *Brown*, black and Mexican parents of children in segregated schools in Corpus Christi took matters into their own hands and filed a suit in 1968 against the practice of busing Mexican children to predominantly black schools to achieve integration, while leaving predominantly white schools alone.[133] For these parents, the question of educational equality for their children was every parent's battle, irrespective of one's race, color, creed, or national origin. Their children were being denied the quality education offered to white children at the predominantly white schools—modern educational facilities, teacher training and experience, updated curriculum, and extracurricular activities.

District judge Woodrow Seals agreed and found that "placing Negroes and Mexican-Americans in the same school does not achieve a unitary system. As contemplated by law, a unitary school district can be achieved here only by substantiated integration of the Negroes and Mexican Americans with the remaining student population of the district."[134] In referring to the *Brown* cases, Seals wrote: "Although these cases speak in terms of race and color, we must remember that these cases were only concerned with blacks and whites. But it is clear to this court that these cases are not limited to race and color alone. In this case, if the proof shows that the Mexican-Americans in the Corpus Christi Independent School District are an identifiable, ethnic-minority group, and for this reason have been segregated and discriminated against in the schools in the manner that *Brown* prohibits, then they are certainly entitled to all the protection announced in *Brown*. Thus *Brown* can apply to Mexican-American students in public schools."[135]

Mexican American and African American parents also joined forces in Denver to file a suit against School District No. 1 for its pattern of drawing attendance boundaries that resulted in the segregation of Mexican and black children in the same schools. The school district made the familiar argument that de facto segregation was a reflection of neighborhood residential patterns and that children are best served when they attend schools in their own neighborhoods. It was not their fault, school officials maintained, that neighborhoods tended to be racially segregated. They further argued that segregation was illegal only when "state action" denied citizens their rights on account of race, color, creed, or national origin, as was the case in the half century before *Brown*.[136]

The highly controversial and complicated case wound its way to the U.S. Supreme Court, which ruled, in effect, that the Denver school system had maintained the equivalent of a dual school system by manipulating school attendance zones, school-site selection, and other means of establishing and maintaining segregated schools. In addition, the court ruled that decisions made by school authorities in assigning faculty, staff, and students to particular schools, choosing construction sites for new schools, and renovating old ones, all constituted "state action" within the meaning of the Fourteenth

Amendment. In a separate opinion, Justice William Douglas declared that de facto segregation was essentially de jure segregation by other means:

> I think it is time to state that there is no constitutional differ-
> ence between *de jure* and *de facto* segregation, for each is the
> product of state actions or policies . . . Where the school district
> is racially mixed and the races are segregated in separate schools,
> where black teachers are assigned almost exclusively to black
> schools, where the school board closed existing schools located
> in fringe areas and built new schools in black areas and in dis-
> tant white areas . . . these actions constitute state action. They
> are of a kind quite distinct from the classical *de jure* type of
> school segregation. Yet calling them *de facto* is a misnomer, as
> they are only more subtle types of state action that create or
> maintain a wholly or partially segregated school system.[137]

Mexican Americans in Corpus Christi and Denver had won their cases to be integrated with whites, but not *as whites.* As an identifiable minority group, many Mexican Americans shed their identities as whites and adopted a "brown" identity, partly as a legal strategy but mostly as a consequence of the Chicano Movement's emphasis on the Indian and mixed-race heritage of Mexican people. As members of a "minority group," Mexicans could no longer be bused to predominantly African American schools as part of a desegregation order.[138]

The fight for equal education lingered long after *Brown v. Board* and *Brown II,* as school districts throughout the South and other parts of the nation sought to preserve de facto segregation by gerrymandering school attendance zones and school selection sites or pairing majority Mexican schools with majority black schools, as was done in Texas and Colorado, to avoid integrating predominantly white schools. More than a half century after *Brown,* between 20 and 30 percent of African Americans continue to live in high-poverty neighborhoods, and young black males have the highest unemployment rates of any other group.[139] Mexican Americans and other Latinos, particularly immigrants, have the highest school dropout rates of any group.[140] The growing shift from pre-*Brown* litigation on voting rights, residential segregation, and labor rights to school integration after *Brown II* did not bring about the changes for which most African Americans or Mexican Americans had hoped, any more than legal challenges to residential segregation have resulted in integrated neighborhoods.

Desegregation turned out not to be the solution to bridging the economic chasm that persists among blacks, whites, and Latinos. As early as 1927, the founder and director of the ACLU, Roger Baldwin, foresaw the problem of relying on the courts to effect meaningful change in American society: "My own view is that such a legalistic approach will fail of its object because the forces that keep the Negro under subjugation will find some way of accomplishing their purposes, law or no law. My personal view is that the whole problem [of discrimination] should be approached from the economic standpoint and primarily that of the union of white and black workers against their common exploiters."[141] In today's globally competitive economy, however, unions represent only a small fraction of the U.S. workforce, while the best jobs require increasingly higher levels of education and training. With among the highest school dropout rates in the country, however, many blacks and Latinos will continue to face economic hardships in this century. If nothing else, economic dislocation and marginalization should be strong incentives for these groups to work together. Why they mostly do not has been attributed to many factors, some of which I explore in the epilogue.

Epilogue

Regional, national, and international politics have presented formidable difficulties for the possibility of cross-racial cooperation between African Americans and Mexican Americans in their struggle for equal opportunity in employment and education. Tenuous attempts to link their struggles amounted to a failed promise—or at least a missed opportunity—in part because Mexican American civil rights leaders (and Mexican consuls) saw little to gain and much to lose in locking arms with African Americans. Yet it would be unfair to expect largely poor and marginalized blacks and Mexicans to form alliances or to express solidarity across lines of race, ethnicity, and class any more than to expect, say, the persecuted Yaqui Indians and Chinese in northern Mexico to cooperatively resist discrimination and eventual deportation. For one thing, marginalized groups often live in highly segregated communities with little opportunity for interaction and coalition building, and are often as wary of each other as they are of those who wield economic and political power over them. The long history of tension between African Americans and immigrants, most recently from Mexico, is a case in point. How can trust be fostered between groups that are largely strangers to one another? Interracial solidarity requires a certain degree of identification with others and a willingness to act on behalf of others who are "not like us." Even within the Mexican community, conflicts over rights often divided Mexican Americans and immigrant "wetback" laborers, while what seemed to matter most to middle-class Mexican Americans was establishing themselves on right side of the color line.[1]

Conservative middle-class black leaders also complicated the prospect of intraracial as well as interracial solidarity, at least in the legal domain, because they favored the "equal" side of the separate but equal doctrine, fearing that integration would end the need for historically black colleges, like Howard University in Washington, D.C. (where Marshall attended law school after being denied admission to the University of Maryland), and Meharry Medical College in Nashville, Tennessee. Carter Wesley, a Houston attorney and important newspaper publisher, carried on a long and at times rancorous exchange with Thurgood Marshall and the NAACP over the strategy of ending segregation rather than building and staffing schools for blacks that were equal to white schools. Although Wesley and other African American attorneys were instrumental in winning the first two "white primary" cases at the Supreme Court, which gave blacks the right to vote in Texas Democratic Party primaries, he and other black leaders opposed the idea that blacks and whites necessarily needed to be in the same schools. What they needed, Wesley believed, was equal facilities. In 1946 he founded the Texas Conference for the Equalization of Educational Opportunities to fight "on the segregated side" for equal but separate schools, thereby effectively enabling Southern states to circumvent *Plessy* while at the same time securing the institutional benefits of enrolling blacks unable to attend graduate and professional schools in the South. Whatever differences in strategies may have prevented closer ties between African Americans and Mexican Americans, at least LULAC and the Legal Defense Fund of the NAACP believed that separate educational facilities were inherently unequal.[2]

In the years after the passage of the Civil Rights Act in 1964, LULAC and other middle-class Mexicans gradually abandoned their decades-long fight to be recognized as "whites" of Mexican ancestry, or "Latin Americans" as they used to refer to themselves. In the sixties and seventies, a younger and more radical generation of Mexican Americans, calling themselves Chicanos and Chicanas, sought empowerment through brown power and, borrowing a page from the black power movement, aligned themselves with third world liberation movements abroad as well as the struggles of nonwhite peoples at home, including those of blacks, Native Americans, and Mexican farmworkers.[3] Two Chicanas, Maria Varela and Elizabeth Sutherland Martínez (aka "Betita"), became charter members of the Student Nonviolent Coordinating Committee (SNCC) and championed the struggles of blacks in the South as well as *la causa* of the United Farm Workers (UFW), founded by César Chávez and Dolores Huerta. Varela and Martínez also participated in the 1964 Mississippi Summer Project (Freedom Summer) to register African American voters, and Martínez later traveled to Cuba as SNCC's representative to a gathering of Latin American revolutionaries.[4]

California, the most multicultural state in the United States in the twentieth century, had long experimented with interracial cooperation, in part because Filipinos, African Americans, Mexicans, Jews, and Japanese Americans had realized the power of coalition politics and labor union organizing to achieve together what they might not accomplish alone. During the Delano Grape Strike of 1965, the San Francisco branch of the NAACP actively called on its membership and others to support César Chávez and the United Farm Workers movement by boycotting all grocers who sold California grapes until the growers agreed to sign contracts with the UFW.[5]

Support the Farm Workers

can **your** family live on
less than $1800
a year ?

DON'T BUY CALIFORNIA GRAPES

CALIFORNIA TABLE GRAPES WERE PICKED BY PEOPLE WORKING 10 HOURS A DAY IN THE FIELDS WITH NO BREAKS AND NO TOILETS. EVEN IF EVERYONE IN THE FAMILY WORKS, THE FAMILY CAN ONLY EARN $1600 - $1800 A YEAR. THE FAMILY IS FORCED TO GO ON WELFARE WHILE THE GROWERS EARN MILLIONS. TO HELP FARM WORKERS GET OFF WELFARE AND GET A LIVING WAGE AND DECENT WORKING CONDITIONS THROUGH RECOGNITION OF THEIR UNION, DON'T BUY CALIFORNIA TABLE GRAPES.

Talk To Your Grocer

Ask him not to sell any California Grapes until the Grape Growers sign contracts with Cesar Chavez's United Farm Workers Organizing Committee, AFL-CIO.

N.A.A.C.P.

948 Market Street - Suite 703
San Francisco, California 94102
(415) 986-6992

Handbill distributed by San Francisco Branch of the NAACP in support of the UFW grape boycott, ca. 1965. The Bancroft Library, "Support the Farm Workers," MSS 78/180 c Bc4:1, University of California, Berkeley.

A few years later, shortly after the assassination of Martin Luther King, Jr., the Reverend Ralph Abernathy of the Southern Christian Leadership Conference (SCLC) and the Chicano leader, Rodolfo "Corky" Gonzalez of the Denver Crusade for Justice, sought to build closer bonds of cooperation during the Poor Peoples' Campaign (PPC) in the spring and summer of 1968 in "Resurrection City," Washington, D.C. Although often regarded as a dismal failure, the PPC represented a new beginning for Latinos (particularly Mexicans and Puerto Ricans) and African Americans to recognize the fundamental basis of their common post–civil rights struggle, namely, chronic systemic poverty. The tenuous beginnings of a shared political community were also forged in the early 1970s between black- and brown-power activists. In 1973 César Chávez and the UFW, for example, endorsed Black Panther Party cofounder Bobby Seale for mayor of Oakland, California.[6]

The larger story of black and brown convergence and divergence thus changed dramatically in the decades after the passage of the Civil Rights Act of 1964, when Chicanos/as increasingly claimed a "brown" identity and rejected the struggle of their elders to assimilate on the basis of their status as respectable middle-class whites. Claiming a white racial status made strategic sense in the Jim Crow era when laws made it legal to discriminate against blacks and other nonwhite peoples, particularly Asian Americans and Native Americans. However, the protections afforded by the Civil Rights Act presented new opportunities for the Chicano Generation to reach out to other marginalized groups, which, as historian Nancy MacLean observes, "made solidarity an option as never before."[7] Whatever progress that has been made in recent decades between Latinos and African Americans at the local and national political level must thus be seen in light of the long history of their segregation from each other, often in the same towns and cities as well as in the countryside.

Only within the last decade have the oldest and largest Mexican American and African American civil rights organizations, LULAC and NAACP, vowed to work together on civil rights and human rights issues, especially the divisive issue of Mexican immigration. In 2002, for the first time in the history of both organizations, the president of LULAC, Hector Flores, addressed the NAACP at its national convention to explore strategic alliances between the two organizations over issues of affirmative action, citizenship and voting, educational equality, equal employment opportunities, racial profiling, hate crimes, and immigration. Flores heralded a "new day" for America when "people of color, brown and black, come together with the common purpose of realizing the dream of all Americans." A few years later the president of the NAACP was invited to address the annual convention of LULAC, rallying the attendees under the banner of *Afro Americano y Latino Juntos*! (Black and Brown Together!)[8]

Today many, perhaps most, Mexican Americans no longer identify themselves matter-of-factly as "people of color," as did former LULAC president Hector Flores. Most Mexican Americans identify themselves simply as Latinos or Hispanics. Although regarded as a minority group since the 1960s, 48 percent of all Latinos in the United States identified their race as white in the 2000 census. Is it possible to be a member of a recognized minority group and still identify oneself as racially white? Despite recent progress in coalition politics (at least between the liberal-minded congressional black and Hispanic caucuses), many rank-and-file African Americans question the fairness of including Latinos within the framework of affirmative action (what's left of it) for jobs in the public and private sectors, or even the establishment of single-member districts that enable

Latinos to be elected to school boards and city councils in cities where African Americans were once the dominant minority group. If Latinos can be both culturally brown and racially white, is it any wonder that many African Americans are suspicious of Latinos for trying to have it both ways? When Latinos sought to be included as a recognized minority in the 1975 struggle over the extension of the Voting Rights Act of 1965, Clarence Mitchell, the chief lobbyist for the NAACP, said, "blacks were dying for the right to vote when you people [Hispanics] couldn't decide whether you were Caucasians."[9] The media further complicated matters with an endless series of articles about the demographic "browning of America" and the fact that African Americans have become, for the first time in our nation's history, the second largest minority group. How are African Americans expected to respond to taking the demographic backseat to Latinos, a group that the U.S. Bureau of the Census now projects will reach 30 percent of the total population by midcentury, compared with 13 percent for blacks? Was this the government's way of saying that blacks, in one author's words, are "no longer such a hot ticket"?[10]

Latinos, on the other hand, like Asian Americans, have long resented how the black-white paradigm of race in America has excluded them from the conversation.[11] Despite decades of immigration from Asia and Latin America and increasing attention from the media, Americans continue to see race in black and white, with Latinos, Asian Americans, and Native Americans cast in supporting roles.[12] When the National Museum of American History in Washington, D.C., for example, celebrated the fiftieth anniversary of *Brown* in an exhibit called "Separate Is Not Equal," some of the African American exhibit advisors opposed the inclusion of school segregation cases involving Chinese Americans and Mexican Americans, including the historically important *Mendez* case. According to the curator for the exhibit, Harry Rubenstein, one African American advisor claimed that including Mexicans and Chinese "would take credit away from the struggles of African Americans."[13]

The exclusion of Latinos and Asians from the national dialogue on race was driven home in a particularly public way when Angela Oh, an Asian American attorney and member of President Clinton's 1997 advisory committee on the President's Initiative on Race, was portrayed in the media as having disagreed with John Hope Franklin, the African American chairman of the advisory board, for simply suggesting that she hoped the board "would include the experiences of people who are neither black or white, let alone mixed race people"; she also urged Franklin and the committee "to talk about multiracialism because I think that's where we are headed." Although Franklin and Oh repeatedly told the press that there was no fundamental disagreement, the media seemed to focus more on the dynamics of race relations among the white, black, Asian, and Latino board members than the issues that brought them together in the first place.[14]

While Latino and African American leaders have disagreed publicly on issues from affirmative action to immigration reform, many Latinos and African Americans in labor unions and the workplace have frequently achieved better results through grassroots cooperation than their elite counterparts, who continually quarrel over the distribution of institutional power and engage in turf-wars over how many slots Latinos get for this and how many slots blacks get for that.[15] In California, for example, the Los Angeles–based grassroots Community Service Organization, in which César Chávez cut his teeth as a labor organizer, developed cooperative relationships in the 1940s and 1950s with organizations that George Sánchez, former LULAC president, disparagingly referred to as "those Jewish-Negro-Anglo-Asiatic groups."[16] Today many labor unions in the service sector (hotels, restaurants, and hospitals) are composed principally of Latino, African American, and Asian American workers, many of them immigrants and women, who seek contracts that include health insurance, better working conditions, and living wages.[17]

But more profound differences than competition for political and economic power inform Mexican American and African American understandings of how race and culture operate in their lives. In an interview published in *Harper's Magazine* in the same year as President Clinton's race initiative, two high-profile public intellectuals, Jorge Klor de Alva, a cultural anthropologist and scholar of Mexico and the Southwest, and Cornel West, a philosopher and scholar of the African American experience, exchanged views that revealed fundamental disagreements and mutual misunderstandings almost from the start. Asked whether he thought Cornel West was a "black man," Klor de Alva explained that West was black only "within a certain reductionist context" and that he could just as well be, from a Latin American perspective, an "Anglo." Klor de Alva wished to make the point that while West might consider himself a "black man" in the United States, where "unambiguous color-coded identities are the rule," in other places, like Africa or Latin America, he might be considered of mixed African descent or even white.[18] Many Mexicans, for example, regard non-Mexicans in the United States as Anglos or *americanos* and thus, from a Latin American perspective, in which culture, class, and nationality—not race—are constitutive of identity, West might be an Anglo of a different color, a moreno, or simply another gringo.[19]

Many African Americans view light-skinned Latinos as "racially" more similar to whites, while dark-skinned Latin American immigrants often regard middle-class African Americans as *culturally* more like non-Hispanic whites. In making the distinction between race and culture as the principal marker of identity, Klor de Alva hoped to convince West that grounding African American identity in essentialist taxonomies of race rather than notions of citizenship, culture, and national belonging would ensure the continued marginalization and alienation of African Americans as the "central metaphor for otherness and oppression in the United States." West continued to insist, however, that part of what it means to be black is the need to come to terms with a history of denigration, Jim Crow, violence, and other forms of oppression, and that claiming and celebrating their common past is a way for black Americans to affirm their agency as subjects in history and not merely its victims. Klor de Alva maintained that a different language was needed to resolve America's enduring problems of poverty and inequality, no matter how much these problems are linked with blacks in the minds of most Americans. He suggested, to West's astonishment, that blacks were "more Anglo than most Anglos, because unlike most Anglos, they can't directly identify themselves with a nation-state outside of the United States. They are trapped in America. However unjust and painful, their experiences are wholly made in America."[20] West was far from convinced that the unique experience of blacks trapped in America made them über Anglos. In calling blacks Anglos, however, Klor de Alva wanted to make the point that "Anglo" was not synonymous with racial whiteness, but rather was a marker of culture, like "Latino":

> Latinos are in a totally different situation, unable to be captured by the government in the 'five food groups' of racial classification of Americans. The Commerce Department didn't know what to do with Latinos; the census takers didn't know what to do with Latinos; the government didn't know what to do with Latinos, and so they said, 'Latinos can be of any race.' That puts

Latinos in a totally different situation. They are, in fact, homologous with the totality of the United States. That is, like Americans, Latinos can be of any race. What distinguishes them from all other Americans is culture, not race. That's where I'm going when I say that Cornel is an Anglo. You can be a Latino and look like Cornel. You can be a Latino and look like you, Earl [Shorris, who is white], or like me. And so, among Latinos, there's no surprise in my saying that Cornel is an Anglo.

Having established how Latinos, particularly Latin American immigrants who haven't learned the racial protocols of the United States, might view some blacks as Latinos and others as americanos or Anglos, Klor de Alva asked West if he thought Latinos were white. West called them brothers and sisters, human beings, and voluntary immigrants who were neither white nor black but rather "brown people," which, West acknowledged, was a cultural rather than a racial identity. He explained that his Ethiopian wife's experience in the United States was closer to that of what brown people experience because she voluntarily came to America to "to be in a place where she can breathe freely" and pursue the American dream. But then, West continued, "I've got to take her, you know, almost like Virgil in Dante's *Divine Comedy*, through all of this other side of America so that she can see the nightmare as well as the dream," to which Klor de Alva responded: "So you are participating in . . . that same song and dance of transforming her into a highly racialized American black."[21] In refusing to identify himself as a Chicano or Mexican American or any other racially marked identity, he told West: "I'm an American citizen trying to get rid of as many categories as possible that classify people in ways that make it easy for them to be oppressed, isolated, [and] marginalized."[22] The "naming game" of race in America has not only impeded the ability of American workers to organize by class but also created, through affirmative action, a tier of middle-class African Americans within the public sphere that have made it difficult for Latinos to make their complaints known. West agreed, but added that blacks get more results than Latinos because "Black people are more likely to raise hell than brown people."[23]

And so the conversation went, a Latino anthropologist and a black philosopher with fundamentally different conceptions of what it meant to be racially black or culturally brown. Blacks cling to their race in order not to forget their history or let others forget or diminish it, while Latinos, lacking the bond of race or even a common culture and history, haven't raised enough hell to get their fair share of the economic pie. Their disagreements extended even to a discussion of good and evil—Klor de Alva preferred the optimistic, epic vision of the United States wherein "evil's defeat, like its creation, can be . . . imagined," whereas for West, such a triumphant, Manichaean vision was "sophomoric" and "childish." He preferred the "more morally mature" tragic view articulated in the works of Unamuno, Melville, Faulkner, Morrison, and Coltrane. Klor de Alva labeled the "indecision and paralysis" of the tragic view the "Hamlet vision," to which West responded, "Better Hamlet than Captain Ahab."[24]

Today pundits would dub Klor de Alva's refusal to be defined by a racial identity, be it Chicano, Mexican American, or Latino, postracial. But another author and public intellectual, Richard Rodriguez, is not so sure that Klor de Alva's commitment to mestizaje ("brownness") is anything more than a convenient Mexican nationalist myth. Despite Mexico's having compiled for centuries a "ravishing lexicon of brown"—"*mestizo, castizo, alvina, chino, negro torno atrás, morisco, canbujo, albarrasado, tente en el aire, canpa mulato, coyote, vorsino, lobo . . . ,*" the "dream of Mexico," he maintained, continues to be "the apotheosis of bleach"—the fetishization of whiteness. Anyone who watches Mexican soap operas or strolls past Mexico City's high-end restaurants and shops in Polanco, Condesa, or nearby Lomas de Santa Fe can see how closely light skin correlates with political and economic power and privilege. Rodriguez, who describes himself as having "dark-skin, thick lips, [and an] Indian nose," recalled that the "whitest dinner party" he had ever attended was in Mexico City where a "Mexican squire of exquisite manner, mustache, and flán-like jowl, expressed himself surprised, so surprised" to learn that Rodriguez was "un escritor . . . ¿Un escritor . . . ?" "You know, in Mexico," he told Rodriguez, "I think we do not have writers who look like you."[25]

Nevertheless, Rodriguez, like Klor de Alva, thinks African Americans need "to speak the truth of themselves" and acknowledge that they too are "brown"—that they are culturally complex and racially mixed. When his African American friend, Darrell, insists, like Cornel West, that not being black is not always an option, that, for one thing, Darrell knows he's black "because *that is what the white cop sees when he looks at me*," Rodriguez responds, "Do you believe you uphold the one-drop theory by your insistence on black, because that is the way a white cop sees you?" To which Darrell responds:

It doesn't matter if my complexion is lemon or redbone or licorice, I'm black . . . You can have black and blue. You can have black and white. You can have *The Red and the Black*. But you can't have reddish black or light black or blackish, as you have reddish brown. Black is historically dense because it is linguistically dense; it overwhelms any more complicated shading . . . There is always a split-second delay between you and me—a linguistic felt-tip line. I am the line in the color book . . . Uphold the one-drop theory? Come on! I don't make this stuff up, you know. And if you'll kindly advise the San Francisco Police

Department their way of thinking is *recherché*, I'll be much obliged and call myself something else.[26]

What Richard Rodriguez offers Darrell, curiously, is what he calls "white freedom," by which he means an absence of culture, an escape from race and the cultural demands of performing blackness. He declares that "the last white freedom in America will be the freedom of the African American to admit brown." But the problem with the brown solution to building racial cross-identification is that, among other things, it fails utterly to acknowledge the large presence of Afro-Latinos within the Hispanic community, particularly in New York and other cities, where relations between Latinos and African Americans are fundamentally different, which is to say, where Puerto Ricans, Dominicans, and other Afro-Caribbean peoples, as well as Afro-descendant South Americans from countries like Venezuela and Colombia, have lived for many decades in close proximity in shared or nearby neighborhoods.[27] More critically, Rodriguez's fetishization of "brown" ignores the long history of Latin American, including Mexican racism toward Afro-descendant peoples.

Rather than counseling blacks to acknowledge their cultural brownness, the author and journalist Ed Morales wonders when Mexican "brownologists" like Rodriguez and others will finally be free to admit their blackness. Immigrants from every country have long understood, Morales reminds us, that "estrangement from blackness is the key to success in America," echoing Toni Morrison's observation that for immigrants, "the move into mainstream America always means buying into the notion of American blacks as the real aliens."[28] Morrison of course did not mean to suggest that American blacks are aliens or "foreigners" in any legal or cultural sense—for they are as native to America as the whites who brought them here—but rather that in many

ways they remain racial outsiders, estranged from the full pano-
ply of rights and opportunities enjoyed by Americans of European ancestry.

Despite the dubiousness of grouping all Latinos under the
rubric of "brown," the fact remains that of the over 45 million
Hispanics in the United States today, almost two-thirds (64.1
percent) are of Mexican descent. Puerto Ricans, who have been
U.S. citizens since 1917, constitute the second largest group at
9 percent, followed by Cubans (3.4%), Salvadorans (3.1%), Dominicans (2.7%), Guatemalans (2.0%), and Colombians (1.8%).
All other immigrants from Central and South American countries comprise the remaining 14 percent of the Hispanic population.[29] This fact is important because the foremost issue that
continues to complicate relations between blacks and Latinos
is immigration, especially undocumented immigration from
Mexico, which would not, for example, have a direct impact on
relations between African Americans and, say, Puerto Ricans
(although that is changing as tens of thousands of Mexican immigrants from the state of Puebla now call New York home).[30]
For many blacks, unchecked immigration from Mexico harms
them more than other Americans, given the large percentage of
African Americans at the lower end of the wage scale where
most Mexican immigrants enter the labor market. For this reason, and because of the constant media attention given to Mexican immigration, including the efforts of the Department of
Homeland Security to construct a fence along almost half of
the U.S.-Mexico border, relations between Latinos and blacks
nationally have been framed mainly within the context of Mexicans and Mexican immigration.[31]

The passage of the Hart-Celler Immigration Act in 1965,
which shifted the main principle of immigration to family re-
unification, set off an unexpected and unprecedented chain
immigration from Latin American and Asia. By the late 1980s,

over 85 percent of all immigrants were coming from Latin America and Asia, including unprecedented numbers of Asian refugees, many seeking asylum from the violent aftermath of the Vietnam War. Many African American leaders, having emerged from the humanitarian struggles of the civil rights movement, supported the right of asylum-seekers to settle in the United States, as well as the rights of immigrants in general. However, mounting pressure from blacks and whites, and many Latinos, to curb illegal immigration resulted in strained relations between the National Council of La Raza, a large umbrella group for Latino organizations, and some African American leaders over the question of illegal immigration. Blacks and whites increasingly supported congressional bills to impose sanctions on employers who hired undocumented workers, while the National Council of La Raza strongly opposed sanctions on the ground that employers would discriminate against all Latinos, regardless of their citizenship status. On the other hand, many blacks, including most members of the Congressional Black Caucus, supported the right of immigrants to escape poverty and oppression in their home countries. African Americans, in short, are divided on the issue of immigration, much as many whites and even Latinos are.[32]

Immigration was not, however, a wedge issue for Mexicans and blacks during World War II and its aftermath in the pre-*Brown* era of the fifties and pre-"brown" (Chicano) era of the sixties and seventies. African Americans, like most whites, were concerned about illegal immigration from Mexico during the 1950s, but so were many Mexican Americans, including LULAC and the G.I. Forum.[33] Mexican Americans' main concern in the 1940s, however, was obtaining defense industry jobs and desegregating schools in the years immediately after the war on the ground that they were white. It was a strategy that worked. Challenging *Plessy* would have been an exercise in futility since nowhere in the United States were Mexicans legally barred from white schools. The middle-class Mexican-American strategy of wrapping themselves in the "Caucasian cloak" nevertheless made it difficult, if not impossible, to cross race and class lines to find common ground with working-class and middle-class African Americans.[34] The NAACP sought support from other, more progressive groups, like the American Jewish Congress, the ACLU, and the National Lawyers Guild, while the efforts of more radical Mexican American groups, like El Congreso de Pueblos de Habla Española and ANMA (Asociación Nacional de México-Americana [National Association of Mexican Americans], which succeeded el congreso after the war), and interracial unions like the International Union of Mine, Mill, and Smelter Workers, were stymied by the anticommunist repression of the 1950s.

Today many African Americans and Latinos have found common ground over issues such as de facto school segregation, unequal school financing, immigration reform, racial profiling, redlining, and the prison-industrial complex, to name a few. But it remains problematic to generalize about the concerns of Latinos, given the heterogeneity of peoples and cultures embraced by the term "Latino." One wonders what a white civil engineer from Buenos Aires and a Zapotec-speaking indigenous farmer from southern Mexico have in common, except that at the moment they cross the border into the United States, they both become "Hispanic." And while African Americans may share a common history and culture, they too represent a wide range of social, economic, and political orientations, like any other group. Underlying differences in organizational strength, political affiliations, class position, level of assimilation, and legal strategies thus complicate the assumption that blacks and Latinos ought to be natural allies. Not surprisingly, then, the two groups mainly pursued their own interests in their own ways, preferring to go it alone, though usually always willing, like the NAACP, to welcome the support of others. People, regardless of race or citizenship, tend to cooperate when they share similar goals and strategies for achieving them, whether organizing to eliminate toxic industries and waste sites from their neighborhoods or demanding better funding for their schools. Put another way, when Latinos and blacks, as well as Asian Americans and whites, appear to share the same objective, as when they voted for the same candidate in the last presidential election, can they be said to be acting in political solidarity with each other, or just voting for the person they think will best represent their interests and those of the nation?

NOTES

INTRODUCTION

1. "Realizan Mexicanos trabajos que ni los Negros quieren: Fox," *La Jornada*, May 14, 2005, www.jornada.unam.mx (accessed October 8, 2008); "Vicente Fox mete las dos patas," May 16, 2005, www.los blogueros.net (accessed November 15, 2008); "Mexican Leader Criticized for Comment on Blacks," May 15, 2005; "Fox 'Regrets' Remark about Blacks," May 17, 2005, www.cnn.com (accessed October 8, 2008). I use the term *Mexicans* to denote citizens of Mexico as well as U.S. citizens of Mexican descent. When it is necessary to distinguish between the two, I refer to Mexican citizens in the United States as *resident Mexican nationals* or *Mexican immigrants*, and to naturalized or U.S.-born citizens of Mexican descent as *Mexican Americans.*

2. José Carreño Carlón, "Unidos, Negros y Mexicanos (contra Fox)," *La Crónica*, May 16, 2004, www.cronica.com.mx (accessed March 22, 2009).

3. Rainbow/PUSH is a progressive organization of workers, women, and people of color advocating social and economic justice. The National Council of La Raza is the largest national Hispanic civil rights and advocacy organization in the United States with a network of nearly 300 affiliated community-based organizations.

4. "Mexican Stamp Fuels 'Racial Stereotypes,'" June 30, 2005, www.msnbc.msn.com (accessed October 9, 2008); "Mexican Stamp Racist, Civil Rights Leaders Say," *Washington Post*, June 30, 2008; Karen Grigsby Bates, "Mexican Stamp Honors Controversial Comic Figure," July 12, 2005, NPR audio story, www.npr.org (accessed October 9, 2008).

5. Memín Pinguín was not the first *negrito* to be celebrated in Mexican culture. According to historian William Beezley, Mexican puppeteers celebrated the heroic resistance and bravery of the Mexican people during the French occupation, 1862–1867, in the character of "El Negrito." The diminutive *negrito* softened the ethnic edge of *el negro* as well as diminished the blackness of the character, reflecting both affection and condescension. See William H. Beezley, "Cómo fue que *El Negrito* salvó a México de los Franceses: Las fuentes populares de la identidad nacional," *Historia Mexicana* 57 (October– December 2007): 405–443.

6. *Memín Pinguín*, "Líos Gordos," Grupo Editorial Vid, No 128, Sept. 27, 2004. On the political, cultural, and moral malignance of the U.S., see Edmundo O'Gorman, *México: el trauma de su historia* (México: Universidad Nacional Autónoma de México, 1977); idem, "Do the Americas Have a Common History?" in *Do the Americas Have a Common History? A Critique of the Bolton Theory*, ed Lewis Hanke (New York: Knopf, 1964); José Vasconcelos, *Breve historia de México*, 4th ed. (México, Ediciones Botas, 1938); Octavio Paz, *Labyrinth of Solitude and Other Essays* (New York: Grove Press, 1985); Américo Paredes, "The Anglo-American in Mexican Folklore," in *New Voices in American Studies*, ed. Ray B. Browne et al. (Lafayette, Ind.: Purdue University Studies, 1966), 113–128.

7. Catherince Bremer, "Defying U.S., Mexicans Flock to Buy 'Racist' Stamps," *Reuters,* July 1, 2005, www.redorbit.com (accessed November 7, 2008). For an insightful analysis comparing Mexico's neglect of the problems of immigrants in the United States with its stubborn insistence that racism does not exist in Latin America, see Claudio Lomitz, "Mexico's Race Problem," November–December 2005, www.bostonreview. net (accessed October 13, 2008).

8. Gonzalo Aguirre Beltrán, *La población negra de México, 1519– 1810: estudio etnohistórico* (México: Ediciones Fuente Cultural, 1946); idem, *Cuijla: esbozo etnográfico de un pueblo negro* (México: Fondo de Cultura Económica, 1958). At the time of independence, Mexico may have had the largest population of free blacks in the

Americas. See Ben Vinson, III, *Bearing Arms for His Majesty: The Free-Colored Militia in Colonial Mexico* (Stanford, Calif.: Stanford University Press, 2001), 25.

9. José Vasconcelos, *The Cosmic Race* (1925; reprint, Baltimore, Md.: Johns Hopkins University Press, 1997); Lelia María Jiménez Bartlett, "Multiculturalismo y derechos indígenas en México" (Ph.D. diss., Universidad Carlos III de Madrid, 2005); Mauricio Tenorio Trillo, *Historia y Celebración, México y sus Centenarios* (Mexico City, Barcelona: Tusquets, 2009), chapter 9.

10. Vasconcelos, *The Cosmic Race*, 32, 72. On his travels to the United States in the late nineteenth century, Justo Sierra noted that Washington, D.C. "is one of the capitals of the black nation, and this burdens it with a dark shade," because [for blacks] liberty has not made them free, but rather, insolent." Justo Sierra, *Viajes en tierra yankee, en la Europa Latina, Obras completas,* vol. 6 (México: Universidad Nacional Autónoma de México, 1948), 111–112. I am indebted to Mauricio Tenorio for bringing this source to my attention.

11. Aguirre Beltrán, *La población negra de México*; Colin A. Palmer, *Slaves of the White God: Blacks in Mexico, 1570–1650* (Cambridge: Harvard University Press, 1976).

12. Bobby Vaughn, an anthropologist who has conducted research among black Mexicans in the Costa Chica, observed that "Mexicans of African descent have no voice and the government makes no attempt to assess their needs, no effort to even count them." "Mexico Finds Its Forgotten Race," *The Guardian,* July 15, 2005.

13. Interview with the Washington Afro-American News Agency, attached to letter from Francisco Castillo Nájera to Secretario de Relaciones Exteriores, July 23, 1943, serie III, lejago 655, expediente 2, Archivo Histórico Genaro Estrada, Secretaría de Relaciones Exteriores, Mexico City (hereafter cited, for example, as III-655-2, SRE).

14. On the anti-Chinese movement in Mexico, see Raymond B. Craib, *Chinese Immigrants in Porfirian Mexico: A Preliminary Study of Settlement, Economic Activity, and Anti-Chinese Sentiment* (Albuquerque: University of New Mexico, 1996); José Jorge Gómez

Izquierdo, *El movimiento antichino en México (1871–1934): Problemas del racismo y del nacionalismo durante la Revolución Mexicana* (Mexico, D.F.: Instituto Nacional de Antropología e Historia, 1991).

15. "Mexican Stamp Fuels 'Racial Stereotypes,' " *The Guardian,* July 15, 2005; Bobby Vaughn, "Afro-Mexico: Blacks, *Indígenas,* Politics, and the Greater Diaspora," in *Neither Enemies Nor Friends: Latinos, Blacks, and Afro-Latinos,* eds. Anani Dzidzienyo and Suzanne Oboler (New York: Palgrave Macmillan, 2005), 117–136; Juliet Hooker, "Indigenous Inclusion / Black Exclusion: Race, Ethnicity, and Multicultural Citizenship in Latin American," *Journal of Latin American Studies* 37 (May 2005): 285–310, especially table 1, 298.

16. "Racism Rears Its Ugly Head in Mexico," *San Francisco Chronicle,* August 3, 2005. Mexican historian and columnist, Enrique Krauze, in defending the stamp, called Memín Pinguín a "thoroughly likeable character" who "touched an authentic chord of sympathy and tenderness among poorer people." Krauze casually acknowledged racism against Mexico's Indian population "in some times and places." "The Pride in Memin Pinguin," *Washington Post,* July 12, 2005.

17. Anthony DePalma, "Racism? Mexico's in Denial," *New York Times,* June 11, 1995, E4. Other expressions one hears in Mexico are *"trabajo como esclavo"* (I work like a slave) and *"trabajo como negro para vivir como blanco"* (I work like a black man to live like a white man). Mexicans insist that these expressions simply mean to "work hard" and that they have no racial connotation whatsoever.

18. Ben Vinson, III, and Bobby Vaughn, *Afroméxico: El pulso de la población Negra en México: Una historia recordada, ovidada y vuelta a recordar* (México, D.F.: Centro de Investigación y Docencia Económicas and Fondo de Cultura Económica, 2004), 11–17.

19. Mexicans rarely used *negro* to refer to Mexico's darkest-skinned citizens, preferring instead *moreno.* Even when referring to *afromestizos* of the Costa Chica, Mexicans prefer the euphemism *costeños* (coastal people) to *negros* or *afromexicanos.* See Ricardo Infante Padilla, "Afromexicanos, excluidos de la historia official," *La Jornada,* February 11, 2007.

20. See, for example, Laura Randall, "Discrimination by Color or Class in Mexico?" *Mexidata.Info*, October 15, 2007, www.mexidata.info (accessed December 12, 2008).

21. Even some Afro-Mexicans who experience racism deny that racism exists in Mexico. See Christina Sue, "'What Racism?' An Ethnographic Study of the Discursive Strategies Surrounding Race in Mexico" (paper presented at the annual meeting of the American Sociological Association, New York, August 11, 2007), www.allacademic.com (accessed October 13, 2008). Numerous scholars have challenged the myth of racial democracy in Latin America, but see Winthrop R. Wright, *Café con Leche: Race, Class, and National Image in Venezuela* (Austin: University of Texas Press, 1990); and Alejandro de la Fuente, *A Nation for All: Race, Inequality, and Politics in Twentieth-Century Cuba* (Chapel Hill: University of North Carolina Press, 2001).

22. On the tensions between Puerto Ricans and Mexicans in New York as a recapitulation of the tensions that once characterized relations between New York blacks and Puerto Ricans, see Arlene M. Dávila, *Barrio Dreams: Puerto Ricans, Latinos, and the Neoliberal City* (Berkeley: University of California Press, 2004).

23. "Los invisibles, la comunidad de Afromexicanos," *El Universal,* March 28, 2007; Vinson and Vaughn, *Afroméxico,* 11–17; Ricardo Infante Padilla, "Afromexicanos, excluidos de la historia oficial," *La Jornada,* February 11, 2007.

24. See, for example, Juan Flores, *From Bomba to Hip Hop: Puerto Rican Culture and Latino Identity* (New York: Columbia University Press, 2000); Raquel Z. Rivera, *New York Ricans from the Hip Hop Zone* (New York: Palgrave Macmillan, 2003).

25. "And Now the Mexicans," editorial, *Pittsburgh Courier,* January 24, 1925. See also D. Hellwig, "Black Leaders and United States Immigration Policy, 1917–1929," *Journal of Negro History* 66 (Summer 1981): 120.

26. William Pickens, "Jim Crow in Texas," *The Nation,* August 15, 1923, 155–156. I am indebted to George Wright for bringing this source to my attention.

27. Ibid.

28. *Plessy v. Ferguson,* 163 U.S. 537 (1896). The African American poet Langston Hughes circumvented segregation statutes by passing for Mexican in San Antonio, Texas, while light-skinned black workers in Chicago also sought to pass as Mexicans to obtain work in factories that did not hire blacks. Arnold Rampersad, *The Life of Langston Hughes,* vol. I (New York and Oxford: Oxford University Press, 1986), 35; Laurencio Sanguino and Mauricio Tenorio Trillo, "Orígenes de una ciudad mexicana: Chicago y la ciencia del Mexican Problem," in Carlos Lira Vázquez and Ariel Rodríguez Kuri, eds. *Ciudades Mexicanas del Siglo XX: Siete Estudios Históricos* (Mexico City: El Colegio de México, 2009), 257-314.

29. Richard Rodriguez, *Brown: The Last Discovery of America* (New York: Viking, 2002), 140.

30. See Zaragosa Vargas, *Labor Rights Are Civil Rights: Mexican American Workers in Twentieth-Century America* (Princeton, N.J.: Princeton University Press, 2005).

31. The War Manpower Commission sought to place the "practical application of established fact" in meeting wartime labor demands over the discriminatory hiring practices of employers engaged in war production. J. H. Bond to Irving W. Wood, September 24, 1942; Irving W. Wood to J. H. Bond, September 22, 1942, box 1, "Minority Discrimination, General Correspondence" folder, RG 211, War Manpower Commission, National Archives, Region X, Fort Worth, Texas (hereafter cited as Region X, NA). Walter White confided to syndicated columnist Jay Franklin that discrimination against Negroes in defense industries in the western United States "is hurting the defense program more than it is hurting the Negro." Walter White to Jay Franklin, December 7, 1940, part 17, reel 23, *A Guide to the Microfilm Edition of the Papers of the NAACP,* ed. Randolph Boehm (Frederick, Md.: University Publications of America, 1982), hereafter cited as NAACP Papers.

32. "Propaganda and the War," *Common Sense* 11 (February 1942): 55.

33. Gunnar Myrdal, *An American Dilemma: The Negro Problem and American Democracy,* vol. 2 (New York: Harper, 1944), 820–821.

34. Winifred Rauschenbush to Governor Stevenson, December 1, 1943, box 4–14/136, "Racial Discrimination" folder, Gov. Coke Stevenson Papers, Texas State Library and Archives, Austin, Texas (hereafter Stevenson Papers, TSLA).

35. Walter White to Mary Taussig Thompkins, September 5, 1944, part 18, series C, reel 26, NAACP Papers.

36. Newspaper clipping, no name, n.d., box 454, Tension files, 1943–1945, "Austin" folder, Records of the Committee on Fair Employment Practice, RG 228, National Archives and Records Administration, College Park, Maryland (hereafter cited as FEPC, RG 228, NA).

37. He signed the letter anonymously because of "the hard feelings against Negroes." A Negro World War II veteran to Governor Stevenson, July 4, 1946, box 4–14/145, "Racial Discrimination 1945" folder, Stevenson Papers, TSLA.

38. Richard M. Garza to Governor Stevenson, n.d., box 4–14/156, "Interracial Discrimination" folder, Stevenson Papers, TSLA.

39. Marciano M. Zamarripa to Manuel Ávila Camacho, March 3, 1941, extracto 21717, exp. 575.1/9, caja 974, Manuel Ávila Camacho Papers, Archivo General de la Nación, Mexico City (herafter cited as Ávila Camacho Papers, AGN).

40. J. Conrad Dunagan to Glenn E. Garrett, February 15, 1960, "Blacklist and Discrimination" folder, box 1989/59–16, Good Neighbor Commission Collection, Texas State Library and Archives, Austin, Texas (hereafter cited as Good Neighbor Commission, TSLA).

41. Of the 9,191 students enrolled at UT in 1948, 114 or 1.2 percent were "Texas-born Spanish-name" students in a state where one out of every six people was of Mexican ancestry. This number does not include non-Texas-born Latinos (mostly Latin Americans from Mexico and Central and South America) or students of Mexican descent without Spanish surnames. Ruth Ann Douglass Fogartie, *Texas-Born Spanish-Name Students in Texas Colleges and Universities,* Inter-American Education Occasional Papers No. 3 (Austin: University of Texas Press, 1948), 14–15.

42. "In Memoriam: The Honorable James DeAnda, 1925–2006," September 8, 2006, www.utexas.edu/law/news/2006 (accessed

November 18, 2008); Judicial Conference of the United States, Bicentennial Committee, *Judges of the United States,* 2nd ed. (Washington, D.C.: Government Printing Office, 1983).

43. See, for example, Natalia Molina, *Fit to Be Citizens?: Public Health and Race in Los Angeles, 1879–1939* (Berkeley: University of California Press, 2006); Scott Kurashige, *The Shifting Grounds of Race: Black and Japanese Americans in the Making of Multiethnic Los Angeles* (Princeton, N.J.: Princeton University Press, 2008).

44. For example, historian Ronald Takaki examines in separate chapters the role of Native Americans, Mexican Americans, African Americans, and other minority groups in World War II. Ronald T. Takaki, *Double Victory: A Multicultural History of America in World War II* (Boston, Mass.: Little, Brown and Co., 2000). See also Tomás Almaguer, *Racial Fault Lines: The Historical Origins of White Supremacy in California* (Berkeley: University of California Press, 1994).

45. Little scholarship exists on this topic, especially for the World War II era, although young scholars are beginning to address moments of convergence and divergence between these groups from the late 1950s to the early 1970s. See especially Lauren Ashley Araiza, "For Freedom of Other Men: Civil Rights, Black Power, and the United Farm Workers, 1965–1973" (Ph.D. diss., University of California, Berkeley, 2006); Brian Behnken, "Fighting Their Own Battles: Blacks, Mexican Americans, and the Struggle for Civil Rights" (Ph.D. diss., University of California, Davis, 2007); and Gordon Keith Mantler, "Black, Brown, and Poor: Martin Luther King Jr., the Poor People's Campaign and Its Legacies" (Ph.D. diss., Duke University, 2008).

1. BRINGING THE GOOD NEIGHBOR POLICY HOME

1. See, for example, Mary Dudziak, *Cold War Civil Rights: Race and the Image of American Democracy* (Princeton, N.J.: Princeton University Press, 2000).

2. On the Good Neighbor policy generally, see Edward O. Guerrant, *Roosevelt's Good Neighbor Policy* (Albuquerque: University of New Mexico Press, 1950).

3. "U.S. Ignorance of Republics to South Deplored," clipping, n.d., attached to letter from Walter White to Committee for Inter-American Cooperation, March 25, 1941, part 14, reel 7, *A Guide to the Microfilm Edition of the Papers of the NAACP,* ed. Randolph Boehm (Frederick, Md.: University Publications of America, 1982), hereafter cited as NAACP Papers.

4. Jay Franklin, "We the People: 'Jim Crow' and the Good Neighbor," typescript attached to letter from Jay Franklin to Walter White, January 27, 1941, part 14, reel 7, NAACP Papers.

5. Quoted in letter from Elis M. Tipton to Walter H. C. Laves, October 9, 1942, "Paul Horgan" folder, box 1717, Office of the Coordinator of Inter-American Affairs, RG 229, National Archives, College Park, Maryland (hereafter cited as OCIAA, RG 229, NA). For an important study of the international consequences of racial injustice in the United States during World War II, see Justin Hart, "Making Democracy Safe for the World: Race, Propaganda, and the Transformation of U.S. Foreign Policy during World War II," *Pacific Historical Review* 73 (February 2004): 49–84.

6. María Emilia Paz, *Strategy, Security, and Spies: Mexico and the U.S. as Allies in World War II* (University Park: Pennsylvania State University Press, 1997), 146–208.

7. Report, "The Military Importance of Northeastern Brazil," August 24, 1942, box 610, folder "Military Importance of N.E. Brazil, 5th Column Activities, Germans in Brazil, the Japanese and Italians in Brazil, Prominent Brazilians in the 5th Column," OCIAA, RG 229, NA. See also Stanley E. Hilton, *Hitler's Secret War in South America, 1939–1945: German Military Espionage and Allied Counterespionage in Brazil* (Baton Rouge: Louisiana State University, 1981).

8. "Axis Tells Brazilians, 'U.S. Negroes Still in Slavery,'" press release, March 13, 1942, part 14, reel 7, NAACP Papers.

9. Robert F. Foerster, report to the secretary of labor, "Racial Problems Involved in Immigration from Latin America and the West Indies to the United States," 1925, attached to letter from Walter White to Mrs. Harry Godfrey Kimball, March 14, 1942, part 14, reel 7, NAACP Papers.

10. Rockefeller was also concerned with the large population of Afro-Latinos in the Caribbean republics and sought to compile a report on "Negroes in the Caribbean Republics, with a special emphasis on their position in relation to the development of hemispheric solidarity and cultural activities." Nelson A. Rockefeller to Walter White, December 9, 1941, part 17, reel 23, NAACP Papers; Antonio Pedro Tota, *The Seduction of Brazil: The Americanization of Brazil during World War II*, trans. Lorena B. Ellis (Austin: University of Texas Press, 2009).

11. Memorandum from Walter White to Nelson Rockefeller, April 22, 1941, part 14, reel 7, NAACP Papers.

12. Ibid.

13. "War and Negro Rights in the Americas—A Discussion of Latin-American Racial Problems," remarks of Rep. John M. Coffee, *Congressional Record,* March 30, 1942, and Charles Anderson Gauld, "Defense and Negro Culture in Latin America," *Negro History Bulletin* (June 1941), part 14, reel 7, NAACP Papers.

14. Memorandum from Walter White to Nelson Rockefeller, April 22, 1941, part 14, reel 7, NAACP Papers; and Walter White, "One Obstacle in Wooing South America," or "Color and Friendship with South America," draft of an article written by Walter White, n.d., ibid.; "Welles Appointed Parley Delegate," *New York Times,* December 24, 1941, clipping attached to letter from Walter White to Summer Welles, December 24, 1941, part 17, reel 23, NAACP Papers; and Summer Welles to Walter White, December 26, 1941, ibid.

15. Walter White to Edward Weeks, September 9, 1940, part 14, reel 7, NAACP Papers; idem to Sue Thurman, September 10, 1940, ibid.; Walter White to Philip Levy, September 18, 1940, part 17, reel 23, NAACP Papers; idem to Sen. Joseph O. O'Mahoney, January 10, 1941, ibid.; idem to Dr. Charles G. Fenwick, March 10, 1941, ibid.; idem to Xavier Cugat, April 22, 1941, ibid.

16. White, "One Obstacle in Wooing South America," part 14, reel 7, ibid.

17. Charles A. Gauld, "Brazil: The Largest Negro Nation," *Negro History Bulletin* (February 1941), article reproduced in the *Congressional Record,* October 2, 1941, A4740, by Rep. John M. Coffee,

extension of remarks, "Racial Problems in Latin America," attached to letter from Walter White to Judge William H. Hastie, April 22, 1942, part 14, reel 7, NAACP Papers; Charles A. Gauld to Walter White, October 4, 1941, part 17, reel 23, ibid.

18. Walter White to Godfrey Lowell Cabot, January 8, 1941, part 14, reel 7, NAACP Papers.

19. "Axis Tells Brazilians, 'U.S. Negroes Still in Slavery,' " press release, March 13, 1942, part 14, reel 7, NAACP Papers.

20. Confidential Report, "Experiences in Negro Employment," Council for Democracy, February 1, 1943, attached to letter from Warren Brown to Victor Borella, February 1, 1943, "Negro file" folder, box 1717, OCIAA, RG 229, NA.

21. "German radio propaganda to Latin America," Inter-Office Memorandum on "Axis Radio Tactics" from Louis T. Olom to Walter H. C. Laves, February 6, 1942, "Negro file" folder, box 1717, OCIAA, RG 229, NA; "Nazi Agitators Try to Influence Brazilian Negroes against U.S.," *La Prensa,* March 17, 1942, ibid.; "Hemispheric Defense," *Pittsburg Courier,* March 21, 1942, copied in memorandum on "The Negro Problem" from Louis T. Olom to Walter Laves, April 7, 1942, ibid.

22. Carter Wesley to Pres. Franklin Delano Roosevelt, June 25, 1943, box 4–14/136, "Racial Discrimination" folder, Gov. Coke Stevenson Papers, Texas State Library and Archives, Austin, Texas (hereafter Stevenson Papers, TSLA). Emphasis in the original.

23. Max Paul Friedman, *Nazis and Good Neighbors: The United States Campaign against the Germans of Latin America in World War II* (Cambridge, Eng.: Cambridge University Press, 2003), 2.

24. *History of the Office of the Coordinator of Inter-American Affairs* (Washington, D.C.: Government Printing Office, 1947), 3–10.

25. Chandler Owen to Nelson Rockefeller, December 23, 1941, "Negro file" folder, box 1717, OCIAA, RG 229, NA; memorandum on "The Negro Problem" from Louis T. Olom to Walter Laves, April 7, 1942, ibid.

26. Kenneth R. Janken, *Rayford W. Logan and the Dilemma of the African-American Intellectual* (Amherst: University of Massachusetts Press, 1993), 139–140.

27. Memorandum from Louis T. Olom to Walter H. C. Laves, "Conference with Negro Leaders in Washington," March 2, 1942, "Negro file" folder, box 1717, OCIAA, RG 229, NA.

28. "The Negro in the Western Hemisphere," notice of lecture series by Rand School of Social Science, attached to letter from Frank R. Crosswaith, American Negro Labor Committee in Harlem, to Walter White, March 3, 1942, part 14, reel 7, NAACP Papers.

29. Ribeiro Couto, "Impressions of a Trip to the United States: The Negro in the U.S.," newspaper account of a speech by Couto to the Brazilian Academy of Letters, April 26, 1942, part 14, reel 7, NAACP Papers; memorandum to executives from Mr. [William] Pickens, April 14, 1941, part 17, reel 23, ibid.

30. Carl N. Degler, *Neither Black nor White: Slavery and Race Relations in Brazil* (New York: Macmillan, 1971), 104–106.

31. Remarks of Luis A. Sarmiento, secretary of the Ministry of National Education, Bogotá, Colombia, at the meeting of Alpha Kappa Delta, University of North Carolina, February 10, 1941, part 14, reel 7, NAACP Papers.

32. "Rio Hotel Hit for Anti-Negro Bias," typescript, *Christian Science Monitor,* March 5, 1947; "Mistake at the Serrador," *Time,* February 24, 1947, part 15, series A, reel 3, NAACP Papers; Ruth Landes to Walter White, December 30, 1941; Walter White to Ruth Landes, December 31, 1941, part 17, reel 23, ibid.

33. Richard Pilant to Roy Wilkins, June 4, 1956; Roy Wilkins to Clarence Mitchell, June 15, 1956, part 24, series B, reel 21, NAACP Papers.

34. Brazil received 73 percent of all Lend-Lease aid to Latin America, followed by Mexico (8 percent) and Chile (5 percent). Donald Marquand Dozer, *Are We Good Neighbors? Three Decades of Inter-American Relations, 1930–1960* (Gainesville: University of Florida Press, 1959), 124. No ground troops from Mexico participated in the war, but the Mexican Expeditionary Air Force, Squadron 201, flew missions under U.S. command in the Philippines in the spring and summer of 1945. Thomas M. Leonard and John F. Bratzel, eds., *Latin America during World War II* (Lanham, Md.: Rowman & Littlefield, 2007), 28–29.

35. Henry Allen Moe to Walter White, April 25, 1941, part 17, reel 23, NAACP Papers; Lesley Byrd Simpson, *Many Mexicos* (New York: Putnam, 1941).

36. Memorandum from W. G. Warnock to F. E. Gannett, president, Gannett Newspapers, October 13, [1941], part 17, reel 23, NAACP Papers.

37. Harry Frantz to Hart Stillwell, January 23, 1943, Central Files, "Spanish and Portuguese-Speaking Minorities in the U.S." folder, OCIAA, RG 229, NA; George I. Sánchez to Nelson A. Rockefeller, Dec. 31, 1941, Box 31, folder 9, George I. Sánchez Papers, Benson Latin American Collection, Austin, Texas (hereafter Sánchez Papers, BLAC.); George Isidore Sánchez, *Forgotten People: A Study of New Mexicans* (reprint, Albuquerque: University of New Mexico Press, 1996).

38. Thomas S. Sutherland to David Saposs, February 16, 1942, "Program for Cooperation of Spanish-Speaking Minorities in the United States" folder, box 1717, OCIAA, RG 229, NA; George I. Sánchez to Nelson A. Rockefeller, February 7, 1942, box 31, folder 9, Sánchez Papers, BLAC.

39. "Recommendations, Rapid Survey of Resident Latin American Problems and Recommended Program," attached to letter from David J. Saposs to Charles P. Taft, September 18, 1942, "OWI— Miscellaneous" folder, box 1717, OCIAA, RG 229, NA.

40. Thomas S. Sutherland to David Saposs, February 16, 1942, "Program for Cooperation of Spanish-Speaking Minorities in the United States" folder, box 1717, OCIAA, RG 229, NA.

41. "The Spanish Americans of the Southwest and the War Effort," p. 2, report attached to letter from R. Keith Kane to Dr. David J. Saposs, July 4, 1942, "OWI—Miscellaneous" folder, box 1717, OCIAA, RG 229, NA.

42. "Spanish-Americans in the Southwest and the War Effort," Report No. 24, Office of War Information, August 18, 1942, Decimal File, 811.4016/444, Records of the Department of State, RG 59, National Archives and Records Administration, College Park, Maryland (hereafter cited as RG 59, NA).

43. Adolfo G. Domínguez, "Memorandum on Racial Discrimination," n.d., attached to letter from Adolfo G. Domínguez, cónsul de México (Houston), to embajador de México, September 10, 1942, legajo 1457–13, Archivo de la Embajada de México en los Estados Unidos de América, in Archivo Histórico Genaro Estrada, Secretaría de Relaciones Exteriores, Mexico City (hereafter cited as Mexican Embassy Archives, SRE).

44. "Mexican Contract Workers in the United States," personal and confidential memorandum prepared by Ernesto Galarza, attached to letter from Francisco Castillo Nájera to secretario de Relaciones Exteriores, October 31, 1944, legajo 1451–23, Mexican Embassy Archives, SRE.

45. *Novedades,* March 26, 1945, clipping attached to letter from David Thomasson to secretary of state, March 27, 1945, Decimal File 811.4016/3–2745, RG 59, NA. Referring to the Pecos incident involving Senador Prado and Deputy Borunda, La Liga Municipal de Organizaciones Populares, Ciudad Juárez, Chihuahua, opposed sending any braceros to Texas. See Cipriano Ramírez D. and Ing. Pedro N. García to Manuel Ávila Camacho, April 7, 1945, exp. 575.1/17, caja 974, Ávila Camacho Papers, Achivo General de la Nación, Mexico City (hereafter cited as Ávila Camacho Papers, AGN); and telegram from Armando Acosta to Manuel Ávila Camacho, March 25, 1945, ibid.

46. "Caucasian Race—Equal Privileges," H.C.R. No. 105, April 15, 1943, in *General and Special Laws of the State of Texas, Passed by the Regular Session of the Forty-Eighth Legislature, Austin, Convened January 12, 1943, and Adjourned May 11, 1943* (Austin: State of Texas, 1943); Jack Danciger to Secretary of State Cordell Hull, June 10, 1943, Decimal File 811.4016/601, RG 59, NA; Thomas A. Guglielmo, "Fighting for Caucasian Rights: Mexicans, Mexican Americans, and the Transnational Struggle for Civil Rights in World War II Texas," *Journal of American History* 92 (March 2006): 1212–1237.

47. Clarence M. Mitchell to Will Maslow, January 18, 1944, reel 66, Records of the Committee on Fair Employment Practice, RG 228,

National Archives and Records Administration, College Park, Maryland (hereafter cited as FEPC, RG 228, NA).

48. Office memorandum from Clarence M. Mitchell to Marjorie M. Lawson, January 18, 1944, reel 66, FEPC, RG 228, NA.

49. H.B. 909, copy in enclosure no. 3, attached to William P. Blocker to Cordell Hull, "Results of a Confidential Survey of the Problem of Racial Discrimination against Mexican and Latin American Citizens in Texas and New Mexico," February 27, 1942, p. 17, Decimal File, 811.4016/337, RG 59, NA.

50. Robert C. Eckhardt to William P. Blocker, May 26, 1945, Decimal File 811.4016/5–2545, RG 59, NA.

51. William P. Blocker to secretary of state, December 23, 1943, Decimal File 811.4016/763, RG 59, NA.

52. Carlos E. Castañeda to Will Maslow, Bi-Weekly Report, May 1–15, 1945, reel 52, FEPC, RG 228, NA.

53. Castañeda was not always free of racial bias. Over a decade earlier he had written to Judge Hardman congratulating him for the apprehension and conviction of two blacks in Freeport, Texas: "I am glad also to hear that you have gotten rid of that entire lot of rotten niggers. There is no question but that Freeport is better off with them away." Carlos E. Castañeda to Judge G. C. Hardman, February 24, 1934, box 22, folder 3, Carlos E. Castañeda Papers, Nettie Lee Benson Latin American Collection, University of Texas Libraries, Austin, Texas (hereafter cited as Castañeda Papers, BLAC); Mario T. García, *Mexican Americans: Leadership, Ideology, and Identity, 1939–1960* (New Haven, Conn.: Yale University Press, 1989), 244.

54. Carlos E. Castañeda to Will Maslow, Bi-Weekly Report, April 15–30, 1945, reel 52, FEPC, RG 228, NA.

55. Carlos E. Castañeda to Will Maslow, Bi-Weekly Report, May 16–31, 1945, reel 52, FEPC, RG 228, NA. In an exceptional case in 1909, F. Flores, of Mexican origin, was charged with violating Texas state law forbidding intermarriage "between a white and a Negro." See Julie Anne Dowling, "The Lure of Whiteness and the Politics of 'Otherness': Mexican American Racial Identity" (Ph.D. diss., University of Texas, 2004), chapter 2.

56. PFC Robert N. Jones to Governor Stevenson, June 29, 1945, box 4-14/145, "racial discrimination 1945" folder, Stevenson Papers, TSLA.

57. Quoted in George Norris Green, *The Establishment in Texas Politics: The Primitive Years, 1938–1957* (Norman and London: University of Oklahoma Press, 1979), 81; idem, "The Felix Longoria Affair," *Journal of Ethnic Studies* 19 (Fall 1991): 24.

58. Radio Program, "What Does It Take to Get the American People Together," March 3, 1941, enclosure no. 2, attached to William P. Blocker to Cordell Hull, "Results of a Confidential Survey of the Problem of Racial Discrimination against Mexican and Latin American Citizens in Texas and New Mexico," February 27, 1942, p. 17, Decimal File, 811.4016/337, RG 59, NA.

59. Gary Gerstle, "The Crucial Decade: The 1940s and Beyond," *Journal of American History* 92 (March 2006): 1292–1299; idem, "Race and Nation in the United States, Mexico, and Cuba, 1880–1940," in *Nationalism in the New World,* ed. Don H. Doyle and Marco Antonio Pamplona (Athens: University of Georgia Press, 2006), 272–303.

60. Quoted in *Common Border, Uncommon Paths: Race, Culture, and National Identity in U.S.–Mexican Relations,* ed. Jaime E. Rodríguez O. and Kathryn Vincent (Wilmington, Del.: Scholarly Resources, Inc., 1997), 46.

61. "Estando prohibida la inmigración de individuos de raza negra a territorio nacional, esta medida se ha hecho extensiva a lo largo de la frontera en tal forma absoluta, que no se permite que ningún ciudadano americano de esa raza, pase algunas horas en viaje de recreo a cualquiera de las poblaciones fronterizas mexicanas." Circular Número 118, issued by Lic. Felipe Canales, November 14, 1929, IV-169-34, SRE; Enrique Santibáñez, consul general de México, to subsecretario de Relaciones Exteriores, October 3, 1929, ibid.; Manuel Collado to subsecretario de Relaciones Exteriores, October 31, 1929, ibid. I am indebted to Juan Manuel Mendoza Guerrero at the Universidad Autónoma de Sinaloa for bringing this circular to my attention.

62. "Increíble: En México les hacen asco a los Negros," *Ultimas Noticias,* July 8, 1943, clipping attached to letter from Genevieve Davis Storey to Walter White, July 9, 1943, part 15, series A, reel 3, NAACP Papers; Guy W. Ray to secretary of state, August 5, 1943, Decimal File 812.4016/128, reel 3, RG 59, NA.

63. Stephen E. Aguirre to secretary of state, May 18, 1943, Decimal File, 811.4016/536, RG 59, NA; R. E. T. to Chris [Fox], n.d., and Ewing Thomason to Chris Fox, May 29, 1943, letters attached to William P. Blocker to secretary of state, June 10, 1943, Decimal File, 811.4016/535, ibid.

64. George S. Messersmith to secretary of state, May 26, 1943, Decimal File, 811.4016/542, RG 59, NA. The deputy chief of staff for the U.S. Army, Lt. Gen. Joseph T. McNarney, stated that the War Department would not send additional black troops to Fort Bliss. William P. Blocker to secretary of state, June 8, 1943, Decimal File, 811.4016/550, ibid.

65. L. S. Armstrong to secretary of state, July 16, 1942, Decimal File 812.4016/120, reel 3, RG 59, NA; William P. Blocker to secretary of state, August 20, 1943, Decimal File 811.4016/664, RG 59, NA.

66. Walter White to Gov. Sidney P. Osborn, November 5, 1942, part 9, series B, reel 12, NAACP Papers; Gov. Sidney P. Osborn to Walter White, November 10, 1942, ibid.; "Governor Renews Plea for Aid of Huachuca Soldiers," *Bisbee Daily Review,* clipping, n.d., ibid.

67. "Eagle Pass Urges No Negroes Be Sent to Near-by Camps," *Dallas Morning News,* July 1, 1942, part 9, series B, reel 12, NAACP Papers; Walter White to Charles T. Brackins, July 13, 1942, ibid.; William Hastie to Walter White, July 15, 1942, ibid.

68. José Jorge Gómez Izquierdo, *El movimiento antichino en México (1871–1934): problemas del racismo y del nacionalismo durante la Revolución Mexicana* (México, D.F.: Instituto Nacional de Antropología e Historia, 1991); Juan Puig, *Entre el Río Perla y el Nazas: la China decimonónica y sus braceros emigrantes, la colonia china de Torreón y la matanza de 1911* (Mexico City: Dirección General de Publicaciones del Consejo Nacional Para la Cultura y las Artes, 1992);

Gerstle, "Race and Nation in the United States, Mexico, and Cuba," 272–303.

69. Marcelo Tadeo Pérez, presidente de Liga Nacional Anti-China y Anti-Judía, to secretario de gobernación, October 23, 1930, Dirección General de Gobierno, 2.360 (29), exp. 1, caja 10, AGN; H. C. Méndez, presidente, Comité Anti-Chino to Presidente Plutarco Elías Calles, May 7, 1928, Dirección General de Gobierno, Exp. 2.360 (29) exp. 15, caja 1, ibid.; R. H. Huerto and Hernando Sotelo, Liga Nacional Pro Raza/Campaña Anti-China, to C. Plutarco Elías Calles, May 24, 1928, Dirección General de Gobierno, 2.360 (29), exp. 15, caja 9, ibid.; "Murder of Chinese in Mexico," n.d.; "Three Chinese Lynched: Riots and Boycott in Chihuahua State," n.d., ibid.; Daniela Gleizer Salzman, "Exiliados incómodos: México y los refugiados judíos del nazismo,1933-1945" (Ph.D. diss., El Colegio de México, 2007).

70. David Thomasson to secretary of state, September 21, 1944, Decimal File 811.4016/9–2144, RG 59, NA.

71. The State Department subsequently requested that the U.S. Navy cancel the assignment. Confidential telegram to secretary of state, April 16, 1943, and Orme Wilson to Cdr. Frank B. Gary, April 17, 1943, Decimal File, 811.4016/526, RG 59, NA; G. W. Westerman, director, National Civil League of Panama City, to James C. Evans, secretary of defense, September 11, 1950, part 15, series A, reel 5, NAACP Papers; Thurgood Marshall to George L. P. Weaver, C.I.O. Committee to Abolish Discrimination, October 30, 1950, ibid.; John L. Yancey, C.I.O. Organizing Committee to Thurgood Marshall, No. 7, 1950, ibid.

72. Descendants of Panamanian slaves, whose language of origin was Spanish, were allowed to retain their citizenship. "70,000 Lose Status under Panama Act," *Detroit News,* January 2, 1941, part 13, series C, reel 3, NAACP Papers; "Panama President Would Castrate Colored Residents," newspaper clipping, n.d., ibid.

73. Quoted in Orlando J. Pérez, "Panama: Nationalism and the Challenge to Canal Security," in *Latin America during World War II,* eds. Thomas M. Leonarde and John F. Bratzel (Lanham, Md.: Rowman & Littlefield, 2007), 59–61.

74. Minutes of NAACP meeting, January 3, 1941, part 13, series C, reel 3, NAACP Papers; Ariel E. Dulitzky, "A Region in Denial: Racial Discrimination and Racism in Latin America," in *Neither Enemies Nor Friends: Latinos, Blacks, Afro-Latinos,* eds. Anani Dzidzienyo and Susanne Oboler (New York: Palgrave Macmillan, 2005), 55, note 21.

75. Capt. John F. Charlton, M. S. Gulfhawk, copy of original notice, November 11, 1940, part 13, series C, reel 3, NAACP Papers; Robert Haskins to Walter White, December 6, 1940, ibid.; Frank P. Corrigan, U.S. ambassador to Venezuela, to secretary of state, restricted memorandum, October 17, 1944, reel 66, FEPC, RG 228, NA.

76. Thurgood Marshall to Cordell Hull, December 11, 1940; idem to Pres. Franklin D. Roosevelt, December 11, 1940; Harold D. Finley, Division of American Republics, Department of State, to Thurgood Marshall, December 20, 1940, part 13, series C, reel 3, NAACP Papers. Hull quietly persuaded the Venezuelan government to allow port privileges to American citizens of African or Asian descent. Harold Finley to Thurgood Marshall, January 13, 1941, ibid.

77. A Mexican journalist defending Mexico against criticism in the Hearst press that Mexico was a lawless society, asked, "Have there been in any race riots in Mexico City? Do we indulge in lynching?" Manuel Carpio, "Intervention—The Mexican Side of It?" *The Public: A Journal of Democracy,* August 23, 1919, 907, clipping in legajo 608/9, Mexican Embassy Archives, SRE.

78. Gerald Horne, *Black and Brown: African Americans and the Mexican Revolution, 1910–1920* (New York: New York University Press, 2005), 4–10.

79. Quoted in Horne, *Black and Brown,* 188–89.

80. Quoted in Horne, *Black and Brown,* 34.

81. *La Prensa,* July 27, 1946, clipping attached to letter from S. Walter Washington to secretary of state, July 29, 1946, Decimal File 811.4016/7–2946, RG 59, NA.

82. N. V. Carlson to George A. Gordon, June 17, 1943, Decimal File 811.4016/622, RG 59, NA.

83. "Mexico's All-American Diplomat," *New York Herald Tribune,* February 14, 1943, clipping attached to letter from Cónsul General Ricardo G. Hill to Lic. Ezequiel Padilla, February 15, 1943, exp. 131/8, caja 117, Ávila Camacho Papers, AGN; Jim Marshall, "Mexico Cuts Off Her Nose," *Collier's,* November 25, 1939, typescript attached to letter from Pedro Boeta de la Serna to LCR, exp. 704.1/124, caja 1301, Lázaro Cárdenas Papers, AGN. On the post–World War II history of the contradiction between the Latin American doctrine of nonintervention and the international protection of human rights, see Robert K. Goldman, "History and Action: The Inter-American Human Rights System and the Role of the Inter-American Commission on Human Rights," forthcoming in *Human Rights Quarterly* 31, no. 4 (November 2009). Copy in author's possession.

84. I am aware that Vicente Guererro, a mestizo of African descent, briefly served as president in the decade following Mexico's independence from Spain and that the much beloved Mexican president, Benito Juárez, was a Zapotec Amerindian from Oaxaca, who inaugurated numerous liberal reforms known as *la reforma* during the mid-nineteenth century. My point here is that it is no more improbable in the twenty-first century for the United States to elect Barak Obama as president than it would be for Mexico to elect an Afro-Mexican. Nevertheless, the election of an Afro-Mexican as president of Mexico would not, I believe, be considered as momentous in Mexico as was the election of the first African-American president of the United States, given the historical persistence of the color line in the U.S. and the ideology of mestizaje in Mexico and other Latin American countries. For such an election to constitute a crucial moment in Mexican history would be to acknowledge, for the first time, the long and profound racial constitution of such a history. I am grateful to Mauricio Tenorio and Erika Gabriela Pani for their insights into the contingent and tangled ways *racismo* is articulated on both sides of the border.

2. The Politics of Race in the Fight for Fair Employment Practices

1. Walter White, "The Right to Fight for Democracy," *Survey Graphic* 31 (November 1942): 272–474; Ronald T. Takaki, *Double Victory: A Multicultural History of America in World War II* (Boston: Little, Brown and Co., 2000), 12.

2. Quoted in Maggie M. Morehouse, *Fighting in the Jim Crow Army: Black Men and Women Remember World War II* (Lanham, Md.: Rowman & Littlefield, 2000), 18.

3. Denton L. Watson, *Lion in the Lobby: Clarence Mitchell, Jr.'s Struggle for the Passage of Civil Rights Laws* (New York: William Morrow and Co., 1990), 122.

4. Quoted in Philip A. Klinkner, *The Unsteady March: The Rise and Decline of Racial Equality in America* (Chicago: University of Chicago Press, 1999), 180.

5. Andrew Edmund Kersten, *Race, Jobs, and the War: The FEPC in the Midwest, 1941–46* (Urbana: University of Illinois Press, 2000), 12.

6. Quoted in Heide Fehrenbach, *Race after Hitler: Black Occupation Children in Postwar Germany and America* (Princeton, N.J.: Princeton University Press, 2005), 22.

7. Hoyt S. Haddock to Cordell Hull, August 10, 1942, Decimal File, 811.4016/428, Records of the Department of State, RG 59, National Archives, College Park, Maryland (hereafter cited as RG 59, NA).

8. The FEPC complaint form listed the following as the reason for discrimination: "Negro, Chinese, Japanese, Filipino; Jew, Catholic, Jehovah's Witness, Seventh Day Adventist; Mexican, German, Italian, Lack of Citizenship." Complaint of Manuel S. Rodriguez, February 27, 1944, box 9, "Phelps-Dodge Corp. 10BN217" folder, FEPC, RG 228, National Archives, Region X, Fort Worth, Texas (hereafter cited as FEPC, RG 228, Region X, NA); Draft, Materials on Final Report, n.d., box 66, "West Coast Material" folder, FEPC, RG 228, National Archives, College Park, Maryland (hereafter cited as FEPC, RG 228, NA).

9. Robert P. Patterson, undersecretary of war, to Nelson A. Rockefeller, OCIAA, April 9, 1942, reel 66, FEPC, RG 288, NA; Victor G. Reuther, UAW-CIO Defense Employment Division, to Will Alexander, Office of Production Management, January 29, 1942, ibid.

10. Two years later FDR issued Executive Order 9346 in response to widespread criticism that the FEPC lacked enforcement powers. Clete Daniel, *Chicano Workers and the Politics of Fairness: The FEPC in the Southwest, 1941–1945* (Austin: University of Texas Press, 1991), 1–3, 132, 142.

11. "The Labor Supply Problem in Southeastern United States," n.d., reel 66, FEPC, RG 228, NA.

12. James A. Neuchterlein, "The Politics of Civil Rights: The FEPC, 1941–1946," *Prologue* 10 (1978): 171–191.

13. Nineteen major unions affiliated with the AFL refused membership to Negroes. "Confidential Report, Experiences in Negro Employment," Council for Democracy, February 1, 1943, attached to letter from Warren Brown to Victor Borella, February 1, 1943, "Negro file" folder, box 1717, Office of the Coordinator of Inter-American Affairs, Record Group 229, National Archives, College Park, Maryland (hereafter cited as OCIAA, RG 229, NA).

14. On the cultural and economic differences within the Spanish-speaking population, see "Spanish-Americans in the Southwest and the War Effort," Report No. 24, Office of War Information, August 18, 1942, Decimal File, 811.4016/444, RG 59, NA; "Report with few benefits and of the Spanish-Speaking Peoples in the Southwest," Field Report, March 14 to April 7, 1942, reel 70, FEPC, RG 228, NA.

15. Lawrence W. Cramer to Ernesto Galarza, September 30, 1941, reel 19, FEPC, RG 228, NA.

16. Ernesto Galarza to Mr. [Mark] Etheridge, September 25, 1941, box 339, Legal Division, Hearings, 1944–1946, "Hearing, Background Material" folder, FEPC, RG 228, NA.

17. Malcolm Ross to Jonathan Daniels, administrative assistant to the president, November 4, 1943, reel 66, FEPC, RG 228, NA; Ernesto Galarza to Mr. [Mark] Etheridge, September 25, 1941, box 339, Legal Division, Hearings, 1944–1946, "Hearing, Background Material"

folder, FEPC, RG 228, NA; Carlos E. Castañeda to Will Maslow, September 16, 1943, reel 41, ibid.; Carlos E. Castañeda to Dr. Francis J. Hass, FEPC chairman, August 27, 1943, ibid.; Carlos E. Castañeda to Clarence M. Mitchell, March 9, 1945, reel 21, ibid.

18. "Spanish-Americans in the Southwest and the War Effort," Report No. 24, Office of War Information, August 18, 1942, Decimal File, 811.4016/444, RG 59, NA.

19. Most shipbuilding and aircraft industries were located in Los Angeles County where African Americans constituted 2.7 percent of the population compared with 12.2 percent for foreign-born white, the majority of whom were undoubtedly Mexican immigrants, although the 1940 census did not classify Mexico-born residents separately from whites. Table 21, "Composition of the Population, By Counties: 1940," *Sixteenth Census of the United States, 1940: Population,* vol. 2, *Characteristics of the Population,* part I, p. 541; R. E. Brown, Jr., examiner-in-charge, to Harry L. Kingman, regional director, Region XII, Weekly Report, October 14, 1944, reel 52, FEPC, RG 228, NA.

20. Lawrence W. Cramer to Pres. Franklin Roosevelt, July 10, 1942, Decimal File 811.4016/405, RG 59, NA; Daniel, *Chicano Workers,* 8–11.

21. Testimony of Bert Corona, FEPC Public Hearings, Los Angeles, October 21, 1941, reel 19, FEPC, RG 228, NA.

22. Gregorio Narvaez to Franklin D. Roosevelt, March 5, 1945, box 6, "International Association of Longshoremen 10UN597" folder, FEPC, RG 228, Region X, NA; Rebecca Anne Montes, "Working for American Rights: Black, White, and Mexican American Dockworkers in Texas during the Great Depression" (Ph.D. diss., University of Texas, 2005), chapter 1, "The Limits of Brotherhood," 20–62.

23. "Conversation with Mr. McGurk and Mr. McLean of the Department of State . . . ," typescript attached to letter from Ernesto Galarza to Joseph F. McGurk, September 9, 1944, legajo 1451–23, Archivo de la Embajada de México en Estados Unidos de América, Archivo Histórico Genaro Estrada, Secretaría de Relaciones Exteriores

México, Mexico City (hereafter cited as Mexican Embassy Archives, SRE).

24. Josefina Fierro de Bright to Manuel Ávila Camacho, June 15, 1942, exp. 546.6/120–4, caja 974, Ávila Camacho Papers, Archivo General de Nación, Mexico City (hereafter cited as AGN); idem to Henry A. Wallace, June 16, 1942, "Spanish-Speaking Congress" folder, box 1717, OCIAA, RG 229, NA; Josefina Fierro de Bright to Nelson A. Rockefeller, June 18, 1942, ibid.

25. R. E. Brown, Jr., examiner-in-charge, to Harry L. Kingman, regional director, Region XII, Weekly Report, October 28, 1944, reel 52, FEPC, RG 228, NA. Moreno also worked with Ignacio L. Lopez, editor of *El Espectador* (Los Angeles) and field investigator for the FEPC, to inform Mexican workers in Los Angeles of their rights and the mission of the FEPC. R. E. Brown, Jr., to Harry L. Kingman, Weekly Report, January 27, 1945, ibid.

26. Carey McWilliams, *North from Mexico: The Spanish-Speaking People of the United States* (1949; reprint, New York: Greenwood Press, 1968), 276.

27. "Discrimination Out, Says Consul," *Los Angeles Times,* December 7, 1943, p. 13; R. E. Brown, Jr., examiner-in-charge, to Harry L. Kingman, regional director, XII, Weekly Report, November 13 and December 11, 1943, reel 52, FEPC, RG 228, NA; "Statement by Mexican Consul Re Discrimination," office memorandum from Robert E. Brown, Jr., to Harry L. Kingman, Region, December 10, 1943, reel 66, ibid.

28. R. E. Brown, Jr., examiner-in-charge, to Harry L. Kingman, regional director, Region XII, Weekly Report, November 27, 1943, reel 52, FEPC, RG 228, NA.

29. Quoted in Daniel, *Chicano Workers,* 5.

30. M. C. Gonzalez to Lawrence W. Cramer, August 18, 1942, reel 66, FEPC, RG 228, NA; Lawrence W. Cramer to Manuel C. Gonzales, September 2, 1942, ibid.; David J. Saposs, "Report on Rapid Survey of Resident Latin American Problems and Recommended Program," April 3, 1942, box 339, Legal Division, Hearings, 1944–1946, "Hearing, Background Material" folder, FEPC, RG 228, NA.

31. Carlos E. Castañeda to Will Maslow, May 21 and July 4, 1944, box 2, Active Cases, "General" folder, FEPC, RG 228, Region X, NA.

32. Statement of Trinidad F. Garcia, April 18, 1944, box 2, Active Cases, "El Paso—American Smelting and Refining Co." folder, FEPC, RG 228, Region X, NA.

33. Ernest G. Trimble to Lawrence W. Cramer, interoffice memorandum, n.d., box 63, "T" folder, FEPC, RG 228, NA.

34. Affidavit of Gilbert Lujan, May 20, 1942, attached to memorandum from Eugene Davidson to Carlos E. Castañeda, February 14, 1944, box 1, Active Cases, "Morenci, AZ" folder, FEPC, RG 228, Region X, NA.

35. Carlos E. Castañeda to Will Maslow, May 21, 1944, box 2, Active Cases, "General" folder, FEPC, RG 228, Region X, NA; "FEPC Investigation of Employment Practices in the Southwest," 1942, box 1, Active Cases, "Arizona" folder, FEPC, RG 228, Region X, NA.

36. Summer Welles to Lawrence W. Cramer, December 1, 1942, Decimal File 811.4016/470, RG 59, NA; William G. MacLean, "Meeting . . . on 'Spanish Speaking Minority Problem' on the Pacific Coast," November 5, 1942, Decimal File 811.4016/468, RG 59, NA; Lawrence W. Cramer to Summer Welles, November 6, 1942, Decimal File 811.4016/469, ibid.

37. William P. Blocker to secretary of state, November 12, 1942, Decimal File 811.4016/473, RG 59, NA; idem to secretary of state, December 27, 1942, ibid.

38. George I. Sánchez to W. W. Alexander, Minority Groups Branch, Office of Production Management, December 4, 1941, reel 66, FEPC, RG 228, NA; J. Edgar Hoover, memorandum for the attorney general, September 17, 1943, ibid.

39. George S. Messersmith to secretary of state, November 12, 1942, Decimal File 811.4016/470, RG 59, NA.

40. Francisco Castillo Nájera, ambassador, to Chairman Malcolm Ross, February 26, 1944, reel 66, FEPC, RG 228, NA; Luis Quintanilla, chargé d'affaires ad interim, Mexican Embassy, to Ernesto Galarza, Pan American Union, September 21, 1942, ibid.; Harold D.

Findley to secretary of state, November 3, 1942, Decimal File 811.4016/466, RG 59, NA.

41. William P. Blocker to secretary of state, September 3, 1942, Decimal File, 811.4016/440, RG 59, NA; William MacLean to Herbert S. Bursley, July 20, 1942, Decimal File, 811.4016/408, ibid.; and William P. Blocker to Ambassador George S. Messersmith, November 22, 1943, Decimal File 811.4016/748, ibid.

42. Lawrence W. Cramer to Pres. Franklin D. Roosevelt, July 10, 1942, RG 59, NA; Summer Welles, undersecretary of state, to Marvin H. McIntyre, secretary to the president, July 24, 1942, Decimal File, 811.4016/405, ibid.

43. See Manuel García y Griego, "The Importation of Mexican Contract Laborers to the United States, 1942–1964: Antecedents, Operation, and Legacy," in *The Border That Joins: Mexican Migrants and U.S. Responsibility,* eds. Peter G. Brown and Henry Shue (Totowa, N.J.: Rowman & Littlefield, 1983), 59–60.

44. See, for example, letters and telegrams from C. Guadarrama and Dámaso E. Sosa to Manuel Ávila Camacho, February 14, 1942, exp. 546.6/120–4, caja 794, Ávila Camacho Papers, AGN; José Hexiquio Ortega to Manuel Ávila Camacho, May 12, 1943, ibid.; Salvador Pérez, presidente de la Cámera de Comercio de la Piedad de Cabadas, Michoacán, to Manuel Ávila Camacho, January 18, 1944, ibid.

45. Daniel, *Chicano Workers,* 106–110.

46. Quoted in Daniel, *Chicano Workers,* 109.

47. Mario T. Garcia, *Mexican Americans: Leadership, Ideology, and Identity* (New Haven, Conn.: Yale University Press, 1989), 231–251.

48. "Statement . . . before Senator Chávez's Subcommittee of the Senate Education and Labor Committee," September 8, 1944, in box 2, Active Cases, "General" folder, FEPC, RG 228, Region X, NA.

49. Neil Foley, *The White Scourge: Mexicans, Blacks, and Poor Whites in Texas Cotton Culture* (Berkeley: University of California Press, 1997).

50. William P. Blocker to secretary of state, December 23, 1943, Decimal File 811.4016/763, RG 59, NA.

51. Francis J. Haas, FEPC chairman, to Ambassador Francisco Castillo Nájera, June 24, 1943, legajo 1457–13, Mexican Embassy

Archives, SRE; Adolfo G. Domínguez, Mexican consul (Houston), to Ambassador Francisco Castillo Nájera, June 8, 1943, ibid.; Emilio Zamora, "The Failed Promise of Wartime Opportunity for the Mexicans in the Texas Oil Industry," *Southwestern Historical Quarterly* 95 (January 1992): 323–350.

52. D. A. Young to Clay L. Cochran, December 7, 1943, box 10, "Sinclair Refining Co. 10BN584" folder, RG 228, FEPC, Region X; A. G. Domínguez to Carlos E. Castañeda, September 13, 1943, ibid.

53. D. A. Young to Clay L. Cochran, December 7, 1943, ibid.

54. "Minutes of Conference Held with Management and Labor of Sinclair Refinery," December 28, 1943, box 10, "Sinclair Refining Co. 10BN584" folder, FEPC, RG 228, Region X, NA.

55. Carlos E. Castañeda to W. R. Lee, November 23, 1943, box 8, "Oil Worker, International Union 10UN133" folder, FEPC, RG 228, Region X, NA. Emphasis in the original.

56. "Minutes of Conference Held with Management and Labor of Sinclair Refinery," December 28, 1943, box 10, "Sinclair Refining Co. 10BN584" folder, FEPC, RG 228, Region X, NA; W. R. Lee to Carlos Castañeda, December 2, 1943, ibid.

57. Carlos E. Castañeda to W. R. Lee, November 23, 1943, box 8, "Oil Worker, International Union 10UN133" folder, FEPC, RG 228, Region X, NA; Carlos E. Castañeda to Will Maslow, July 4, 1944, box 2, Active Cases, "General" folder, ibid.

58. Carlos E. Castañeda to A. G. Domínquez, December 6, 1943, box 8, "Oil Worker, International Union 10UN133" folder, FEPC, RG 228, Region X, NA.

59. A. S. Sánchez to Carlos E. Castañeda, December 19, 1943, box 8, "Oil Workers International Union 10UN133" folder, FEPC, RG 228, Region X, NA.

60. Robert Meza to Richard M. Kleberg, M.C., July 27, 1942, reel 66, FEPC, RG 228, NA. Emphasis in the original.

61. Castañeda used the terms *Latin Americans* and *Mexicans* interchangeably, often in the same paragraph. Carlos E. Castañeda to Clarence M. Mitchell, Monthly Report, September 15–October 15, 1945, reel 52, FEPC, RG 228, NA.

62. "Spanish-Americans in the Southwest and the War Effort," Report No. 24, Office of War Information, August 18, 1942, Decimal File, 811.4016/444, RG 59, NA.

63. "Investigation Conducted by Carlos E. Castañeda . . . of Alleged Complaints against the American Smelting and Refining Company," November 18, 1943, Corpus Christi, reel 19, FEPC, RG 228, NA.

64. W. R. Lee to O. A. Knight, August 19, 1943, box 8, "Oil Worker, International Union 10UN133" folder, FEPC, RG 228, Region X, NA.

65. O. A. Knight to W. R. Lee, July 27, 1943, box 8, "Oil Worker, International Union 10UN133" folder, FEPC, RG 228, Region X, NA; W. R. Lee to P. Kendall, August 3, 1943, ibid.; Ernest G. Trimble to Father Francis J. Haas, July 9, 1943, box 10, "Sinclair Refining Co. 10BN584" folder, ibid.

66. G. L. Farned to Lawrence W. Cramer, January 26, 1943, box 4, "Humble Oil Co. 10BN83" folder, FEPC, RG 228, Region X, NA; Leonard M. Brin, Final Disposition Report, February 9, 1944, box 4, "Humble Oil Co. 10BN81" folder, ibid.

67. G. L. Farned to Lawrence W. Cramer, January 26, 1943, box 4, "Humble Oil Co. 10BN83" folder, FEPC, RG 228, NA, Region X, Fort Worth, Texas.

68. Employees Federation Bulletin No. 63, n.d., part 13, series A, reel 15, NAACP Papers, telegram from Lawrence W. Cramer, FEPC, to Baytown Employees Federation, October 27, 1942, ibid.; memorandum, Ernest G. Trimble to Lawrence Cramer, September 13, 1943, box 4, "Humble Oil Co. 10BN81" folder, FEPC, RG 228, Region X, NA; W. B. Taylor to Father Haas, July 5, 1943, ibid.

69. G. L. Farned to Clay L. Cochran, December 29, 1943, box 4, "Humble Oil Co. 10BN82" folder, FEPC, RG 228, Region X, NA; Clay L. Cochran to Carlos E. Castañeda, October 25, 1943, box 11, "Texas Oil Co 10BR85" folder, ibid.

70. W. Don Ellinger to Will Maslow, October 20, 1944, reel 41, FEPC, RG 228, NA; Will Maslow to W. Don Ellinger, October 16, 1944, ibid.

71. Confidential memorandum from Leonard M. Brin to Will Maslow, January 27, 1944, reel 41, FEPC, RG 228, NA.

72. W. Don Ellinger to Clarence Mitchell, July 14, 1945, box 10, "Shell Oil Co. 10BN64" folder, FEPC, RG 228, Region X, NA; memorandum, W. Don Ellinger to File, July 30, 1945, ibid.

73. W. Don Ellinger to O. W. Knight, May 24, 1945, box 10, "Shell Oil Co. 10BN64" folder, FEPC, RG 228, Region X, NA.

74. W. Don Ellinger to Malcolm Ross, May 23, 1945, box 10, "Shell Oil Co. 10BN64" folder, FEPC, RG 228, Region X, NA; typescript, Bi-Weekly Report, May 26, 1945, ibid.

75. Carlos Castañeda to Will Maslow, Weekly Report, January 1, 1944, reel 52, FEPC, RG 228, NA.

76. "Important Unadjusted Cases in Region X," office memorandum from Clarence M. Mitchell to Will Maslow, January 25, 1944, reel 41, FEPC, RG 228, NA; "Opening Statement," n.d., box 348, "Shell Oil Company Hearings" folder, FEPC, RG 228, Region X, NA; Carlos E. Castañeda to Bruce Hunt, November 21, 1944, box 339, Legal Division, Hearings, 1944–1946, "Southwest Hearings" folder, FEPC, RG 228, NA.

77. Carlos E. Castañeda to O. A. Knight, January 1, 1944, box 10, "Shell Oil Co. 10BN64" folder, FEPC, RG 228, Region X, NA.

78. "Stipulation Agreed to by Respondents and Terms of Directive in the Matter of Shell Oil Co. and Oil Workers International Union, Local 367, C.I.O., Case No. 68, Exhibit 5," December 30, 1944, reel 21, FEPC, RG 228, NA; "Findings of Fact and Conclusions, FEPC, in the Matter of Shell Oil Company," December 30, 1944, box 10, "Shell Oil Co. 10BN64" folder, FEPC, RG 228, Region X, NA.

79. C. E. Belk to Harold J. Stafford, December 30, 1944, box 1, "Hearing FEPC v. Shell Oil Co.—Houston, TX" folder, War Manpower Commission, Record Group 211, National Archives, Region X, Fort Worth, Texas (hereafter cited as RG 211, Region X, NA); "Shell Case May Be Settled Privately," clipping, *Houston Press,* December 28, 1944, ibid.; memorandum from Carlos Castañeda to Will Maslow and W. Don Ellinger, August 30, 1944, box 10, "Shell Oil Co. 10BN64" folder, FEPC, RG 228, Region X, NA.

80. *Houston Chronicle,* clipping, April 28, 1945, box 454, Tension files, 1943–1945, "Adequacy of Housing" folder, FEPC, RG 228, NA; Carlos E. Castañeda to Will Maslow, Bi-Weekly Report, May 1–15, 1945, reel 52, FEPC, RG 228, NA.

81. W. Don Ellinger to Malcolm Ross, May 1, 1945, box 10, "Shell Oil Co. 10BN64" folder, FEPC, RG 228, Region X, NA.

82. Carlos E. Castañeda to Will Maslow, July 4, 1944, box 2, Active Cases, "General" folder, FEPC, RG 228, Region X, NA.

83. W. Don Ellinger to Malcolm Ross, May 1, 1945, box 10, "Shell Oil Co. 10BN64" folder, FEPC, RG 228, Region X, NA.

84. Carlos E. Castañeda to Will Maslow, Bi-Weekly Report, June 16–31, 1945, reel 52, FEPC, RG 228, NA.

85. Teletype from Will Maslow to W. Don Ellinger, June 4, 1945, box 10, "Shell Oil Co. 10BN64" folder, FEPC, RG 228, Region X, NA.

86. Recorded from telephone conversation with OWIU official, n.a., n.d., box 10, "Shell Oil Co. 10BN64" folder, FEPC, RG 228, Region X, NA.

87. J. E. Arnold to Lindley Beckworth, M.C., August 15, 1944, box 340, Legal Division, Hearings, 1944–1946, "Southwest Hearings" folder, FEPC, RG 228, NA.

88. Adolfo Domínguez, "Memorandum on Conference Held Friday, May 14, 1943, at Mexican Consulate in Houston, Texas, Relative to Discrimination of Mexican Workers at Shell Oid and Refining Company," attached to letter from Francisco Castillo Nájera, ambassador, to Lawrence W. Cramer, May 24, 1943, reel 70, FEPC, RG 228, NA.

89. W. Don Ellinger to Malcolm Ross, May 20, 1945, reel 21, FEPC, RG 228, NA; idem to Malcom Ross, May 23, 1945, box 10, "Shell Oil Co. 10BN64" folder, FEPC, RG 228, Region X, NA.

90. Frank P. Graham, Case No. 2898-C8-D, June 5, 1943, National War Labor Board, box 4, "Humble Oil Co. 10BN81" folder, FEPC, RG 228, Region X, NA.

91. C. M. García to War Production Board, December 29, 1944, box 8, "Pantex Ordinance Plant 10BN438" folder, FEPC, RG 228, Region X, NA; C. M. García to Carlos E. Castañeda, January 8, 1945, ibid.

92. Carlos E. Castañeda to Will Maslow, July 4, 1944, box 2, Active Cases, "General" folder, FEPC, RG 228, Region X, NA.

93. Ida Wren to President Roosevelt, August 28, 1944, box 1, Active Cases, "Miami, AZ" folder, RG 228, FEPC, Region X, NA; "Complaint of Ida Wren," October 7, 1944, ibid.; Complaint of Ruby Lee Wyatt, October 2, 1944, ibid.

94. Complaint of Helen E. Phillips, October 7, 1944, box 1, Active Cases, "Miami, AZ" folder, FEPC, RG 228, Region X, NA.

95. Memorandum, Frank D. Reeves to Bruce Hunt, November 1, 1944, box 1, Active Cases, "Morenci, AZ" folder, FEPC, RG 228, Region X, NA; Carlos E. Castañeda to Will Maslow, May 8, 1944, box 2, Active Cases, "General" folder, ibid.; "Final Disposition Report," April 27, 1945, box 8, "Pantex Ordinance Plant 10BN438" folder, ibid.

96. W. Don Ellinger to C. F. Favrot, March 20, 1945, box 9, "R. J. Dorn Co. 10BR169" folder, FEPC, RG 228, Region X, NA; memo, W. Don Ellinger to files, March 15, 1945, ibid. For other examples of the refusal of companies to hire or upgrade black women workers, see Carlos E. Castañeda to Will Maslow, Weekly Report, March 24, 1945, reel 52, FEPC, RG 228, NA; Carlos E. Castañeda to Will Maslow, Weekly Report, March 17, 1945, ibid.

97. Carlos E. Castañeda to Will Maslow, Bi-Weekly Report, May 16–31, 1945, reel 52, FEPC, RG 228, NA.

98. Carlos E. Castañeda to Will Maslow, Bi-Weekly Report, June 1–15, 1945, reel 52, FEPC, RG 228, NA.

99. Leonard M. Brin to commanding officer, January 20, 1944, box 2, "Camp Plauche 10GR170" folder, FEPC, RG 228, Region X, NA.

100. C. E. Belk [state director, WMC Texas] to John R. Reagor [acting chief, WMC, Region X], December 9, 1943, box 1, "Minority Discrimination, General Correspondence" folder, War Manpower Commission, RG 211, Region X, NA.

101. J. H. Bond to Irving W. Wood, September 24, 1942, box 1, "Minority Discrimination, General Correspondence" folder, War Manpower Commission, RG 211, Region X, NA; Irving W. Wood to J. H. Bond, September 22, 1942, ibid.

102. Leonard M. Brin to Butane Equipment Company, April 26, 1944, box 2, folder "Butane Equipment Co. 10BR300" folder, FEPC, RG 228, Region X, NA; Signey S. Smith to Leonard M. Brin, May 12, 1944, ibid.

103. Freeman Everett to Lula White, April 12, 1945, box 6, "International Association of Longshoremen 13UR516" folder, FEPC, RG 228, Region X, NA; W. Don Ellinger to Lulu B. White, April 9, 1945, ibid.; Lulu B. White to W. Don Ellinger, April 13, 1945, ibid.

104. Will Maslow to Leonard M. Brin, January 25, 1944, reel 41, FEPC, RG 228, NA; Leonard M. Brin to Will Maslow, January 28, 1944, ibid.; Carlos Castañeda to Will Maslow, Weekly Report, December 6, 1943, reel 52, ibid.; Carlos Castañeda to Will Maslow, Weekly Report, December 18, 1943, ibid.

105. Harry L. Kingman, region director, to Clarence Mitchell, February 2, 1944, reel 66, FEPC, RG 228, NA.

106. "Federal Bureau Asks Newspaper Ads Omit Any Mention of Race," *Dallas Morning News,* May 18, 1944.

107. "Misguided Bureaucrats," *Dallas Morning News,* May 18, 1944.

108. "Bureau Order on Ads Called Lawless Act," *Dallas Morning News,* May 20, 1944.

109. John S. Gibson, "FEPC Order Merely Violates Constitution," *Dallas Morning News,* May 23, 1944.

110. W. H. Wingo, "Unspecific Enough," *Dallas Morning News,* May 23, 1944.

111. Leonard Brin submitted his resignation, although he claimed that he was resigning for personal reasons and not because of the controversy over want ads. "Brin Resigns FEPC Post," *Dallas Morning News,* June 10, 1944.

112. "FEPC Attempts to Explain Action in *Dallas News* Case," *Dallas Morning News,* June 1, 1944. Brin was forced to write a letter of apology to the American Beauty Cover Company. "O'Daniel Told Brin Apologized for FEPC Order to Dallas Firm," *Dallas Morning News,* June 6, 1944.

113. "Brin Quizzed on FEPC Work by Governor," *Dallas Morning News,* June 9, 1944. Brin declined to respond to Governor Stevenson's letter. "Brin in Washington," ibid., June 12, 1944.

114. H. P. Willis to Governor Stevenson, June 9, 1944, box 170, "Fair Employment Practices Committee" folder, Gov. Coke R. Stevenson Papers, Texas State Library and Archives, Austin, Texas (hereafter cited as Stevenson Papers, TSLA).

115. J. E. Jones to Governor Stevenson, June 13, 1944, box 170, "Fair Employment Practices Committee" folder, Stevenson Papers, TSLA.

116. C. W. Gibson [Corpus Christi] to Governor Stevenson, June 10, 1944, box 170, "Fair Employment Practices Committee" folder, Stevenson Papers, TSLA.

117. Will F. Evans to Governor Stevenson, June 10, 1944, box 170, "Fair Employment Practices Committee" folder, Stevenson Papers, TSLA.

118. W. Don Ellinger to Will Maslow, September 6, 1944, reel 41, FEPC, RG 228, NA; Clarence M. Mitchell to W. Don Ellinger, September 19, 1944, ibid.

119. Edgar F. Kaiser to Harry L Kingman, region director, Region XII, December 1, 1943, reel 41, FEPC, RG 228, NA.

120. *San Francisco Chronicle,* March 28, 1946, clipping, box 443, Tension files, 1943–1945, "San Francisco" folder, FEPC, RG 228, NA.

121. George I. Sánchez to John J. Herrera, May 13, 1955, box 19, folder 5, George I. Sánchez Papers, Nettie Lee Benson Latin American Collection, University of Texas Libraries, Austin (hereafter cited as Sánchez Papers, BLAC).

122. *Labor Herald,* San Francisco, February 16, 1945, clipping, box 443, Tension files, 1943–1945, "San Francisco" folder, FEPC, RG 228, NA.

123. Statement of Alexander Pierce, June 5, 1945, box 12, "Todd Johnson Dry Dock 10BR129" folder, FEPC, RG 228, Region X, NA.

124. Carlos E. Castañeda to Will Maslow, Bi-Weekly Report, April 1–15, 1945, reel 52, FEPC, RG 228, NA.

125. Malcolm Ross to editor, *Atlanta Journal,* July 17, 1944, box 5, "Negroes and Other Minorities" folder, War Manpower Commission, RG 211, NA.

126. Untitled document by FEPC Chairman, Mark Etheridge, n.d., reel 66, FEPC, RG 228, NA.

127. "Confidential Report: Experiences in Negro Employment," Council for Democracy, p. 4, February 1, 1943, attached to letter from Warren Brown to Victor Borella, February 1, 1943, "Negro file" folder, box 1717, OCIAA, RG 229, NA.

128. Ibid., p. 17.

129. "Statement by Joseph James, chairman of the Negro Shipyard Workers Committee . . .", n.d., attached to memorandum from Harry L. Kingman, regional director, Region XII, June 28, 1945, reel 41, FEPC, RG 228, NA.

130. "Motion of J. Strom Thurmond, Governor's Conference," February 7, 1948, box 4–14/93, "Southern Governors' Conference, Wash., D.C., March 12–13, 1948" folder, Gov. Beauford H. Jester Papers, TSLA.

131. See Risa Lauren Goluboff, *The Lost Promise of Civil Rights* (Cambridge, Mass.: Harvard University Press, 2007).

3. BLACK V. BROWN AND *BROWN V. BOARD OF EDUCATION*

1. Some Texas school districts provided no school for African Americans in towns with only a few black families. Thurgood Marshall to A. Maceo Smith, September 17, 1948, part 3, series B, reel 4, *A Guide to the Microfilm Edition of the Papers of the NAACP,* ed. Randolph Boehm (Frederick, Maryland: University Publications of America, 1982), hereafter cited as NAACP Papers; idem to Dr. H. Boyd Hall, October 1, 1948; ibid.; L. A. Woods to J. F. Harbin, September 1, 1948, ibid.

2. *Mendez v. Westminster School District,* 64 F. Supp. 544 (D. Cal. 1946); *Delgado v. Bastrop Independent School District,* Civ. No. 388 (W.D. Tex. June 15, 1948); *Sweatt v. Painter* 339 U.S. 629 (1950); Motion and Brief of Amicus Curiae NAACP (No. 11,310), *Westminster*

School District et al. v. Gonzalo Mendez et al., 161 F.2d 774 (9th Cir. 1947). Hereafter cited as "NAACP Amicus Curiae, No. 11,310."

3. Juan Williams, *Thurgood Marshall: American Revolutionary* (New York: Three Rivers Press, 1998), 15–51; Mark V. Tushnet, *Making Civil Rights Law: Thurgood Marshall and the Supreme Court, 1936–1961* (New York: Oxford University Press, 1994), 7–15; *University of Maryland v. Murray*, 169 Maryland 478 (1936).

4. Ruben Flores, "States of Culture: Relativism and National Consolidation in Mexico and the United States, 1910–1950" (Ph.d. diss, University of California, Berkeley, 2006), chapter 4; Mario T. Garcia, *Mexican Americans: Leadership, Ideology, and Identity, 1930–1960* (New Haven, Conn.: Yale University Press, 1989), 252–272.

5. *Mendez v. Westminster School District*, 64 F. Supp. 544 (D. Cal. 1946). Gonzalo Mendez was raised in California since he was six years old and later became a naturalized U.S. citizen. Christopher Arriola, "Knocking on the Schoolhouse Door: *Mendez v. Westminster*, Equal Protection, Public Education, and Mexican Americans in the 1940s," *La Raza Law Journal* 8 (Fall 1995): 166–207; Charles Wollenberg, "*Mendez v. Westminster*: Race, Nationality, and Segregation in California Schools," *California Historical Quarterly* 55 (Winter 1974): 317–332.

6. See *Independent School District v. Salvatierra*, 33 S.W. 2d 790 (Tex. Civ. App. 1930); and *Alvarez v. Owen*, No. 66625 (San Diego County Super. Ct. filed April 17, 1931).

7. "Segregation Case Is before U.S. Court Here," *San Francisco Chronicle*, December 10, 1946, clipping attached to letter from N. W. Griffin to Thurgood Marshall, December 10, 1946, part 3, series B, reel 1, NAACP Papers.

8. *Mendez v. Westminster School District*, 64 F. Supp. 544 (D. Cal. 1946).

9. *Brown v. Board of Education*, 347 U.S. 483 (1954).

10. Michael Kotlanger, S.J., "U.S. Stamp Honors Former Student," www.siprep.org, accessed May 2, 2009.

11. See, for example, *Murray v. Maryland*, 182 A. 590 (1936); *Missouri ex rel. Gaines v. Canada*, 305 U.S. 337 (1938); *Sipuel v. Oklahoma*

State Board of Regents, 332 U.S. 631 (1948); and *Sweatt v. Painter,* 339 U.S. 629 (1950).

12. Telegram from Robert L. Carter to Judge Albert Stevens, August 20, 1946, part 3, series B, reel 1, NAACP Papers; Paul P. O'Brien, clerk, Ninth Circuit Court, to Robert L. Carter, August 21, 1946, ibid.; Robert L. Carter to David C. Marcus, September 13, 1946, ibid.; idem to Loren Miller, September 13 and 14, 1946, ibid.; telegram from Thurgood Marshall to Paul P. O'Brien, October 4, 1946, ibid.; "Pacific States: Segregation of Mexicans Stirs School-Court Fight," *New York Times,* December 22, 1946.

13. Robert L. Carter to David C. Marcus, September 13, 1946, part 3, series B, reel 1, NAACP Papers. On the San Bernardino swimming pool case, see *Lopez v. Seccombe,* 71 F. Supp. 769 (S.D. Cal. 1944).

14. Quoted in Gilbert G. Gonzalez, *Chicano Education in the Era of Segregation* (Philadelphia: Balch Institute Press and London and Toronto: Associated University Presses, 1990), 28; Richard Kluger, *Simple Justice: The History of* Brown v. Board of Education *and Black America's Struggle for Equality* (New York: Alfred A. Knopf, 2004), 252–253; Ruben Flores, "Social Science in the Southwest Courtroom: A New Understanding of the NAACP's Legal Strategies in the School Desegregation Cases" (B.A. thesis, Princeton University, 1994), chapters 3 and 4. Six of the seven works on the harmful psychological effects of segregation cited in footnote 11 of *Brown v. Board* were published *after* 1947 when the NAACP submitted its amicus brief in *Mendez.*

15. Carey McWilliams, "Is Your Name Gonzales?" *The Nation,* March 15, 1947, clipping attached to letter from Office of Jewish Information, American Jewish Congress, to NAACP, April 1, 1947, part 3, series B, reel 1, NAACP Papers.

16. Thurgood Marshall to Carl Murphy, December 20, 1946, part 3, series B, reel 1, NAACP Papers.

17. "NAACP Amicus Curiae, No. 11,310."

18. Ibid.

19. Ibid.

20. Ibid.; Kluger, *Simple Justice,* 169.

21. Robert L. Carter to Claude G. Metzler, December 26, 1946, part 3, series B, reel 1, NAACP Papers; idem to Leon Silverman, March 24, 1947, ibid.

22. Quoted in Carey McWilliams, "Is Your Name Gonzales?" *The Nation,* March 15, 1947, 302–303, clipping attached to letter from Office of Jewish Information, American Jewish Congress, to NAACP, April 1, 1947, part 3, series B, reel 1, NAACP Papers.

23. "Is Your Name Gonzalez?" ibid.

24. *Mendez v. Westminster School District,* 64 F. Supp. 544 (S.D. Cal. 1946), 161 F. 2d 774 (1947). Emphasis added.

25. *Westminster School District of Orange County v. Mendez et al.,* 161 F.2d 774 (1947).

26. Charles Wollenberg, *All Deliberate Speed: Segregation and Exclusion in California Schools, 1855–1975* (Berkeley: University of California Press, 1976), 132. A few years later Texas Gov. Beauford Jester marveled at how Warren came to Laredo, met with Mexican governors, and left with a contract to receive 10,000 workers for the citrus industry in southern California. Memorandum, William McGill to Governor Jester, June 1, 1948, box 4–14/52, "Mexican Labor" folder, Beauford Jester Papers, Texas State Library and Archives, Austin, Texas (hereafter cited as Beauford Jester Papers, TSLA).

27. "Protest Negro Classmates," *Daily News,* March 18, 1947, clipping attached to letter from assistant secretary, NAACP, to Thomas L. Griffin, president, Los Angeles Branch, part 3, series B, reel 1, NAACP Papers.

28. James A. Ferg-Cadima, "Black, White, and Brown: Latino School Desegregation Efforts in the Pre– and Post–*Brown v. Board of Education* Era," *MALDEF* (May 2004): 21; Kluger, *Simple Justice,* 400.

29. "Press Release Re: *Westminster School District of Orange County et al. v. Gonzalo Mendez et al.,*" memorandum from Robert L. Carter to Public Relations Department, April 24, 1947; "Court Upholds Decision against Discrimination," press release, May 9, 1947, part 3, series B, reel 1, NAACP Papers.

30. *Open Forum* (Los Angeles), May 3, 1947, quoted in Wollenberg, *All Deliberate Speed,* 131.

31. Jorge C. Rangel and Carlos M. Alcala, "Project Report: De Jure Segregation of Chicanos in Texas Schools," *Harvard Civil Rights-Civil Liberties Law Review* 7 (March 1972): 314.

32. *Independent School District v. Salvatierra,* 33 S.W. 2d 795.

33. George I. Sánchez to Dr. Hector P. García, November 18, 1948, box 4, folder 9, George I. Sánchez Papers, Nettie Lee Benson Latin American Collection, University of Texas Libraries, Austin (hereafter cited as Sánchez Papers, BLAC).

34. "Complaint to Enjoin Violation of Federal Civil Rights and for Damages, in the United States District Court for the Western District of Texas," box 79, folder 4, Sánchez Papers, BLAC; Gus C. García to A. L. Wirin, August 22, 1947, box 16, folder 17, ibid.; idem to George I. Sánchez, November 28, 1947, ibid.

35. Steven H. Wilson, "*Brown* over 'Other White': Mexican Americans' Legal Arguments and Litigation Strategy in School Desegregation Lawsuits," *Law and History Review* 21 (Spring 2003): 145–194.

36. Cristobal P. Aldrete to L. A. Woods, January 5, 1949, box 12, folder 7, Sánchez Papers, BLAC; C. P. Aldrete, "Interviews with Del Rio School Officials, May 1948 to December 1948," ibid.; statement of L. A. Woods, state superintendent of Public Schools, April 23, 1949, ibid.; Pilar Garza to George I. Sánchez, January 13, 1949, ibid.; Maria Luisa Camarillo to L. A. Woods, February 3, 1949, ibid.; Hector P. García to Gus García, March 9, 1949, ibid.

37. "Latin Segregation," *Texas Observer,* January 22, 1957, box 1989/59–18, "Nueces County" folder, Good Neighbor Commission Collection, Texas State Library and Archives, Austin, Texas (hereafter, Good Neighbor Commission, TSLA); *Hernandez et al. v. Driscoll Consolidated Independent School District,* Civil Action 1384, U.S. District Court for the Southern District of Texas (1957).

38. Final Judgment, *Delgado v. Bastrop Independent School District,* Civ. No. 388 (W.D. Tex. June 15, 1948), box 79, folder 5, Sánchez Papers, BLAC.

39. Quoted in Jorge C. Rangel and Carlos M. Alcala, "Project Report: De Jure Segregation of Chicanos in Texas Schools," *Harvard Civil Rights-Civil Liberties Law Review* 7 (March 1972): 337.

40. *Gong Lum v. Rice,* 275 U.S. 78 (1927).

41. Quoted in Martha Casas, "An Historical Analysis of the United States Supreme Court and Its Adjudication of *Gong Lum v. Rice* (1927) and *Keyes v. Denver School District No. 1* (1973)," *Journal of Thought* 41 (Winter 2006): 93. In 1944 an official of the Chinese Embassy, Victor Kwong, objected to the Mississippi practice of "classifying Chinese with negroes as non-whites" and indicated that the embassy "would be loath to take action which would tend to associate the Chinese in the public eye with the negro race . . . in the South." Memorandum of conversation, Division of Chinese Affairs, April 24, 1944, Decimal File 811.4016/820, Records of the Department of State, RG 59, National Archives and Records Administration, College Park, Maryland (hereafter cited as RG 59, NA).

42. *Hernandez v. Driscoll CISD,* 2 Race Rel. L. Rptr. 329 (S.D. Tex. 1957); George I. Sánchez to Roger Baldwin, January 4, 1942, and September 21, 1942, box 2, folder 17, Sánchez Papers, BLAC.

43. George I. Sánchez to Dr. Hector P. García, April 14, 1949, box 4, folder 9, Sánchez Papers, BLAC.

44. George I. Sánchez to Joe R. Greenhill, assistant to the attorney general, May 8, 1947, box 32, folder 15, Sánchez Papers, BLAC; Joe R. Greenhill to DeWitt County Attorney Wayne L. Hartman, April 8, 1947, ibid.; George I. Sánchez to Gov. Beauford Jester, May 15, 1947, ibid.; Gus C. García to Atty. Gen. Price Daniel, August 13, 1947, ibid.

45. Cristobal P. Aldrete, American Veterans Anti-Discrimination Committee, to Price Daniel, July 28, 1947, box 32, folder 15, Sánchez Papers, BLAC.

46. George I. Sánchez to Gus García, April 20, 1949, box 16, folder 19, Sánchez Papers, BLAC.

47. "School Trouble Laid to Race Segregation," *Houston Post,* September 21, 1947, clipping attached to letter from Heman M. Sweatt to Thurgood Marshall, September 21, 1947, part 3, series B, reel 16, NAACP Papers.

48. C. G. *Jennings v. Board of Trustees of the Hearne ISD,* Complaint, Civil Action 822, n.d., part 3, series B, reel 4, NAACP Papers; "LaGrange High School Girl Refused Registration in 'White' High School: Father Brings Suit," press release, Southwest Region NAACP, December 6, 1947, ibid.

49. "Hearne Case Results in Declaratory Judgment," press release, Southwest Region NAACP, September 2, 1948, part 3, series B, reel 4, NAACP Papers.

50. Thurgood Marshall to U. Simpson Tate, February 7, 1949, part 3, series B, reel 4, NAACP Papers.

51. Lulu B. White to Thurgood Marshall, November 24, 1947, part 3, series B, reel 4, NAACP Papers. I was unable to find any record of Marshall meeting with the Mexican consul.

52. Thurgood Marshall to George I. Sánchez, July 1, 1948, box 24, folder 8, Sánchez Papers, BLAC; George I. Sánchez to Thurgood Marshall, July 6, 1948, ibid.; A. L. Wirin to George Sánchez, July 1, 1948, box 62, folder 15, ibid.

53. Gus C. García, "Memorandum of Points and Authorities in Support of Plaintiffs' Application for Injunction, Pendente Lite [*Delgado v. Bastrop Independent School District* (1948)]," n.d., box 32, folder 14, Sánchez Papers, BLAC; Mark V. Tushnet, *NAACP's Legal Strategy against Segregated Education, 1925 to 1950* (Chapel Hill: University of North Carolina, 2004), 62. Sánchez often sought political rather than costly, drawn-out legal solutions, such as getting a ruling from the state attorney general on the illegality of segregated schools or public housing for Mexicans. George I. Sánchez to A. L. Wirin, October 30, 1951, box 62, folder 16, Sánchez Papers, BLAC.

54. George I. Sánchez to Thurgood Marshall, July 6, 1948, box 24, folder 8, Sánchez Papers, BLAC (also in NAACP Papers, part 3, series B, reel 4); U. Simpson Tate, NAACP counsel for the Southwest, to Thurgood Marshall, January 21, 1949, part 3, series B, reel 4, NAACP Papers; Monthly Report of Regional Special Counsel, Southwest Region NAACP, January 31, 1949, ibid.; "Hearne Case Results in Declaratory Judgment," press release, September 2, 1948, ibid.

55. *Smith v. Allwright,* 321 U.S. 649 (1944).

56. Quoted in Amilcar Shabazz, *Advancing Democracy: African Americans and the Struggle for Access and Equity in Higher Education in Texas* (Chapel Hill: University of North Carolina Press), 69.

57. Kluger, *Simple Justice*, 260.

58. Thurgood Marshall to Carl Murphy, editor of *The Afro-American*, September 30, 1947, part 3, series B, reel 16, NAACP Papers; idem to W. Robert Ming, Jr., NAACP Legal Committee, April 22, 1947, reel 15, ibid.

59. J. H. Morton, president of the Austin branch of the NAACP, to Gloster B. Current, director of Branches, December 10, 1946, part 26, series A, reel 20, NAACP Papers; Lulu [B. White] to Thurgood Marshall, December 11, 1946, ibid.; A. Maceo Smith to Thurgood Marshall, January 17, 1947, ibid.; Thurgood Marshall to William H. Hastie, April 3, 1947, ibid.; "Summary of University of Texas Fund Drive for Marion Sweatt Case," n.d., attached to memorandum from Thurgood Marshall to Ollie Harrington, January 24, 1947, part 3, series B, reel 15, ibid.

60. Herb. [no last name] to Lulu [B. White], May 17, 1947, part 26, series A, reel 20, NAACP Papers. See also the student flyer, "Join the NAACP," March 7, 1950, part 3, series B, reel 16, ibid.

61. Donald Logan to Gov. Beauford Jester, March 14, 1948, box 4–14/96, "Civil Rights (against the Govs. Stand)" folder, Beauford Jester Papers, TSLA.

62. President's Committee on Civil Rights, *To Secure These Rights* (Washington, D.C.: Government Printing Office, 1947); A. L. Burden to Gov. Beauford Jester, March 25, 1947, box 4–14/67, "Communist Party" folder, Beauford Jester Papers, TSLA.

63. Quoted in Charles H. Thompson, "Separate but Not Equal: The *Sweatt* Case," *Southwest Review* 33 (Spring 1948): 107.

64. W. Lee O'Daniel to Gov. Beauford Jester, February 13, 1948 (speech attached to letter), box 4–14/93, "Civil Rights (Favoring the Govs. Stand)" folder, Beauford Jester Papers, TSLA.

65. Homer P. Rainey, *The Tower and the Dome: A Free University versus Political Control* (Boulder, Colo.: Pruett Publishing Co., 1971), 6–7, 33, 43, 83–84 (quotes); Henry Nash Smith, *The Controversy at*

the University of Texas, 1939–1946: A Documentary History ([Austin]: Student Committee for Academic Freedom, Students' Association, University of Texas, [1945]), 7–9.

66. H.C.R. No. 50, *House Journal,* 51st Legislature [1949], Vol. 1, 909, 955, 988, 1098, box 4–14/103, "Communist Legislation" folder, Beauford Jester Papers, TSLA.

67. Carl Modglin to Gov. Beauford Jester, February 9, 1948, box 4–14/82, "University of Texas 1948" folder, Beauford Jester Papers, TSLA; Winston Bode, *A Portrait of Pancho: The Life of a Great Texan, J. Frank Dobie* (Austin: Pemberton Press, 1965), 78.

68. Wendell Addington, secretary of the Communist Party in Austin, Texas, to Governor Jester, July 14, 1948, box 4–14/112, "John Roe Case-D.P.S." folder, Beauford Jester Papers, TSLA; "Texas Plantation System," handbill, n.d., ibid.

69. *San Antonio Express,* March 25, 1949, clipping attached to letter, J. R. Smith to Gov. Beauford Jester, March 25, 1949, box 4–14/103, "Communist Legislation" folder, Beauford Jester Papers, TSLA.

70. "Dixie Fans Cheer Negro," n.d., newspaper clipping, attached to envelope, P. B. Maunde to Gov. Beauford Jester, box 4–14/93, "Southern Governors' Conference, Wash., DC, Mar. 12–13, 1948" folder, Beauford Jester Papers, TSLA.

71. Wm. M. Tuck to Gov. Beauford Jester, February 25, 1948, statement attached, box 4–14/93, "Southern Governors' Conference, Wash., DC, Mar. 12–13, 1948" folder, Beauford Jester Papers, TSLA.

72. Donald S. Smith to Gov. Beauford Jester, November 24, 1948, box 4–14/52, "Negro Football Players" folder, Beauford Jester Papers, TSLA.

73. Of the 9,191 students enrolled at UT in 1946, 114, or 1.2 percent, were "Texas-born Spanish-name" students, although one out of every six persons in the state was of Mexican ancestry. The number does not include non-Texas-born Latinos, mostly Latin Americans from Mexico, Central and South America, or students of Mexican descent with non-Hispanic surnames. Ruth Ann Douglass Fogartie,

Texas-born Spanish-Name Students in Texas Colleges and Universities, Inter-American Education Occasional Papers No. 3 (Austin: University of Texas Press, 1948), 14–15.

74. PFC Robert N. Jones to Governor Stevenson, June 29, 1945, box 4-14/145, "Racial Discrimination 1945" folder, Stevenson Papers, TSLA.

75. "Latin Americans State *Sweatt* Case Neutrality," *Daily Texan,* December 8, 1946, clipping in part 3, series B, reel 15, NAACP Papers.

76. See, for example, Olga Freidt et al. to Thomas S. Sutherland, March 5, 1950, box 1989/59-18, "Discrimination Correspondence, 1949–1950" folder, Good Neighbor Commission, TSLA.

77. Thompson, "Separate but Not Equal," 105–106; "Charles H. Thompson," *Journal of Negro Education,* www.journalnegroed.org, accessed February 4, 2009.

78. Typescript of "Press Conference for Heman M. Sweatt Held in the Offices of the Association," April 4, 1950, part 3, series B, reel 16, NAACP Papers; Thurgood Marshall to the editor, *New York Times,* April 19, 1950, ibid. Emphasis added.

79. "Negro Discovered in Class at U.T.," *Austin Statesman,* October 20, 1938, clipping attached to letter from A. Maceo Smith to Thurgood Marshall, October 22, 1938, part 3, series A, reel 18, NAACP Papers.

80. "Scott Cancels Concert Because of Segregation," *Daily Texan,* November 22, 1948, part 15, clipping in series A, reel 5, NAACP Papers.

81. Thurgood Marshall to Carl Murphy, December 20, 1946, part 3, series B, reel 1, NAACP Papers; Tushnet, *NAACP's Legal,* 126–127.

82. Thompson, "Separate but Not Equal,"105–106.

83. Thurgood Marshall to Heman Sweatt, September 30, 1947, part 3, series B, reel 15, NAACP Papers; Thurgood Marshall to editor, *Dallas Morning News,* February 5, 1948, ibid.; Shabazz, *Advancing Democracy,* 70–71.

84. "Inaugural Address of Gov. Beauford H. Jester," January 21, 1947, box 4-14/66, "Inauguration" folder, Beauford Jester Papers,

TSLA; Hector Perez Martinez, secretario de Gobernación, to Gov. Beauford Jester, September 2, 1947, box 1989/59–16, "Discrimination, General File, 1946–1956" folder, Good Neighbor Commission, TSLA.

85. "Jester Apologizes to Aleman," *Amarillo Daily News,* April 25, 1949, attached to letter from Alfonso Guerra, oficial mayor, to secretario de Relaciones Exteriores, May 12, 1949, exp. 130/280, caja 117, Miguel Alemán Papers, AGN; "Jester Plans Mexican Tour," *Amarillo Globe,* April 25, 1949, ibid.

86. Gov. Beauford Jester to George C. Marshall, June 7, 1948, box 4–14/52, "Mexican Labor" folder, Beauford Jester Papers, TSLA.

87. Quoted in letter from William McGill to M. A. Urbina, September 17, 1947, box 4–14/122, "Good Neighbor Commission, 1947" folder, Beauford Jester Papers, TSLA.

88. Price Daniel, attorney general, to Hon. Gus García, August 21, 1947, box 32, folder 15, Sánchez Papers, BLAC.

89. Palmer wrote on behalf of the executive committee of the Texas Association of the Improved Benevolent Protective Order of Elks of the World. J. E. Palmer et. al., April 4, 1948, box 4–14/93, "Civil Rights (Favoring the Govs. Stand)" folder, Beauford Jester Papers, TSLA.

90. Lulu B. White to Gov. Beauford Jester, July 21, 1947, box 4–14/52, folder "National Association for the Advancement of Colored Peoples," Beauford Jester Papers, TSLA.

91. Leon Guitry to Governor Jester, March 19, 1947, box 4–14/117, "Correspondence, G–H" folder, Beauford Jester Papers, TSLA; C. M. Simpson to Gov. Beauford Jester, February 9, 1948, box 4–14/96, "Civil Rights (against the Govs. Stand)" folder, ibid.

92. Thurgood Marshall to the editor, *New York Times,* April 19, 1950, part 3, series B, reel 16, NAACP Papers. The case summary does not list the Council of Churches, the CIO, or the AFL as having submitted briefs. *Sweatt v. Painter* 339 U.S. 629.

93. "Daniel Seeks 'United South' on Segregation," *Corpus Christi Caller Times,* December 21, 1949, clipping attached to letter from Dr. H. Boyd Hall to Thurgood Marshall, part 3, series B, reel 15, NAACP Papers.

94. *Sweatt v. Painter,* 339 U.S. 629 (1950).

95. "End of Jim Crow Seen by Marshall," NAACP press release, June 8, 1950, part 3, series B, reel 16, NAACP Papers.

96. Thurgood Marshall to Pauli Murray, June 9, 1950, part 3, series B, reel 16, NAACP Papers.

97. George I. Sánchez to A. L. Wirin, November 18, 1949, box 62, folder 15, Sánchez Papers, BLAC.

98. George I. Sánchez to John J. Herrera, June 16, 1953, box 3, folder 5, Sánchez Papers, BLAC.

99. Gus Garcia to George E. Rundquist, ACLU, March 3, 1949, box 16, folder 19, Sánchez Papers, BLAC; idem to Rowland Watts, March 3, 1949, ibid.

100. Quoted in telegram from Dr. Hector P. García to Gov. Beauford Jester, January 11, 1949, box 4–14/82, "Three Rivers Case" folder, Beauford Jester Papers, TSLA.

101. "GI of Mexican Origin, Denied Rites in Texas, To Be Buried in Arlington," *New York Times,* January 13, 1949.

102. Hector García to Gerald Saldana, March 13, 1954, box 141, folder 13, Hector P. García Papers, Texas A&M University, Corpus Christi, Texas (hereafter cited as Hector García Papers).

103. Hector P. García to editor, *Lubbock Morning Avalanche,* July 18, 1956, Hector García Papers.

104. Philip M. Hauser to Dr. Hector P. García, February 23, 1950, box 1989/59-18, "Discrimination Correspondence, 1949–1950" folder, Good Neighbor Commission, TSLA; Hector P. García to president of Lubbock School Board, June, 2, 1950, ibid.; "Where Do I Belong," clipping, n.d., attached to letter, Donald M. Woodward to Tom Sutherland, May 23, 1950, ibid.

105. Hector P. García to Homer Garrison, April 17 and 26, 1950, box 1989/59-18, "Discrimination Correspondence, 1949–1950" folder, Good Neighbor Commission, TSLA.

106. Hector P. Garcíal to commanding officer, December 1, 1950, box 1989/59-18, "Mexicans Burned to Death in Fisher County" folder, Good Neighbor Commission, TSLA.

107. Efraím Domínguez, Jr., to G. F. Dohrn, April 13, 1948, box 1989/59–16, "Discrimination, General File, 1946–1956" folder, Good Neighbor Commission, TSLA.

108. Sánchez and García demonstrated their support of workers rights mainly by adamantly opposing the Bracero Program and endorsing "Operation Wetback," the quasi-military campaign in 1954 to round up "wetbacks" for deportation. George I. Sánchez to Ernesto Galarza, October 12, 1948, box 16, folder 13, Sánchez Papers, BLAC.

109. Manuel Avila, Jr., to Ed Idar, February 7, 1956, box 26, folder 28, Hector García Papers; *News Bulletin* 4, nos. 1 and 2 (September–October) 1955, ibid.

110. Manuel Avila, Jr., to Ed Idar, February 7, 1956, box 46, folder 28, Hector García Papers; Isaac P. Borjas to Hector P. García, June 2, 1940, ibid.; newspaper clipping, *Caracas Daily Journal,* n.d., box 114, folder 22, ibid.

111. Quoted in Brian Behnken, "On Parallel Tracks: A Comparison of the African-American and Latino Civil Rights Movements in Houston" (M.A. thesis, University of Houston, 2001), 98–99.

112. *Brown v. Board of Education of Topeka,* 98 F. Supp. 797 (1951).

113. George I. Sánchez to A. L. Wirin, October 14, 1953, box 62, folder 18, Sánchez Papers, BLAC.

114. George I. Sánchez to Roger N. Baldwin, August 27, 1958, box 31, folder 8, Sánchez Papers, BLAC (emphasis in the original); Neil Foley, "Over the Rainbow: *Hernandez v. Texas, Brown v. Board of Education,* and Black v. Brown." *Chicano-Latino Law Review* (UCLA) 25 (Spring 2005): 139–152.

115. George I. Sánchez to Nicholas T. Nonnenmacher, research specialist for the American Legion, September 17, 1952, box 3, folder 5, Sánchez Papers, BLAC

116. Roger N. Baldwin to A. L. Wirin, June 8, 1951, box 62, folder 16, Sánchez Papers, BLAC.

117. George I. Sánchez to A. L. Wirin, June 25, 1952, box 62, folder 17, Sánchez Papers, BLAC; George I. Sánchez to A. L. Wirin, October 28, 1953, box 62, folder 18, ibid.

118. George I. Sánchez to Lyle Saunders, November 4, 1952, box 3, folder 5, Sánchez Papers, BLAC. Lyle Saunders was a professor of sociology at the Colorado School of Medicine at the time.

119. Roger Baldwin to George Sánchez, December 18, 1952, box 3, folder 5, Sánchez Papers, BLAC.

120. A. L. Wirin to George I. Sánchez, June 20, 1952, box 62, folder 17, Sánchez Papers, BLAC.

121. A. L. Wirin to James Marshall, September 30, 1953, box 62, folder 18, Sánchez Papers; A. L. Wirin to Roger Baldwin, October 9, 1953, ibid.

122. David G. Gutiérrez, *Walls and Mirrors: Mexican Americans, Mexican Immigrants, and the Politics of Ethnicity* (Berkeley: University of California Press, 1995), 168–173.

123. Thomas H. Krenek, *Mexican-American Odyssey: Feliz Tijerina, Entrepreneur and Civil Leader, 1905–1965* (College Station: Texas A&M University Press, 2001), 204.

124. Phil J. Montalbo to Felix Tijerina, May 27, 1957, box 11, folder 9, LULAC Council #60 Collection, RG E 21, Houston Metropolitan Research Center (hereafter cited as HMRC); Krenek, *Mexican-American Odyssey,* 204–205.

125. A. G. Ramirez to Felix Tijerina, May 30, 1957, box 11, folder 9, HMRC. Ramirez also told LULAC regional director, Pete Tijerina, "My District does not want to be affiliated with the Negro group." Idem to Pete Tijerina, May 30, 1957, ibid.

126. A. G. Ramirez to LULAC Council 2 (San Antonio), May 30, 1957, ibid.

127. Quoted in Krenek, *Mexican-American Odyssey,* 206; Brian Behnken, "On Parallel Tracks," 98–100.

128. Quoted in Krenek, *Mexican-American Odyssey,* 209.

129. Feliz Salazar, Jr., to Luciano Santoscoy, April 7, 1958, box 14, folder 7, LULAC Council #60, RG E 21, HMRC.

130. Luciano [Santoscoy] to Feliz Salazar, Jr., April 17, 1958, ibid.

131. "Address Delivered by Gus C. García at his Testimonial Dinner," Feb. 13, 1952, San Antonio, Tex., box 1, folder 2, Gus García Papers, Nettie Lee Benson Latin American Collection, University of

Texas Libraries, Austin, Tex. (hereafter cited as García Papers, BLAC); "International Assembly to Hear S.A. Attorney," *San Antonio Express*, Jan. 27, 1952, ibid.; Michael A. Olivas, "*Hernandez v. Texas*: A Litigation History," in idem, ed., *"Colored Men" and "Hombres Aquí": Hernandez v. Texas and the Emergence of Mexican-American Lawyering* (Houston, Tex.: Arte Público Press, 2006), 209–222.

132. "Segregation of Children and Racial Assignment of Teachers in El Centro (Calif.) Challenged in U.S. District Court," press release, February 7, 1955, part 3, series C, reel 2, NAACP Papers; "Sue to End Jim Crow Schools in Southern California City," press release, February 10, 1955, ibid.

133. Brief for United States, U.S. Court of Appeals for the Fifth Circuit, *Jose Cisneros v. Corpus Christi Independent School District*, box 1, folder 2, Hector García Papers; Texas State Advisory Committee, *School Desegregation in Corpus Christi: A Report* (Washington, D.C.: U.S. Commission on Civil Rights, 1977).

134. *Jose Cisneros v. Corpus Christi Independent School District*, 324 F. Supp. 599 (S.D. Tex. 1970).

135. *Jose Cisneros et al. v. Corpus Christi Independent School District*, 324 F. Supp. 599 (1970).

136. *Keyes v. School District No. 1, Denver, Col.*, 413 U.S. 189 (1973).

137. Opinion of Justice Douglas, ibid.

138. Guadalupe San Miguel, *Brown, Not White: School Integration and the Chicano Movement in Houston* (College Station: Texas A&M University Press, 2001).

139. William Julius Wilson, *More than Just Race: Being Black and Poor in the Inner City* (New York: W. W. Norton and Co., 2009), 57–60.

140. Richard Fry, *Hispanic Youth Dropping Out of U.S. Schools: Measuring the Challenge*," Pew Hispanic Center Report (Washington, D.C.: Pew Hispanic Center, 2003), 1–18; Anne K. Driscoll, "Risk of High School Dropout among Immigrant and Native Hispanic Youth," *International Migration Review* 33 (Winter 1999): 857–875.

141. Quoted in Tushnet, *NAACP's Legal Strategy*, 7–8; Risa Lauren Goluboff, "'Let Economic Equality Take Care of Itself': The

NAACP, Labor Litigation, and the Making of Civil Rights in the 1940s," *UCLA Law Review* 52 (2005): 1393–1486.

EPILOGUE

1. For an excellent theoretical discussion of "racialized solidarity," see Juliet Hooker, *Race and the Politics of Solidarity* (New York: Oxford University Press, 2009), chapters 1 and 2. See also Lani Guinier and Gerald Torres, *The Miner's Canary: Enlisting Race, Resisting Power, Transforming Democracy* (Cambridege, Mass.: Harvard University Press, 2002).

2. Thurgood Marshall to Carter Wesley, October 3, 1947, part 3, series B, reel 15, *A Guide to the Microfilm Edition of the Papers of the NAACP*, ed. Randolph Boehm (Frederick, Md.: University Publications of America, 1982) (hereafter cited as NAACP Papers); Thurgood Marshall to Carl Murphy, editor of *The Afro-American,* September 30, 1947, ibid.; Heman M. Sweatt to Thurgood Marshall, September 21, 1947, ibid.; Richard Kluger, *Simple Justice: The History of* Brown v. Board of Education *and Black America's Struggle for Equality* (New York: Alfred A. Knopf, 2004), 167; Mark V. Tushnet, *NAACP's Legal Strategy against Segregated Education, 1925 to 1950* (Chapel Hill: University of North Carolina, 2004), 107.

3. The literature on the Chicano Movement is extensive, but to understand the sharp transformation of Mexican youth into radical persons of color, see Ian Haney López, *Racism on Trial: The Chicano Fight for Justice* (Cambridge, Mass.: Harvard University Press, 2003).

4. Elizabeth Sutherland Martínez, ed., *Letters from Mississippi* (New York: McGraw-Hill, 1965); Lauren Ashley Araiza, "For Freedom of Other Men: Civil Rights, Black Power, and the United Farm Workers, 1965–1973" (Ph.D. diss., University of California, Berkeley, 2006), 1–54; "Veterans of the Civil Rights Movement," www.crmvet .org (accessed June 1, 2009).

5. Araiza, "For Freedom of Other Men," 1–54. On networks of interracial cooperation in California during this period and earlier, see

Shana Bernstein, *The Struggle for Civil Rights in Multiracial Los Angeles* (Oxford University Press, forthcoming).

6. Gordon Keith Mantler, "Black, Brown, and Poor: Martin Luther King, Jr., the Poor People's Campaign, and Its Legacies" (Ph.D. diss., Duke University, 2008).

7. Nancy MacLean, "The Civil Rights Act and the Transformation of Mexican American Identity and Politics," *Berkeley La Raza Law Journal* 18 (2007): 125; idem, *Freedom Is Not Enough: The Opening of the American Workplace* (Cambridge, Mass.: Harvard University Press, 2006), 155–184.

8. www.lulac.org/advocacy/press/2002/ (accessed February 19, 2009); www.naacp.org/advocacy/ (accessed October 10, 2006).

9. Quoted in Charles Kamaski and Raul Yzaguirre, "Black-Hispanic Tension: One Perspective," *Journal of Intergroup Relations* 21 (Winter 1994–1995): 19.

10. Richard Rodriguez, *Brown: The Last Discovery of America* (New York: Viking, 2002), 117; U.S. Census, table 4, "Projections of the Population by Sex, Race, and Hispanic Origin for the United States: 2010 to 2050," www.census.gov (accessed May 11, 2009).

11. See Angela Oh's disagreement with John Hope Franklin over President Clinton's Race Initiative in which Oh argued that it was time to move beyond the "black-white paradigm," "In Harmony's Way," *Wired,* August 25, 1997, www.wired.com/politics/law/news/1997/08/6301 (accessed February 23, 2009).

12. See, for example, Andrew Hacker, *Two Nations: Black and White, Separate, Hostile, Unequal* (New York: Ballantine Books, 1995).

13. Telephone conversation with Harry Rubenstein, chair and curator of the Division of Politics and Reform, National Museum of American History, Washington, D.C., April 29, 2009.

14. Patricia Williams, "What Happened to the National Race Dialogue?" *ColorLines* (Spring 1999) www.colorlines.com/article.php ?ID=110&p=2 (accessed February 23, 2009); Jonathan Tilove, "Strange Bedfellows, Unintended Consequences, and the Curious Contours of the Immigration Debate," in *Debating Immigration,*

ed. Carol M. Swain (New York: Cambridge University Press, 2007), 217.

15. See, for example, William W. Sales, Jr., and Roderick Bush, "African American and Latino Coalitions: Prospects for New Social Movements in New York City," in *Race and Politics: New Challenges and Responses for Black Activism,* ed. James Jennings (London; New York: Verso, 1997), 135–148.

16. George I. Sánchez to Lyle Saunders, November 4, 1952, box 3, folder 5, George I. Sánchez Papers, Nettie Lee Benson Latin American Collection, University of Texas Libraries, Austin (hereafter cited as Sánchez Papers, BLAC).

17. On the transformation of organized labor to "social movement unionism" that includes transnational and immigrant workers as well as U.S. workers from a broad range of racial-ethnic backgrounds, see Bruce Nissen, ed., *Unions in a Globalized Environment: Changing Borders, Organizational Boundaries, and Social Roles* (Armonk, N.Y.: M. E. Sharpe, 2002), esp. chapters 5 and 6.

18. Cornel West, Jorge Klor de Alva, and Earl Shorris, "Our Next Race Question: The Uneasiness between Blacks and Latinos," *Harper's Magazine* 292 (April 1996): 55–63.

19. Legal scholar Tanya Katerí Hernández prefers to call African Americans "Anglo-Blacks" to recognize their cultural difference from Afro-Latinos because the term " 'Anglo-Blacks' refrains from negating the influence of the geographic space of the Americas on Afro-Latino/ as that the terms 'Black-American,' 'Afro-American,' and 'African-American' do by exclusively associating 'America' with Anglo-Blacks." Hernández, " 'Too Black to Be Latino/a:' Blackness and Blacks as Foreigners in Latino Studies," *Latino Studies* 1 (March 2003): footnote 3, 154–155.

20. West, Klor de Alva, and Shorris, "Our Next Race Question."

21. Ibid.

22. Ibid.

23. Ibid.

24. Ibid.

25. Rodriguez, *Brown*, 131–132.

26. Ibid., 137–138.

27. John J. Betancur and Douglas C. Gills, eds. *The Collaborative City: Opportunities and Struggles for Blacks and Latinos in U.S. Cities* (New York: Garland, 2000); Paula McCain, "Coalition and Competition: Patterns of Black-Latino Relations in Urban Politics," in *Politics of Minority Coalition,* ed. Wilbur C. Rich (Westport, Conn.: Praeger, 1996), 53–64.

28. Ed Morales, "Brown Like Me," *The Nation,* March 8, 2004; Toni Morrison, "On the Backs of Blacks," *Time,* December 2, 1993.

29. "Statistical Portrait of Hispanics in the United States," Pew Hispanic Center, table 5, "Detailed Hispanic Origin, 2006," www.pewhispanic.org/factsheets (accessed September 3, 2008); U.S. Census, Population Estimates, "Annual Estimates of the Population by Sex, Race, and Hispanic Origin for the United States: April 1, 2000 to July 1, 2007 (NC-EST2007-03)," www.census.gov (accessed May 13, 2009).

30. Robert C. Smith, *Mexican New York: Transnational Lives of New Immigrants* (Berkeley: University of California Press, 2006); Regina Cortina and Mónica Gendreau, *Poblanos en Nueva York: Migración Rural, Educación y Bienestar* (Puebla, México: Universidad Iberoamericana Puebla, 2004).

31. See, for example, Nicolás Vaca, *Presumed Alliance: The Unspoken Conflict between Latinos and Blacks and What It Means for America* (New York: Rayo, 2004); Tatcho Mindiola, Jr., Yolanda Flores Niemann, and Nestor Rodriguez, *Black-Brown Relations and Stereotypes* (Austin: University of Texas Press, 2002).

32. Aristide R. Zollberg, "Reforming the Back Door: The Immigration and Reform Act of 1986 in Historical Perspective," in *Immigration Reconsidered: History, Sociology, and Politics,* ed. Virginia Yans-McLaughlin (New York: Oxford University Press, 1991), 315–339; Jeff Diamond, "African-American Attitudes towards United States Immigration Policy," *International Migration Review* 32 (Summer 1998): 451–470.

33. In the midfifties, the American G.I. Forum and the Texas State Federation of Labor (AFL) copublished the controversial pamphlet

What Price Wetbacks? (Austin, Tex.: The Forum, [1953]) that blamed "wetbacks" for displacing American workers and threatening the security of the United States.

34. The phrase is taken from Appellant's Brief, *Pete Hernandez v. State of Texas,* Court of Criminal Appeals, No. 25,816, at 17; *Hernandez v. Texas,* 251 S.W. 2d 531, rev'd, 347 U.S. 475 (1954).

INDEX

Abernathy, Ralph, 144
Addington, Wendell, 116
African Americans: assimilation of, 13–14; post-World War II activism, 16–18; stereotypical views of Mexicans, 12. *See also* Black/brown convergence and divergence; Employment discrimination; Good Neighbor policy; School segregation
Afro Americano y Latino Juntos! (Black and Brown Together!), 145
Aguilar, Manuel, 61
Aircraft industry, employment discrimination, 59–62, 181n19
Aldrete, Cristóbal, 111
Alemán, Miguel, 120–121
Allen, George, 119
Allianza Hispano-Americana (Allianza), 131, 132, 136
American Beauty Cover Company, 87, 190n112
American Civil Liberties Union (ACLU), 15, 102, 108, 156
American Council of Spanish-Speaking People (ACSSP), 131–133
American Council on Race Relations, 90

American Federation Labor (AFL), 12, 57, 63, 122, 180n13
American Federation of Teachers, 122
American G.I. Forum, 15, 34, 126–128, 132, 155
American Jewish Congress (AJC), 15, 156; *Mendez* and, 102, 104–105, 106
American Veterans Committee, 122
"Anglo-Blacks," 209n19
ANMA (Asociación Nacional de México-Americana), 156
Antimiscegenation laws, 41, 50
Arias, Arnulfo, 47
Arizona: employment discrimination, 62; stationing of African American soldiers, 45–46
Avila, Manuel, 128–129

Baldwin, Roger, 130, 131, 132, 139
Baytown Employees Federation, 73–74
Beezley, William, 160n5
Belk, C. W., 84
Bermudez, Antonio M., 44

Hernández, Tanya Katerí, 209n19
Hernandez v. Texas, 135
Herrera, Ernest, 83
Herrera, John, 126, 133
Heurta, Dolores, 142
Honduras, 48
Houston, Charles, 67, 96
Howard University, 67, 96, 141
Hughes, Langston, 30, 50–51,
164n28
Hull, Cordell, 44, 48–49, 65, 66,
177n76
Hull House, 90
Humble Oil and Refinery Com-
pany, 68, 72–73

"I, Too" (Hughes), 30
Illegal immigration. *See*
Immigration
Immigration: as divisive issue,
20–21, 145–147, 153, 154–155;
of free-blacks from Texas to
Mexico, 43; Latin America and,
48; U.S. and, 46
Indians. *See* Native Americans
Informer, 76
International Longshoremen and
Warehouseman's Union, 15,
59–60, 86
International Union of Mine,
Mill, and Smelter Workers, 15,
62, 156

Jackson, Jesse, 4
James, C. L. R., 54
James, Joseph, 91

Japanese American Citizenship
League (JACL), 102
Jennings, C. G. and Doris Fay, 112
Jester, Beauford, 114–115, 117,
195n26
Johnson, Jack, 51
Johnson, Lyndon Baines, 126
Jones, Robert, 41–42
Juárez, Benito, 178n84
Junco, Alfonso, 51

Kaiser, Edgar F., 89
Kaiser Corporation, 89
Kazen, Abraham Jr., 133
Kelly Air Force Base, 83–84
Kelly Katies, 83
Kennedy, T. W., 126
Kenney, Robert W., 102
Kleberg, Richard M., 70
Klor de Alva, Jorge, 148–152
Knight, O. A., 72
Krauze, Enrique, 162n16
Kwong, Victor, 197n41

Lafayette College, 117
"Language handicap," *Delgado*
and, 108–111, 113
Latin America. *See* Good Neighbor
policy; *specific countries*
Latin-American Union, at
University of Texas, 118
Latinos/Latinas: black-white
paradigm of race and, 146–147;
race and culture and, 148–152;
whiteness issue, 145–146
Laveaga, Rafael, 4, 6